SAN'YA
BLUES

SAN'YA
BLUES

*Laboring Life in
Contemporary Tokyo*

EDWARD FOWLER

CORNELL UNIVERSITY PRESS

ITHACA AND LONDON

First published 1996 by Cornell University Press
First printing, Cornell Paperbacks, 1998

San'ya Blues
by OKABAYASHI NOBUYASU
© 1968 by FUJIPACIFIC MUSIC INC. & BelAir Music Publishing, Ltd.

Used by permission of JASRAC
License no. 9593003-501

English translation of "San'ya Blues" by Edward Fowler
© 1996 by FUJIPACIFIC MUSIC INC.

Cornell University Press strives to use environmentally responsible suppliers
and materials to the fullest extent possible in the publishing of its books. Such
materials include vegetable-based, low-VOC inks and acid-free papers that are
recycled, totally chlorine-free, or partly composed of nonwood fibers. For
further information, visit our website at www.cornellpress.cornell.edu

Library of Congress Cataloging-in-Publication Data

Fowler, Edward.
  San'ya blues : laboring life in contemporary Tokyo / Edward Fowler.
    p.   cm.
  Includes bibliographical references and index.
  ISBN-13: 978-0-8014-3247-7 (cloth : alk. paper)
  ISBN-10: 0-8014-3247-2 (cloth : alk. paper)
  ISBN-13: 978-0-8014-8570-1 (pbk.: alk. paper)
  ISBN-10: 0-8014-8570-3 (pbk.: alk. paper)
    1. Day laborers–Japan–Tokyo. 2. Working class–Japan–Tokyo. 3. San'ya
(Tokyo, Japan)–Social conditions.   I. Title.
HD5854.2.J3F68 1996
305.5'62—dc20   96-13898

Cloth printing

      1   3   5   7   9   10   8   6   4   2

Paperback printing

      1   3   5   7   9   10   8   6   4

To Hiroko
in memoriam

SAN'YA BLUES

by Okabayashi Nobuyasu

Had a rough time on the job today,
Now I'm gonna drink my cares away.
There's nothin' else for me to do—
I'm stuck in San'ya, and it makes me blue.

Sitting here at the bar alone,
I dream of days forever gone.
I know my tears won't bring them back;
San'ya's home now, and that is that.

When the job is done, that's all she wrote;
I'll be out of work and soon flat broke.
But cursing my fate won't help, I know—
I'm a Yama man with no place to go.

San'ya's the pits, or so people say,
But guess what'd happen if we all went away?
No buildings go up, no roads go in—
But no one seems to get it, so you just can't win.

There's no use cryin' 'bout might-have-been's
Our time is coming, we'll get our due then.
And when we do, just wait and see—
I'll cry tears of joy for you and me.

CONTENTS

CONTENTS

MAPS

ILLUSTRATIONS

PREFACE

No two people are alike, we often tell ourselves. Yet we tend to ignore that common wisdom when directing our attention beyond our own generation or gender, race or culture. Not only do we relegate those we do not know to the category of indefinable Other, we assume that they are all utterly the same in their otherness. If this is true for the way one group looks at another inside our own country, it is all the more true when we look beyond our borders to another country such as Japan.

Westerners visiting Tokyo—a huge metropolis, a seemingly endless sea of humanity—are often so conscious of the obvious physical and cultural disparities between their host country and their own that they overlook the diversity within Japanese society. It is especially easy to overlook when, despite some excellent recent books demonstrating irrefutably just how varied and complex Japanese society is, bureaucrats and cultural pundits alike are busy promoting the notion of the country's ethnic and cultural homogeneity. Confronted with this notion, which easily escalates into myth, many Westerners are tempted to apply the label of homogeneity, which seems at first glance to characterize the monotonous urban landscape stretching before them, to the population that inhabits it.

Tokyo's distinguishing features—and there are many—become apparent to the long-term resident. One place, however, is immediately recognizable as different from any other: San'ya, the day-laborer community straddling Taitō and Arakawa wards where workers—mostly construction workers—get their jobs off the street. In contrast to the rest of the city, moreover, San'ya leaves a disquieting impression of neglect, poverty, and outright misery. Yet in the midst of the misery is a certain almost-refreshing ebullience and chutzpah. The compulsion toward outward conformity, so regularly at work in the rest of the city, is either absent or stood on its head. Codes of behavior do exist, but they clearly differ from those of mainstream society. There is a freedom, too, that is not to be observed in any other part of Tokyo. Only in San'ya people seem to be doing more or less what they want when they want, and saying what they want to whomever they want—even to total strangers like me.

This freedom, however, cannot mask a malaise that deeply afflicts the neighborhood. It is disturbing indeed to see so many human beings visibly hurting, both physically and psychically, a hurt that lingers in the memory far more tenaciously than does the ever-present filth and stench. Yet even more disturbing than the occasionally gruesome scenes one witnesses in San'ya is the realization of just how much one has been conditioned to see the difference between this part of Tokyo and the rest of the city in terms of inhospitable otherness—which is to say through the eyes of one's mainstream Japanese hosts.

This book, based on my own experience of San'ya, first as a frequent visitor during a sixteen-month period in 1989–1990 and then as a resident during the summer of 1991, has a fourfold purpose: (1) to provide a thorough physical description of San'ya and its inhabitants and, through it, an account of Japan that is somewhat at odds with popular conceptions; (2) to supplement that description with portraits of day laborers and other groups living and working in the community; (3) to focus on San'ya as a *yoseba*, or site of job procurement, rather than as a site of homelessness (the emphasis in most journalistic reporting), in order to underscore the primacy of work to the day laborer; and (4) to offer a personal account of life in San'ya in an effort to put a human face on a community too often obscured by statistics and dry studies.

I attempt to let the members of a marginalized community speak directly to the reader. Of course, the reader is not getting an unadulterated or unmediated account—far from it, as a perusal of both the frame of Prologue/Epilogue/Interviewing and the main text itself will reveal. The reader will also note that I have been unable to contain my presentation of San'ya within a single format. I juxtapose oral history (the "lives" of San'ya residents) with my own journal (in "Work") and other personal accounts in an effort to thicken the description of a neighborhood—and of a chapter in Japanese history—that is usually given short shrift.

Every format has its trade-offs, but it became clear to me as I began writing that my own approach to San'ya could not claim to be detached or "objective"—that is, an account that pretended to the sort of distance which those of us who are particularly privileged members of society (and endowed with a sometimes altogether different sensibility) generally impose on an area like San'ya and its residents. The result is a record of vulnerability as well as bravado on the parts of both observer and observed.

What this book lacks in scholarly dispassion it gains, I hope, in immediacy—the kind I trust will not lose its urgency over time. The people I came to know in San'ya face dilemmas that continue long after any written account comes to an end and that, more important, touch on our own lives, often in ways we do not care to admit. If this book has any value, it will perhaps lie not so much in revealing the plight of a little-known neighborhood far removed from our own circumstances and cultural memory as in suggesting that an appreciation of what we commonly think of as the universal human condition comes only through an awareness of just how differently people's lives can be led.

Times have changed since my frequent visits to San'ya in the late 1980s and early 1990s. In 1995 I returned to find that jobs off the streets were down to less than half of what they were in boom times. Japan's deepest recession since World War II was hurting nearly everyone, but it was hurting those at the bottom of the economic pyramid the most. Here once again was evidence of what people have told me about time after time: the existence of a buffer zone that absorbs the brunt of economic exigencies. It is the last area to feel the effects of a boom, the first to feel the bust.

I have tried to write not so much a critical as a symphonic essay, a series of interlocking movements straining noisily against their own boundaries and constantly at war with their own linearity. Its aim in theory, however limited in practice, is to be multivocal—and to incorporate, rather than suppress, a cacophony of voices that have spoken to me over the years. To this end I have benefited enormously from the work of others. Some antecedents are clear enough, although they may not recognize themselves: the late Alan Booth (*The Roads to Sata*), the late Asada Tetsuya/Irokawa Takehiro (*Mājan hōrōki* and *Kyōjin nikki*), Masao Miyoshi (*As We Saw Them*), Donald Richie (*The Inland Sea*), and Edward G. Seidensticker (*Genji Days*); more recently, Cathy N. Davidson (*Thirty-six Views of Mount Fuji*), and Norma Field (*In the Realm of a Dying Emperor*); and finally, Henryk Górecki, whose incantatory music struck a responsive chord in me when I was in the thick of writing. Others may recognize themselves in the text even though I do not. To those mentioned, all but the first of whom I have had the privilege to know personally, and to many, many others I owe a debt of gratitude: I have found my own voice through theirs.

EDWARD FOWLER

Durham, Irvine, London, Tokyo, 1989–1995

ACKNOWLEDGMENTS

My first and greatest debt is to the more than one hundred men and women I have talked to in the course of my association with San'ya and whose conversations provide the material for "Lives." This book would simply not have been possible without their participation, and I hope at the very least that their candor and articulateness come through in these pages. The many conversations not reproduced here also contributed immensely to my historical and economic understanding of San'ya and other yoseba.

This book began in 1989 as a series of "letters from Tokyo" to James Fujii, friend and now colleague at the University of California, Irvine. I thank him for responding in a way that moved this project from a series of idle musings to more dynamic involvement. I am grateful to him, Cathy N. Davidson, Godfrey Herndon, and Lucy North for reading the book in manuscript (the first two people twice) and offering important suggestions for its improvement. Special thanks go to Cathy Davidson for further reviewing the manuscript and offering astute advice and generous support at critical stages. Two outside readers for Cornell University Press also provided a wealth of useful comments.

Many others have helped this project. To Paul Waley I am in debt for his expert advice on several crucial details, not to mention his important book on Tokyo (see Suggested Readings). I am grateful as well for the encouragement of Masao Miyoshi, who was the first to tell me that I had the makings of a book (although he may be surprised by the kind of book it has turned out to be); to Tetsuo Najita, for insisting that I come to grips with San'ya's history; and to Edward G. Seidensticker, who repeatedly encouraged me to write something about Tokyo and who made some valuable criticisms of the final draft but one. Tony Guzewicz, Jeffry Hester, Ben Jones, and especially James Roberson have unselfishly provided me over the years with indispensable archival materials as well as backdrops for discussions about the yoseba. I have also benefited from the work of Koide Izumi and her staff at the Tokyo International House Library and the staff of the Tokyo Central Library in securing further research materials.

My initial visits to San'ya took place during my stay in Tokyo as a Fulbright Research Fellow; my thanks go to the CIES/Japan–United States Educational Commission for its support and for providing a venue for presenting material on San'ya and Shitamachi. The Asiatic Society of Japan provided another venue, as well as a medium for publication of an article, "San'ya: Scenes from Life at the Margins of Japanese Society," which appeared in its *Transactions* (4th ser., vol. 6, 1991), 141–198, and which the society has kindly permitted me to incorporate in revised form into this book.

Many academic institutions provided venues for presentations on San'ya, including Cambridge University, Duke University, Harvard University, Princeton University, the University of London's School of Oriental and African Studies (SOAS), the Tōhō Gakkai, the University of California, Irvine and Santa Barbara campuses, the University of Chicago, the University of Essex, the University of Maryland, and the University of Wisconsin. SOAS also provided me with space and facilities for writing up my research when I was a visiting professor in the fall of 1993.

I wish to express particular appreciation to the members of Santōrō, the San'ya-based labor union, who no doubt looked at this observer of their activities with mild amusement at first but who indulged his frequent intrusions with an alacrity for which I am eternally grateful. Thanks are due as well to Hayashi Kōichi, Itō Tatsuyuki, Machida Kazuyuki, Matsuzawa Tessei and other members of the Yoseba Gakkai (a group of very "hands-on" scholars of day-laborer life), Miyashita Tadako, Mizuta Megumu, and Yamada Akira, as well as to Sheri Blake, Charles McJilton, and Tadashi Ōrui for putting up with repeated questionings and sharing information on numerous aspects of the yoseba. Finally, Shimizu Eijun has taught me much about Asakusa, while Jay A. Kranis and Peter P. Smith have expanded my knowledge of the homeless in the United States.

I owe a special debt of gratitude to Hiroko Fowler for allowing her spouse, no doubt against her better judgment, to play the truant husband and make a temporary escape from familial obligation one summer into yoseba life.

I am indebted as well to the University Research Council and the Asian/Pacific Studies Institute of Duke University, and on two occasions to the Research and Travel Committee of the University of California, Irvine's School of Humanities, for research support. The Northeast Asia Conference of the Association for Asian Studies provided travel funds during my stay in Tokyo in the summer of 1991 and generously provided further funding for a follow-up trip in the summer of 1995, which allowed me to revise and update my manuscript after a lengthy illness. During that illness, I was very fortunate to be surrounded by family, friends, and colleagues whose solicitous concern was indispensable in helping to revive body and spirit. Finally, a word of appreciation goes to Roger Haydon, my editor at Cornell University Press, for his unflagging interest in my work on San'ya from its inception. To all I owe an immense debt of gratitude for keeping faith in a project that seemed destined to languish indefinitely.

E. F.

A NOTE ON LANGUAGE
AND MONEY

Most Japanese words and phrases appearing in this book are listed and identified in the Glossary. Vowels in Japanese are pronounced similarly to those in Italian, although somewhat more clipped. There are no silent vowels. Transliteration follows the modified Hepburn system, which uses macrons to indicate elongated vowels (except the long "i" sound, as in Iidabashi). Macrons have been eliminated only from those words, mostly place names, where custom has dictated ease of reading in English. Thus: daimyo, Hokkaido, Honshu, Kobe, Kyoto, Kyushu, Osaka, Tokyo, and so on, for daimyō, Hokkaidō, Honshū, Kōbe, Kyōto, Kyūshū, Ōsaka, and Tōkyō.

Personal names are given in the Japanese order: family name first, followed by the given name, as is the custom throughout East Asia.

Monetary figures are generally given in Japanese yen (¥). The rate of exchange at the time of most of my visits to San'ya (1989–91) was roughly ¥120 to the U.S. dollar. At the time this book goes to press, it is roughly ¥100 to the dollar.

SAN'YA
BLUES

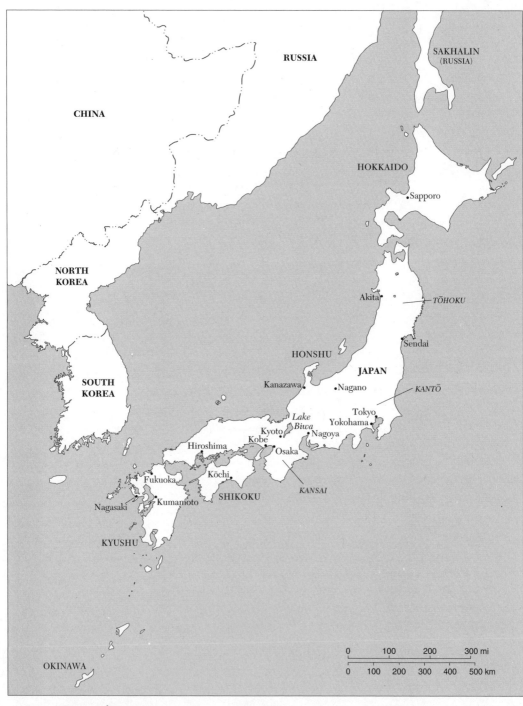

Japan and environs

※

PROLOGUE

If you really wish to write about San'ya, don't weep with the workers. Shedding tears in their company is all too easy, and when you cry, you lose sight of where they're going. That's what I was told. But I *will* weep with them when I wish. Only then can I truly view their world clear-eyed. That was my reply.
—Miyashita Tadako, *San'ya nikki* (San'ya diary)

Remember—you can't spell "bum" without a "u" in it.
—Bowery man (anonymous)

My active engagement with San'ya, the Tokyo backwater that is home to some seven or eight thousand day laborers, was inaugurated with a punch in the face.

I had long known about San'ya and its sordid reputation. The name alone conjures up in the minds of most Japanese unsavory images of moral lassitude and physical decay. I did not actually set foot in it, however, until the spring of 1989, during one of a series of walks I was making through the plebeian sections of Tokyo on the city's eastern side known as Shitamachi or "Low City" (to borrow Edward G. Seidensticker's rendering from his *Low City, High City*), where San'ya is located.

The incident I refer to took place several visits later in early fall of the same year. The weather that October was clear and crisp—a welcome change from the muggy heat of August and the incessant rains of September. A perfect day, in short, for exploring the city, which is what I had been doing since morning, working my way block by block, as was my habit, away from Asakusa, Shitamachi's principal amusement center—this time toward the site of Yoshiwara, the fabled pleasure quarter that survived until 1958 and that lies just beyond San'ya's western edge. On this day alone I had shot several rolls of film, capturing whatever street scene I thought notable and then, conscious of the miles left to trek, moving on to the next block.

The sun had already set as I crossed the street dividing the former

Yoshiwara (now Senzoku 4-chōme) and Nihonzutsumi, one of the administrative districts making up San'ya. The gathering dusk increased the air of unsavoriness, and I reflected on the concerns of some of my Japanese friends about the area's possible hazards ("It's dirty!"; "It's dangerous!"; "It's different!"). The three or four self-guided tours I had undertaken since the spring, however, had been without incident. Tokyo is a very safe city. Yet as I ambled for the first time after dark down the dilapidated, tunnel-like shopping arcade that leads into the heart of San'ya, I wondered if I should have taken my friends' concerns more seriously.

During previous walks through the neighborhood I had not encountered any hostility among the street people except for an occasional drunken epithet or scowl—perhaps brought on as much by surprise or embarrassment as by disdain for the outsider in their midst. On the contrary, I frequently met with displays of affable disbelief at my presence and even with open-armed welcomes by more than a few men, distilled spirits in hand, who seemed ready for any excuse to socialize. Looking back on my very first encounters, I recall that I rarely availed myself of opportunities to associate with people whom I looked upon more as subjects for my camera than as partners in conversation.

I proceeded east through the dilapidated arcade, known as the Iroha, which bustled with evening shoppers. San'ya is home to entrepreneurs, office workers, shopkeepers, and housewives as well as to day laborers, and the teeming arcade serves the entire community. The farther east you walk, however, the drearier the surroundings become. Disheveled men sit in lazy circles drinking and chatting. Others lie on the street, sleeping off their liquor. More line up in front of two or three tiny take-out stalls, waiting to buy dinner. Still others imbibe at a stand-up bar opening onto the street.

The bar is called Sen'nari, a mere hole in the wall near the arcade's east end which holds barely six or eight people and serves grilled pig guts (*horumon-yaki*), a cheap and nutritious dish popular in day-laborer neighborhoods. The bar was filled to capacity that evening, and the men were jovial. They would have just returned from their jobs at various construction sites. Thanks to good weather and a general construction boom, work was plentiful. The gaiety and camaraderie contrasted pleasantly with the bar's dismal surroundings. The scene was an ideal subject for a picture. There was still a frame or two left on the roll, and my flash unit was already mounted. I did not want to disturb the men. I certainly did not want them to disturb me. I snapped the picture, barely slowing down to focus, and moved on.

I did not get five steps past the bar before being surrounded by half a dozen drunken men whose faces were no longer smiling. One tall, sinewy man, a characteristic worker's towel twisted around his head, grabbed me by the arm before I could even think of making a run for it. Who was I to be taking pictures without their permission? he yelled. There were to be no reporters spying on them! His words were seconded by a volley of heckles. The group closed in on me. Then it came: a punch in the face along with a thick-tongued curse about the "damned foreigner" to augment the blow. I reeled back but did not go down, being hemmed in on all sides, and could only steel myself for whatever else might come.

The scuffle was quickly brought to a halt when the leader forced himself between me and the man coming at me and reminded him that they weren't looking to start an international incident. They were, however, wary of media exposure of any kind and did not take kindly to strangers walking up unannounced and snapping pictures. All they wanted was an apology and possession of the incriminating film.

I was hardly in a position to negotiate. But taking courage from the leader's gesture of conciliation, I rubbed my jaw and hazarded an objection in hopes of saving the film. To give it up would mean losing the rest of the pictures on the roll, which had nothing to do with San'ya. I was sorry to have offended anyone, but perhaps there was a way to give up the last picture without losing all the others?

The leader reminded me that he would be calling the shots. He then announced to the other men his plan to escort me to a nearby camera shop where we two would work everything out. He could handle me alone just fine, he said as he yanked me away from the others. We walked in the direction I had come from, to a tiny photo studio on the arcade's west end.

This man (I will call him Shiga after the prefecture in western Japan from which he hails), who first grabbed me and then saved me from further injury, did not let go until we had walked halfway through the arcade, which is to say well out of the other men's sight. Even after leading his captive safely out of harm's way, however, he did not mince his words.

"You're a damned fool, you know." Shiga spat out the sentence in a piercing, throaty voice. "Listen to you. You can speak Japanese. Speak it real good. So what happens? You go and bring this whole business on yourself because you were too damned arrogant to open your mouth when it counted. All you had to do was ask, you know. Why didn't you just ask to take our picture? If any of the men didn't like the idea, they'd have told you so or moved out of the way. But no, you just had to barge right in and shoot us."

"But I didn't want to bother you," I protested. "You all looked so merry in there. I didn't want to spoil the mood."

"You don't think a camera flashing in our faces spoils the mood? Next time do the decent thing and ask us before you go snapping away. We had every right to be upset. You butted into our lives and then tried to walk away from us. You can't get away with that—at least not around here."

Iroha Arcade, east entrance. San'ya Workers' Hall (under construction) is on the right.

Before I could reflect on or rebut Shiga's words, we had reached the studio. After a brief exchange with the clerk, it was decided that Shiga would have first viewing rights of the developed slides so that he could remove the source of embarrassment. I could come anytime afterward to pick up the remaining slides. Shiga and I then went our separate ways: he east through the arcade back to Sen'nari, I north along the avenue that bisected Nihonzutsumi and Senzoku to the nearest subway station home.

I spent several restless days and sleepless nights. I told no one of the incident, not even my wife, who is Japanese. Doing so, I was convinced, would confirm her worst suspicions about the area. Hadn't I visited San'ya enough already to satisfy my curiosity? she had complained to me more than once before. Wasn't I risking an ugly confrontation or worse? More to the point, wasn't I wasting my precious research time in Japan? If I had that many free hours on my hands, why couldn't I spend more of them with her and our young child?

Why couldn't I, indeed? I had no obligations, scholarly or otherwise, in San'ya. Two year-long literary projects had brought me to Tokyo, I reminded myself, and I was bound to them if to nothing else. I had emerged from a potentially disastrous situation relatively unscathed; I should count my blessings, cut my losses, and wash my hands entirely of the area.

And yet I knew that I could not simply walk away from events now. There was too much at stake in reading correctly the message that had been hurled at me. I had to return to San'ya not just to retrieve my slides but also to revisit the site of that ill-fated photograph. I had to confront the guests of Sen'nari again and let them know, if only by my presence without a camera, that I had understood the message. I set out four days later.

The story of that return trip is better told later in this book. Suffice it to say that reflection on the incident had made me see Shiga and the other men's side of the issue in a more sympathetic light. I had indeed been the instigator, the intruder. In fact, I had violated something these men obviously held very dear—their freedom to be not simply undisturbed but unobserved—forced them, in effect, into exposing their vulnerable and unreflecting presence. I was putting them on display, moreover, while concealing my own identity—a voyeur safely cloaked in anonymity.

With a single swing of his fist, a drunken day laborer had shaken up the easy formula of San'ya resident as pictorial commodity and foreign observer as picture-snapping consumer. I brushed off my pride and began visiting San'ya regularly to learn as much as I could. I went at all hours of the day and sometimes stayed the night. I spoke with day laborers, bureaucrats, missionaries, and shopkeepers and took part in many activities, some of which are described in these pages. I returned to Japan without my family in the summer of 1991 for a six-week stay, during which I lived in San'ya and worked as a day laborer. In the process I came to realize how important this dingy Tokyo neighborhood is to the Japanese economy as a whole. The narratives that follow are the result of these various investigations and experiences. The detail will, I hope, not detract from my initial impression, which struck me with such unexpected force, of the area: its inhabitants collectively give the lie to so much of what is being said and written about Japan.

The common view of this powerful East Asian nation, held by academics and journalists alike, is that the Japanese are a breed apart; that their customs are not simply alien from our own but, in the extreme view, border on the nonhuman; that they are a colorless people who look alike, dress alike, and think alike, performing their social and economic roles mindlessly and mechanically in the manner of so many interchangeable parts. In searching for the reasons behind Japan's spectacular economic success, we in the West have fastened on the country's supposed social and ethnic homogeneity, as if this quality were as natural to the Japanese landscape as its mountainous terrain and island topography.

The diversity that is habitually concealed in mainstream society, however, is often graphically revealed in San'ya and other day-laborer communities like it throughout urban Japan. It turns out that the Japanese, who have been described (in the words of James Fallows) as categorically "different from you and me," are in fact very different from one another. The people in San'ya do not, and should not, represent the country at large. Neither should any other single group. It just so happens that the differences that manage to persist in many parts of Japan despite rigorous centralization and social control are particularly pronounced in San'ya. There I encountered people who came from virtually every social and ethnic group living in Japan. Some people I met were generous, others stingy; some were warm and garrulous, others aloof and morose. I encountered a good many decent people and I ran into a few scoundrels. Hardly any were what might be described as "colorless."

Not only did the day laborers I met in San'ya not fit any stereotype, they reminded me again and again of the many other people I know in mainstream society who fit the stereotypes no better than they. For the closer I looked, the more I realized that the line dividing San'ya and the rest of society is a thin one indeed. The story of San'ya as I tell it is in fact the flip side of the well-known hymn to economic success in Japan, for it describes the heavy price paid by a great many for that success. It is the story of lost hopes and failed dreams; it is about the wrenching migration from country to city; it is about a city's (and by extension a nation's) attempt to modernize at the expense of its cultural memory; it is about the discrepancy between Japan's immense corporate wealth and the unenviable living condi-

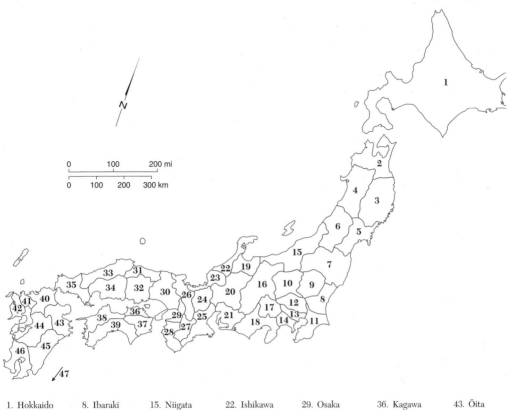

1. Hokkaido	8. Ibaraki	15. Niigata	22. Ishikawa	29. Osaka	36. Kagawa	43. Ōita
2. Aomori	9. Tochigi	16. Nagano	23. Fukui	30. Hyōgo	37. Tokushima	44. Kumamoto
3. Iwate	10. Gumma	17. Yamanashi	24. Shiga	31. Tottori	38. Ehime	45. Miyazaki
4. Akita	11. Chiba	18. Shizuoka	25. Mie	32. Okayama	39. Kōchi	46. Kagoshima
5. Miyagi	12. Saitama	19. Toyama	26. Kyoto	33. Shimane	40. Fukuoka	47. Okinawa
6. Yamagata	13. Tokyo	20. Gifu	27. Nara	34. Hiroshima	41. Saga	
7. Fukushima	14. Kanagawa	21. Aichi	28. Wakayama	35. Yamaguchi	42. Nagasaki	

21. Aichi	7. Fukushima	22. Ishikawa	26. Kyoto	15. Niigata	24. Shiga	19. Toyama
4. Akita	20. Gifu	25. Mie	43. Ōita	33. Shimane	28. Wakayama
2. Aomori	10. Gumma	36. Kagawa	46. Kagoshima	45. Miyazaki	32. Okayama	18. Shizuoka	6. Yamagata
11. Chiba	34. Hiroshima	39. Kōchi	16. Nagano	47. Okinawa	9. Tochigi	35. Yamaguchi
38. Ehime	1. Hokkaido	14. Kanagawa	42. Nagasaki	29. Osaka	37. Tokushima	17. Yamanashi
23. Fukui	30. Hyōgo	44. Kumamoto	27. Nara	41. Saga	13. Tokyo
40. Fukuoka	8. Ibaraki		12. Saitama	31. Tottori

Prefectures of Japan

tions of those mobilized to support it; and it is about the statist goals, oblivious to individual aspirations, that underwrite this discrepancy. The story of San'ya, in many surprising ways, is the story of Japan today.

At the same time, it is the story of one person's very particular and no doubt highly idiosyncratic experience of San'ya and of Japan. It is told out of an acute awareness of the reciprocal relationship between portrayer and portrayed—thanks to my memorable encounter in a run-down arcade one autumn evening in 1989. What follows, then, is not simply a description of an economically essential yet largely disenfranchized segment of Japanese society, but a meditation on why the existence of this segment should matter at all to one non-Japanese who happened to spoil an evening for half a dozen workers just returned from a hard day on the job.

CHAPTER I

❋

SETTING

San'ya is the largest of several Tokyo yoseba, or gathering places for casual laborers who get work off the street. The workers are called, with varying degrees of condescension, by many names—*hiyatoi rōdōsha* (lit., "laborer employed by the day") being the most neutral, but also *dokata* ("ground side," i.e., unskilled or common laborer who does roadwork or other construction work), *ninpu* or *ninsoku* (coolie/navvy), *pūtarō* ("child of the wind," i.e., transient), *tachinbo* (from *tachinbō* or "standby," i.e., one who awaits a job on the street), or, if you are in Osaka or elsewhere in the Kansai region, *anko* (from *ankō* or "angler fish," i.e., one who idly awaits a job—typically dock work—to snap up).

San'ya's reputation as an urban blight far exceeds its actual area, officially, 1.66 km.² or just over a half square mile, which is to say a mere dot on the vast Tokyo landscape. (San'ya is situated in the districts of Kiyokawa and Nihonzutsumi and parts of Hashiba and Higashi Asakusa in Taitō Ward, and parts of Minami Senjū in Arakawa Ward.) Home to as many as fifteen thousand day laborers during its heyday in the late 1950s and early 1960s, it had in the early 1990s about half that number living among a permanent population of some thirty-five thousand. More than two-thirds of the day laborers come from Japan's eastern half—the island of Hokkaido and the Tōhoku and Kantō regions of Honshu—of which the sprawling Tokyo metropolis is the major hub. The great majority make their home in

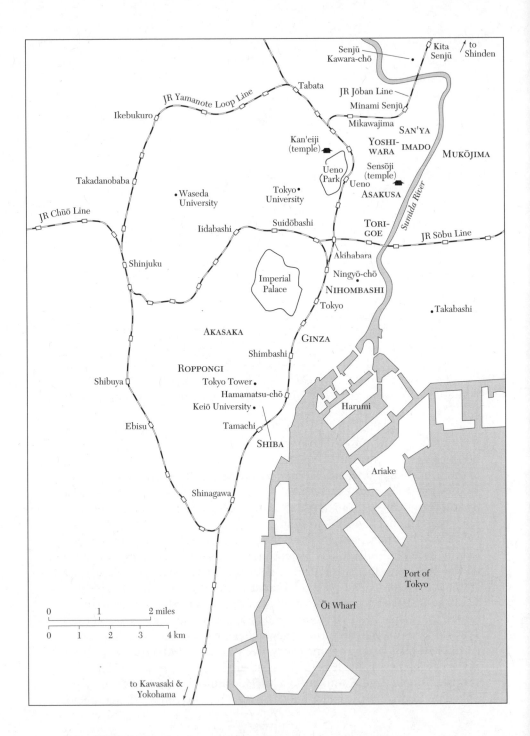

Central Tokyo

the *doyagai* or lodging-house district, a compact, densely populated area covering barely a quarter square mile. This is the site of the cheap accommodations (*doya*—the argot for *yado* or lodging house, the two syllables being reversed) for which San'ya is famous.

More even than the other Tokyo yoseba active in this century, such as Ikebukuro (named after the train station, to the west of San'ya), Takadanobaba (also named after the station, to the southwest), Senjū Kawara-chō (to the north), and Takabashi (to the south), San'ya is at once thoroughly isolated from and yet very close to the center of things. It is situated less than ten minutes away by train or subway from Ueno, one of Tokyo's major terminals. At the same time, being the only yoseba in the city with a lodging district and a variety of businesses that cater to the day laborer, it is a realm unto itself, into which a man on the down and out can withdraw for as long as desire or necessity dictates—from a few months or years to decade upon lonely decade.

Hidden though it may be from the ordinary citizen, the yoseba is in fact ubiquitous. Day-laborer centers once dotted the country's urban landscape, from Hokkaido to Okinawa, and can still be found in most major cities. Immediately to the south of Tokyo is the yoseba of Harappa, in the heavily industrial Kawasaki. To the south of that is Kotobuki-chō, a major yoseba in the port city of Yokohama with some five or six thousand day laborers, many of them migrant workers from abroad (notably Korea and the Philippines). Go farther west and you will find others, in Nagoya, Hiroshima, Fukuoka, and of course Osaka, where Kamagasaki, the largest yoseba by far, is home to twenty-five thousand day laborers. Altogether, it is estimated that between one and two hundred thousand men earn their wages by the day in Japan.

The equivalent of the yoseba can be found all over the world, including in the United States, from the Bowery (notably its pre–World War II incarnation) on Manhattan's Lower East Side, to a site scarcely a mile inland from California's famous Laguna Beach, where scores of migrant workers gather each morning. You will find few places on the scale of San'ya, however, and of its even larger counterpart, Kamagasaki; both are virtually autonomous communities, ostracized by the rest of society yet offering anonymity and freedom of movement—for those who can find work.

Each yoseba differs markedly from the others in its physical aspect and way of life; generalizations based on conditions in San'ya must therefore be made with caution. Yet broad similarities are apparent. First, the major yoseba—San'ya, Kotobuki-chō, and Kamagasaki—are self-contained ghettos rarely penetrated by outsiders. All differ visibly from their immediate surroundings, and all have doyagai where the men live as well as pick up work. Second, yoseba are inhabited by a dual population: a more or less

The doyagai in Kiyokawa. Men are gambling on the street in the distance.

stationary group of shopkeepers, light- and cottage-industry entrepreneurs, and low-income white-collar workers; and a highly mobile group of day laborers who are prepared to travel about the country to wherever work is available, be it another yoseba or a *hanba* (construction site with barracks on the premises). Finally, yoseba offer the nation a ready supply of manpower through their day-laborer populations, ensuring that jobs of vital economic importance get done. If you have walked the streets of Tokyo—a city that seems as though it is being constantly rebuilt—and have passed by a building going up or a sewer being dug or a street being torn up for a subway, chances are you have seen a day laborer at work.

Some day laborers work on the docks, although the number has decreased considerably in recent years with the rise of containerization. Others work in warehouses or in factories, and a small number work as drivers or as security guards. The vast majority, however, are engaged in construction, a huge industry that employs a greater proportion of Japan's total labor force (nearly 10 percent, or half again the proportion employed in the United States) than that of nearly any other country in the developed world, including France, Germany, and Great Britain. Most of Japan's half million construction firms are tiny operations, but the "Big Six"—Kajima, Kumagaigumi, Ōbayashi-gumi, Shimizu, Taisei, Takenaka Kōmuten—are among the world's largest.

The success of these general contracting firms, ironically, has much to do with their ability to keep as many workers as possible off the payrolls, and they do so with the help of an intricate system of subcontracting which farms out work through a network of subcontractors, sub-subcontractors, foremen, labor brokers, and finally yoseba like San'ya. Unlike U.S. corporations, in which trade unions are firmly entrenched, general contractors in Japan can take advantage of an extremely fluid labor supply that yields workers promptly on an as-needed basis. This multitiered system provides the shock absorber that buffers the larger firms against fluctuations in the business cycle, which is particularly violent in the construction industry. The men at the bottom are forced to take up the most slack, and the jobless rate on any given day in the yoseba, except in the very best of times, is typically 50 percent or higher.

The high rate of unemployment contributes to the shabby appearance of a yoseba like San'ya, for it is the men who cannot get work who end up drinking on the street during the day. And yet, while San'ya has often been called a slum, it is almost pristine as slums go compared to those found not just in other parts of Asia but in the United States as well. To take as an example New York, the U.S. city that comes closest to approaching Tokyo in size, there are far grimmer neighborhoods in, say, the South Bronx, and many more hard-core street drunks (not to mention drug addicts) on the Lower East Side than there are anywhere in Japan's capital.

Several observers have commented on the San'ya doyagai's dearth of families and its relative lack of violence. The quiet atmosphere, however, is by no means a sign of healthiness. Indeed, San'ya's diurnal lethargy (there is little to see except a few idle men lying about on the streets), in such stark contrast to the bustling, almost frenetic, activity seen throughout the rest of the city, suggests a kind of moral degeneracy to mainstream Japanese which is anathema to their way of life. An acquaintance became visibly disturbed when I told him that I was frequenting this section of Tokyo. "I wouldn't waste my time there if I were you," he told me. "You don't want to get dragged down in the mire." In the eyes of my Japanese acquaintance, San'ya was not simply an eyesore, a blot on Tokyo's image, but a festering wound capable of infecting any passerby foolish enough to come in contact with it.

San'ya, then, might just as well be considered a state of mind as a slum. Or, more properly, "states of mind," for the meaning of this neighborhood is clearly not the same for the resident (or even the different categories of residents) and nonresident. For the latter, who rarely if ever sets foot in the area and is left simply to imagine it, San'ya is a filthy repository for men whose personal world has gone awry, the result of individual excess or error; for the former (at least for the day-laborer resident), it is a refuge—a symbol of defeat, perhaps, but at the same time a cradle of opportunity which holds the possibility, however slim, of a second chance in a society that is most stingy with its second chances. Located in an easily accessible section of town, it beckons the laid-off worker, or the stray migrant from the provinces, or the man on the run from creditors, or the gambling addict or ex-con or ex-gangster, with its lures of liquor, gambling, casual sex, anonymity, and most important, a ready income.

Without this last, of course, the other attractions would not be viable. For although the outside world typically regards San'ya as a kind of skid row, workers based here know it first and foremost as a labor market, albeit one of last resort, where a job can be had with no questions asked. And although many jobs require only minimal skills, a goodly number demand extensive technical expertise in electrical work, masonry, carpentry, or scaffolding and offer a very high wage. None of the work is easy, however, and none of the jobs offers security. That is why San'ya as a labor market can be said to be located at the intersection of personal choice and corporate/statist exploitation. The individual worker freely elects to come here, it is true, but he makes this choice knowing that there is no place else to go in a land where the welfare system tends to be restrictive rather than inclusive and where panhandling is strongly frowned on.

In a very important sense, day laborers have been funneled into the yoseba by an ongoing process of often traumatic economic restructuring which has been part and parcel of Japan's supposedly "miraculous" (and by inference painless) postwar rise to affluence. The tremendous dislocation caused by that economic success is all too easily forgotten. When whole farming communities in the provinces lost their livelihood in the national rush to industrialize after the Second World War, men ended up in San'ya and other yoseba. Likewise, when small businesses took a direct hit from a draconian postwar austerity program (the so-called "Dodge Line," introduced in 1949), men went to San'ya; when the mines closed down in response to a shift in energy dependence from domestic coal to foreign oil in the late 1950s, men went to San'ya; when the nation's once-mighty steel industry collapsed in the face of foreign competition, men went to San'ya; when its gargantuan shipbuilding industry shut down after the 1973 Oil Shock and giant tankers were no longer in demand to transport Arabian crude, men went to San'ya; and when its heavy metal and aluminum industries shrank in the 1970s and 1980s as capital moved offshore in search of cheaper wages and less environmental consciousness, men went to San'ya.

San'ya and other yoseba are also homes for groups with long histories of discrimination because of their national, ethnic, or social origins: a disproportionate number of Koreans, Chinese, other Asians, Okinawans, Ainu, and the descendants of the outcastes now known collectively as *hisabetsu burakumin* (henceforth *burakumin*), live here. Of these groups, Koreans and *burakumin* are particularly overrepresented, not just as day laborers but also as labor brokers; both exploiter and exploited may well have the same ethnic or social background. A disproportionate number have some type of disability. Not a few men are missing an eye or a limb or suffer from radiation sickness or mental illness. In short, men from all social groups and all walks of life, having fallen through the cracks of society and family, drift to Tokyo and enter the day-laborer community that is San'ya.

For mainstream society, San'ya and the other yoseba thus provide a dual safety valve, relieving both economic and social pressures on the majority population, as many observers have pointed out. The yoseba, along with the extensive, multitiered system of subcontractors in manufacturing and construction (of which the yoseba can be viewed as the lowest tier), provide an otherwise rigid social economy with much-needed elasticity; without them, lifetime employment and other corporate benefits of the good life at the top which we hear so much about in the West would be far less secure. During a recession, the stress of economic contraction is shifted to the subcontractor, the sub-subcontractor, and so on down to the street, where day laborers absorb the brunt of hard times.

Even as it relieves pressure on the majority population, this safety valve increases pressure on the yoseba. Indeed, like pits of quicksand, San'ya and other yoseba have a way of pulling workers ever deeper into a quagmire of alcoholism, debt, disease, and premature death. And yet more than the poverty and malnutrition, which are rampant here, it is the sense of sheer isolation which plagues the men most. Whether resolutely or resignedly, the men leave something behind by coming here: jobs, families, creditors, prison records, gangster connections, failed businesses—the list is perhaps nearly as long as the combined rosters of the area's two hundred lodging houses. They may indeed gain anonymity and freedom of movement, but the price they pay for these is very dear: a loss of contact with the outside world. It is a price that newcomers pay perhaps more willingly than veterans of the yoseba; the latter know that the tally of loneliness adds up over the years with compound interest.

San'ya is thus physically and psychologically segregated from the rest of Tokyo. And yet unlike the South Bronx, for example, which may receive attention in election years by American politicians promising reform only to be forgotten when the television cameras move on to the next photo opportunity, San'ya figures on a daily basis in Tokyo's and Japan's economic agenda with no political posturing whatsoever. Its own vitality is depleted during the day precisely because its day-laborer population is out on the job and adding significantly to the quality of life in other sections of the city and surrounding prefectures. Surprisingly few workers are welfare recipients (less than 15 percent in the early 1990s according to government statistics, although the figure has no doubt risen in the early 1990s recession), and medical care is as much the province of private as public funding. The difference between San'ya and a true slum is that San'ya is home to thousands of unattached "derelicts" who manage nonetheless to contribute substantially to the society that has largely ignored them.

A Tour of San'ya

Alight at Minami Senjū Station, a mere twenty-three-minute ride on the Hibiya Subway Line from the Ginza (Tokyo's most fashionable shopping district), then ascend the stairs of a pedestrian bridge that traverses half a dozen railroad tracks leading to the JR (Japan Railways) Shioiri switchyard, and a panorama of San'ya's flat, gray expanse spreads before you, belying its claim (the Chinese characters for San'ya read "mountain-valley") to topographic diversity. You will be serenaded by the screeching of subway trains going into a curve on the elevated tracks above you (they plunge into the earth just west of the station) and by the grating and lurching of slow-moving freight trains in the switchyard below. The entranceway to the heart of San'ya lies about a five-minute walk to the south: Namidabashi, or "Bridge of Tears," an intersection named after the spot over a canal, filled in long ago, where criminals in the Edo (1603–1868) and early Meiji (1868–1912) periods are said to have bade grieving loved ones a last farewell before being led away to their deaths at an execution ground known as Kozukappara, located next to the temple (Ekōin) behind the bridge.

Unlike the even more compact and densely populated Kamagasaki in Osaka, which is more or less contiguous and unbroken by large roads, San'ya is divided by the Namidabashi intersection into four quadrants, giving the area a more diffuse and disjointed feel to it. To the east and west of the intersection runs Meiji Boulevard (Meiji-dōri, after the first post-Restoration emperor in whose name the modern Japanese state was formed), a major thoroughfare that circles the city. To the north and south runs Old Streetcar Boulevard (Kyū Toden-dōri), named after the trolley that used to run down the middle and connecting the Nikkō Highway to the Sumida River. A stretch of Old Streetcar Boulevard north of the intersection, still known by its nick-name "Street of Bones" (Kotsu-dōri), was lined in the Edo Period with the decapitated heads and shallow graves of some two hundred thousand criminals from the aforementioned execution ground.

The northern half of San'ya, lying in Arakawa Ward, has little to distinguish itself from other less affluent sections of Tokyo's "Low City." Perhaps the most notable landmark in its northwest quadrant is the large bronze statue of Jizō, the Buddhist guardian deity of children and the underprivileged, which stands on the execution ground site adjacent to Ekōin as a memorial to the thousands executed there; and in its northeast quadrant, the Shioiri switchyard—a vast, creaking, century-old expanse of rust, dilapidation, and occasional train movements—marked for eventual removal by city planners and abutting the property of Tokyo Gas and its three huge, hospital-green fuel tanks.

San'ya's center of gravity is located to the south of Namidabashi in Taitō Ward. More than three-quarters of the area's lodging houses are concentrated in these two quadrants, as well as several buildings and institutions to be found nowhere else in the city: the Mammoth (*Manmosu*), a three-story police box that accommodates up to fifty officers; the Tamahime Shokuan, a ward-administered hiring office where hundreds of men gather each morning in search of work arranged by the city and apply for unemployment compensation (*abure teate*) when they can get none; the Jōhoku ("north-of-the-castle") Welfare Center, a drab, four-story facility housing a hiring office, consultation rooms, recreation area, pawn shop, and a medical clinic that will treat those who can stay off alcohol, at least for the day;

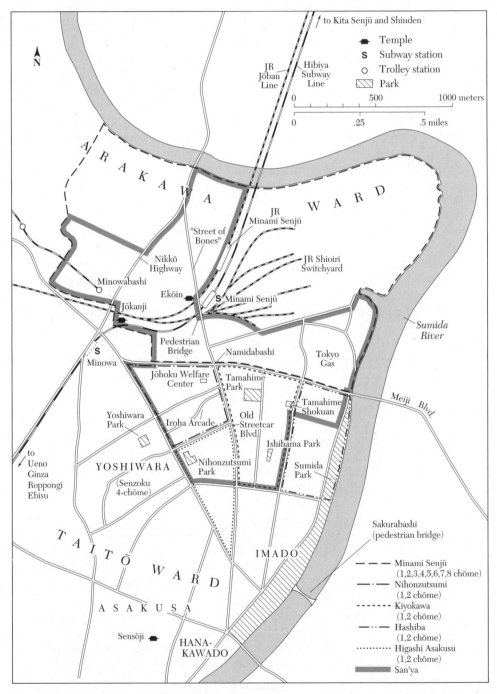

Map labels (reading within the figure):

to Kita Senjū and Shinden

Temple
S Subway station
○ Trolley station
Park

0   500   1000 meters
0   .25   .5 miles

N

JR
Jōban
Line

Hibiya
Subway
Line

A R A K A W A   W A R D

JR
Minami Senjū

"Street of
Bones"

JR Shioiri
Switchyard

Nikkō
Highway

Minowabashi

Ekōin

Jōkanji

S Minami Senjū

Sumida
River

Pedestrian
Bridge

Namidabashi

Tokyo
Gas

S
Minowa

Jōhoku Welfare
Center

Tamahime
Park

Meiji Blvd.

Yoshiwara
Park

Iroha Arcade

Old
Streetcar
Blvd

Tamahime
Shokuan

to
Ueno
Ginza
Roppongi
Ebisu

YOSHIWARA

(Senzoku
4-chōme)

Nihonzutsumi
Park

Ishihama Park

Sumida
Park

T A I T O   W A R D

I M A D O

Sakurabashi
(pedestrian bridge)

A S A K U S A

Sensōji

HANA-
KAWADO

Minami Senjū
(1,2,3,4,5,6,7,8 chōme)
Nihonzutsumi
(1,2 chōme)
Kiyokawa
(1,2 chōme)
Hashiba
(1,2 chōme)
Higashi Asakusu
(1,2 chōme)
San'ya

San'ya and environs

San'yūkai, a private clinic, staffed largely by volunteers, which treats the many men who cannot stay off even for the day or who want nothing to do with bureaucracies; two independent, local labor unions, one moderate (Santōrō) and the other more militant (Sōgidan), which periodically confront the bureaucracy, the police, the labor brokers, and the gangsters known as *yakuza* who control the area; the headquarters of a nationally known yakuza gang (Kanamachi Ikka), which was responsible for the slaying of two men connected with the militant labor union; Tokyo's seediest shopping arcade (the Iroha Kai or simply Iroha); a public park (Tamahime Kōen) with a caged playing field that is permanently under lock and key to prevent day laborers from occupying it; and finally, the doyagai itself, with prices for a bunk or room ranging (in the early 1990s) from seven hundred to twenty-seven hundred yen per night.

In San'ya as in other lower-class Tokyo neighborhoods, you will find the same rude dwellings and many of the same conveniences. It has its share of barbers and shoemakers, paint shops and automobile repair shops, coffee houses and minimarts—not to mention karaoke bars, *pachinko* (pinball) parlors, and mahjong dens. Yet you will also find two Denny's-like drive-in restaurants, replete with upholstered booths, carpets, and color-picture menus, standing practically opposite each other on Meiji Boulevard to the east of Namidabashi. Day laborers are rarely among the customers. The families, young couples, and businessmen who make up the clientele often come by car, sometimes from far away (and thus diners appear on both sides of the boulevard to catch traffic going in either direction); and they pay prices close to double the neighborhood average for set dinners, which are well beyond the means of the typical "Yama" man (which is what the San'ya day laborer calls himself, after the alternate reading of the first Chinese character in "San'ya"). The empty space between tables is truly vast by local standards and is an extravagance that is of course included in the price of a meal. Each group of customers here is isolated by this physical space in a way that is impossible and undesirable in an ordinary San'ya eatery. There are no cross-table exchanges of any sort. The diners serve beer and wine, but there is not a bottle of *shōchū* (distilled spirits) or *umeshu* (plum brandy) in sight. Franchises of well-known chains, they actually make it possible to stop over in San'ya without ever knowing you were there.

The typical San'ya dining spot is a far more modest affair: a stand-up bar—just a counter with a few stools—which may serve up hors d'oeuvres along with the alcohol; or the more substantial tavern, with tables and chairs (sometimes spilling out onto the street in warm weather) and serving a choice of entrees (*horumon-yaki* being a prominent item on the menus). No color-picture menus, however; and no food models in the windows, which appear in other sections of town. All entrees are written out by hand on pieces of paper or on slats of wood pegged to the walls. Not that all modern conveniences found in the rest of the city are lacking. Most taverns boast at least one color television set. Watching TV in San'ya is a revelation—a viewer cannot help comparing the immaculate attire of the studio newscasters, for example, with the day laborers' rough, soiled garb. Some of the taverns have karaoke bars where a patron can sing to a professionally recorded background of popular or folk music and see each song's lyrics and dramatization on the high-resolution laserdisc monitors that are the envy of the world.

During its peak years San'ya boasted some five hundred eating and drinking establishments—from restaurants to take-out shops, taverns to stand-up bars—not to mention fifty liquor stores, nearly all with vending machines installed outside. These numbers have diminished along with the population of day laborers, but they still speak to an obvious truth: the Yama man nearly always dines out. Another obvious truth is that, whether the men imbibe at Sekai, on the southwest corner of Namidabashi, or at Nodaya, just outside the Iroha Arcade's east end, or at Masumoto, on Asahi Street (to mention just three of the neighborhood's best-known stand-up bars), they do not do so to savor the decor, with the possible exception of Nodaya, where the cases of beer sometimes stacked nearly to the ceiling lead the eye to the tavern's pride: dark, massive beams hewn in the prewar style. Most stand-up bars have a publike atmosphere, where you used to be able to order *shōchū* by the half-glass if you were low on cash, and brown-bag your own morsels to go with the drinks. The bars are now stocked with an assortment of tinned fish and fruit as well as peanuts, pickled scallions, boiled eggs, and dried cuttlefish, among other items popular with men in the yoseba.

The neighborhood has a goodly number of both coin laundries—with their inevitable signs, "Absolutely, positively no washing of *jikatabi* (split-toed footwear) allowed"—and coin lockers, some of which charge by the month as well as by the day. Also to be found are the many small construction-firm offices that get their work from the big contractors. Most are legitimate operations, others little more than fronts for yakuza organizations. Then there are the yakuza haunts themselves, the most prominent being that of Kanamachi Ikka, the House of Kanamachi (a branch of Dai Nippon Kokusuikai [The Greater Japan Society of National Purity] and named after a section of Tokyo on the eastern extremity near Chiba Prefecture), located in a swanky, three-story brick and stucco structure just south of Meiji Boulevard in Kiyokawa, which is to say San'ya's southeast quadrant. It is hard to miss. The organization's name is prominently lettered in silver, alongside its gold coat of arms, over the entranceway. This publicity is not at all atypical; yakuza operations are far more openly conducted than, say, those of the Mob in the United States. The passerby who chances to get a glimpse through the door will see a row of black leather sofas where some of the members are manning the telephones. The middle floor has a nondescript appearance, at least from the outside; but the top floor is done in the penthouse style with a bubble roof. The windows on the first two floors are glazed and barred.

Perhaps more telling is what cannot be found in San'ya: no commercial banks (and only a couple of credit-union–type institutions [shinyō kumiai and shinyō kinko] that make small loans to local businesses), no high schools or institutions of higher learning, no theaters, no hospitals. As noted above, San'ya has two medical clinics, one public and one private, which tend to the men's simpler ailments, but the nearest hospital lies a mile away across the Sumida River. The last cinemas and stage theaters went out of business in the 1960s. Although cash is plentiful in this neighborhood, because every day is payday, frugality is not a virtue among most day laborers, and gambling soaks up much of the income. Some day laborers deposit their money in the Jōhoku Welfare Center credit union, which reportedly held a total of ¥400 million in savings accounts in 1990. Unlike other financial institutions, it restricts the amount that can be withdrawn on any given day. A bureaucrat working for the San'ya Countermeasures Bureau (San'ya Taisaku Shitsu), a Tokyo Metropolitan Government agency established in 1968 to keep tabs on the neighborhood, told me that one credit-union member had ¥20 million (approx. $200,000 at the current exchange rate) in his account—a tidy sum for any citizen. "You see, it is possible to save there if you put your mind to it," he assured me. True enough; but such exceptions no doubt prove the rule.

Even more surprising, however, is that although San'ya has many drinking spots, it has not a single hostess bar, night club, or cabaret. Nor are there any "love hotels" of the kind seen clustered around certain train stations in other parts of the city. On the surface, at least, San'ya proper is not just a "cultureless" (in the mainstream sense of the word) but a sexless town. Typically without spouse or female companionship of any kind, the Yama man is on his own here, unless he is inclined toward same-sex relationships; yet there are no gay bars of the sort that dot certain areas of Shinjuku. And just because Yoshiwara (the former licensed quarter and current bathhouse district) lies but a short walk down the street does not mean that the average Yama man's sexual (to say nothing of his emotional) needs are being met. Yet it would be hasty to conclude that women play no part in this neighborhood; indeed, you get the sense that its dynamic is formed by their very absence. In many an alcohol-laden tale of a man's woes in the yoseba, you can hear between the lines a complementary tale of the strength, hope,

The San'ya doyagai

Legend:
- ∵ Pachinko parlor
- ♨ Public bath
- 🍶 Eatery
- 🍶 Drinking spot
- ⛩ Shrine

0 — 100 m
0 — 300 ft

N

MEIJI BLVD.

OLD STREETCAR BLVD.

ASAHI STREET

Namidabashi (intersection)

Tokyo Gas

NTT Tower

Santōrō H.Q.

Parcel Post Distribution Center

Tamahime Shokuan

Public Apts.

Taitō Ward Annex

Masumoto

Tamahime Park

WC

Caged Area

Tamahime Shrine

Kanamachi Ikka H.Q.

San'yukai

Hifumi

Tatsumi

Hōrai Middle School

Hōju Inari Shrine

Palace House

Sekai

Maria

Iseya

Mammoth Box

Yamagataya

Sōgidan H.Q.

Jōhoku Welfare Center

Mitoya

Nodaya

Makotoya

Takara

San'ya Workers' Hall

Sen'nari

Jōhoku Credit Union

Tanaka Elementary School

or deep disappointment of a woman back home—a wife struggling to manage the family in her husband's absence, a mother praying in vain for her son's triumphal return, a daughter fearing her father's occupation will spoil her chances at marriage—and of the emotional burden that these expectations and disappointments place on the man.

That most ubiquitous entertainment spot, the *pachinko* parlor, is well represented, as might be expected, as is the liquor store and its offspring, the liquor vending machine, which offers beer, saké, *umeshu*, and other spirits to anyone eighteen hours a day. (Machines on the street have automatic timers that shut them down from eleven at night until five in the morning.) Ten such machines line one corner of the Namidabashi intersection alone outside Sekai. Other amusements, such as off-track betting, have a more streetwise feel. Tokyo has several designated centers for officially sanctioned gambling (such as Asakusa and Kōrakuen, near Suidōbashi); bets placed elsewhere are illegal. Illegality, however, is hardly a concern of the gangsters who control the action in San'ya. A common sight on one tiny intersection in the Kiyokawa doyagai is that of a local gang member walking down the street from his headquarters sporting a fistful of ten-thousand-yen bills—the payoff for that session's betting. Men also bet on the races at one of the tiny sushi stalls closer to the main drag. The police do not seem to mind; in fact, the police are nowhere in sight. Although based a mere stone's throw away (in the Mammoth box) on the western edge of Kiyokawa, they rarely venture into the back streets. This is strictly gangster turf.

Not that the presence of gangsters necessarily means danger. On the contrary, the House of Kanamachi, which achieved ascendance in the early 1980s, brings a certain order to the area. It and the other gangs also bring the area its livelihood, having as they do virtually total control over how the day laborer both earns and spends his money. Working as labor brokers (*tehaishi*), yakuza and those connected with yakuza offer the Yama man both jobs for the day and provision for jobless days, the latter through unemployment-insurance stamps sold on the black market. (These are procured through unethical corporations, which, unlike individuals, are entitled to buy them direct, and which net the gangsters an income in the tens of millions of yen per month.) Working as entrepreneurs, they offer him a variety of entertainments such as gambling on San'ya street corners and prostitution in nearby Yoshiwara—and thus keep him occupied after hours. Money changes hands rapidly here, yet rarely leaves the neighborhood.

Kanamachi Ikka is by no means the only gang in San'ya (or in Yoshiwara, which is far too lucrative a quarter for any single group to monopolize), only the most prominent. Branches of several regional and national syndicates, including the Nihon Gijintō, with which the late Kodama Yoshio (a former

Class-A war criminal implicated in the 1970s Lockheed scandal) was affiliated and which formerly dominated San'ya into the 1970s, the Sumiyoshi Rengō, the Iijima Ikka Rengō, and the enormous Yamaguchi-gumi are also here, with representatives and subsidiary groups doing their bidding. The House of Kanamachi has its own subsidiary groups, including the Kinryūkai and Nishido-gumi. The latter spearheaded the clash with Sōgidan, the more militant San'ya labor union.

The yoseba labor unions' principal mission has been to improve working conditions, particularly at the *hanba,* which are notoriously dismal. (The worst *hanba* are referred to as *takobeya,* which are more like labor camps than construction sites.) Because these conditions are governed to a large extent by gangsters and others associated with the gangs, the unions must in effect confront the yakuza, whose control of the laborers' lives in such important areas as job procurement and leisure activity is virtually complete. So, too, they have occasional run-ins with the police, who constantly monitor union activities and who generally turn a blind eye to the yakuza so long as no violence breaks out. At times the unions' efforts have been directed against each other.

The history of union activity in San'ya and other yoseba is too complex to review here in much detail. Suffice it to say that the two currently active unions have antecedents in the student movement going back more than two decades, in particular to the nationwide demonstrations against the 1970 United States–Japan Security Treaty extension and the regional demonstrations against the building of Tokyo International Airport in Narita before it opened, incomplete and far behind schedule, in 1978.

Several day-laborer activists, Kaji Daisuke being the most conspicuous, attracted attention from the early 1960s. The leaders of the most prominent 1970s activist group, the Akushitsu Gyōsha Tsuihō Genba Tōsō Iinkai (Work Site Struggle Committee against Corrupt Labor Bosses; abbrev. Gentōi), had all met their demise by the end of the decade: one, Suzuki Kunio, died in jail under mysterious circumstances; another, Funamoto Shūji, set fire to himself at an Okinawan base to protest the crown prince's (which is to say, current emperor's) visit to an international exposition; and a third, Isoe Yōichi, was imprisoned for life for stabbing to death a policeman in front of the Mammoth box. The vacuum was eventually filled by the present groups: Santōrō (1977) and Sōgidan (1981).

Sōgidan (more formally, San'ya Sōgidan) is part of a nationwide organization called Hiyatoi Zenkyō (the abbreviation for Zenkoku Hiyatoi Rōdō Kumiai Kyōgikai [National Council of Day Labor Unions]), which has chapters in Yokohama, Nagoya, Osaka, and Fukuoka as well as Tokyo. It has engaged in the more aggressive campaign against yakuza intimidation and extortion, but not without a price. Two men connected with the union became victims of yakuza-hired assassins. Both murders were committed in reaction to a film (*San'ya: Yararetara yarikaese,* the subtitle meaning "Eye for an eye") produced by Sōgidan about the yoseba and yakuza involvement in day laborers' lives. Satō Mitsuo, a Sōgidan sympathizer, wrote the film's script and had begun shooting when he was stabbed to death in late 1984; Yamaoka Kyōichi, a union officer, carried on Satō's work but was himself gunned down in early 1986. The first killing was a deliberate attempt to disrupt production; the second, which occurred after the film's completion in December 1985, can be described only as a desperate act of revenge. Assassinations of this sort, committed by proxy, are not always treated as the serious crimes they are, thanks to legal loopholes. Satō's killer, hired by Kanamachi Ikka, is reported to have turned himself in to the police immediately after the deed and confessed to having done away with someone named other than Satō—which is to say that he admitted to the crime of murder, but of the wrong person. He was thus able to get off the hook for first-degree homicide and receive a lighter sentence.

Be that as it may, there was a general realization at this point that things had gone too far, and no major clashes have occurred since. But as late as 1990 the riot police were present nearly every morning to monitor the yoseba and the movements of Sōgidan during its early-morning demonstrations, making sure that members did not cross the street from Nihonzutsumi, where it has its headquarters, into Kiyokawa, the home of Kanamachi Ikka. What run-ins did occur typically resulted in the arrest of Sōgidan members but no gangsters. The film in question was released and distributed despite these various setbacks, and it continues to be shown occasionally in Tokyo and around the country.

Sōgidan's frequent early-morning marches and other activities are regarded by permanent local residents, who simply wish for more peace and quiet, as counterproductive, and by the police themselves as reprehensible. The police maintain a policy of neutrality in the interest of protecting both sides—the unions and the gangsters—but it is clear that they are not merely straddling the fence. The fact that the situation in San'ya is not unique but part of a nationwide pattern was demonstrated, if it was not before, in October 1990, when the officer in charge of yakuza surveillance in Kamagasaki was found to be on the take of gangsters, sparking violent, collective outrage on the part of day laborers there.

Santōrō (more formally, San'ya Tōitsu Rōdō Kumiai), while equally committed to social reform, has lately devoted more energy to doing battle with local ward-assembly incumbents than with gangsters. One of its officers campaigned twice for office as an independent in the 1980s. He lost both times, racking up at best less than a third of the votes needed for election, and has withdrawn from future candidacy because of poor health. In the spring of 1991 another officer ran in his place for the same ward-assembly seat, this time with the backing of a national party, the Shakai Minshu Rengō (abbrev. Shaminren). Because most day laborers, who are the union's natural constituency, do not establish residency with the ward and therefore cannot vote, Santōrō has looked to the wider community for support. The second officer ran on a platform calling for more public housing and increased social services, particularly for single residents and the aged, lighter taxation for small residences in the face of Tokyo's skyrocketing land prices, and expanded environmental protection. He garnered over nine hundred votes, or roughly two hundred shy of the minimum needed for election. The union regards this figure as a major step forward and is preparing vigorously for the next campaign.

Two San'ya Landmarks

Like any Tokyo neighborhood, San'ya has its shopping center and its park. Both are unique, and their like is not found in any other section of the city. The Iroha ("A-B-C") is a roofed arcade running nearly a quarter mile from the western edge of Nihonzutsumi northeast into to the heart of San'ya just shy of Old Streetcar Boulevard. It competes with two other commercial areas, the Asahi Shōtengai, a shop-lined street (with metal awnings on the shop fronts but no roof) located a five-minute walk to the southeast; and Minowa Joyful (near Minowabashi Station), a venerable but well-kept arcade located a fifteen-minute walk to the northwest. Unlike Asahi Street, the Iroha Arcade is not open to automobile traffic, and unlike the Minowa Arcade and most Tokyo shopping centers, it is not fed by any commuter train (in the case of the latter, Tokyo's last trolley line). It is patronized by day laborer and permanent resident alike, as well as by shoppers from farther afield.

The Iroha is well populated by Yama men but can hardly be said to be overrun by them, with the exception of the eastern-most stretch, which spills out into the street leading to Old Streetcar Boulevard—a small open area lined with liquor store, tavern, and several used-clothing shops that do business only in the morning, when day laborers are about in large numbers. Day and night small children can be seen romping about the arcade's west end, which is bisected down the middle by a long row of bicycles—the patrons' parking lot. Housewives chat animatedly. Businessmen run errands. Merchants call out their wares. For all the grime, the variety of shops is impressive. In addition to a modest supermarket there are meat, fish, and vegetable markets, along with bakeries, tea shops, and shops specializing in prepared foods; stores selling furniture, appliances, electrical goods, dry goods, hardware, ceramic ware, haberdashery, shoes, men's and women's clothes; and, of course, the usual complement of dry cleaners, stationery stores, bookstores, toy stores, tobacconists, beauty salons, photo studios, pharmacies, and flower shops.

The arcade thus caters to the general population and not to the day laborer. The latter's needs are better served by the businesses, most of them open only in the morning, that line the south side of Meiji Boulevard east of Namidabashi. Here the Yama man can find all the gear necessary for his work, including *shichibu* (flared knickers), *jikatabi*, boots, socks (both regular fit and fit for the split-toed *jikatabi*), gloves, hats, towels in all colors and tools of all sorts, belts, soap, tote bags, and certain provisions—hard-boiled eggs and fruit being the most popular. The fruit is served in single portions and is expensive (especially larger fruit, like melon, which must be cut up); it sells anyway because few men have a place to store food.

Many homeless Yama men live in the arcade, thanks to a corrugated plastic roof that protects the street below. The men seek cover here, as well as beneath the metal awnings along Asahi Street, the concrete eaves of the Tamahime Shokuan, and the few trees dotting the local parks and shrine grounds. Once in a while you will find someone sleeping right on the street pavement. Late one night I witnessed a man comfortably bedded down on a thin mattress and pillow in the middle of a narrow street that runs alongside the Palace House (San'ya's largest and best-known lodging facility) into Old Streetcar Boulevard, blocking the path of an expensive-looking, late-model car that was inching its way around him. (There was a time when drivers had to be wary of men who were looking to get hit—lightly, of course—by a car and then demand hefty compensation, preferably on the spot.) This man, however, seemed far too well organized to be thought of as a mere drunk. It is the thoroughly inebriated who are in the most danger of bodily harm, for they can fall prey to criminals known as *mogaki*, who rob sleeping men on the street or in the parks after jabbing their feet or other bare-skinned areas with sharp objects or lit cigarettes to determine whether they are too intoxicated to resist.

The Iroha is not as attractive a refuge for the homeless as it might first appear. The roof can be winched open, and often is, section by section, by merchants who would rather let the rain or cold air in at night during the monsoon or winter season than have men sully their store fronts. Still, it is a place where men like to gather. As the evening progresses and the crowds of shoppers thin out, men form circles to drink, sleep, and chat—especially to chat, among themselves and to anyone who will lend an ear.

Hailed myself innumerable times over the months during my walks through the arcade, I finally succumb one chilly fall evening and join a group of four men. The man who first beckoned me immediately offers his hand. Its thick, leathery skin bespeaks years of toil. The mood is friendly and the talk is of baseball. The Yomiuri Giants are playing, but no one can determine which side is ahead. "I can't keep track of the score—I'm too damned drunk," one of them remarks. I fill them in as best I can from what I have seen earlier at a nearby tavern on the TV. One man hands me his bottle of potato *shōchū.* Another passes me his pint-sized can of beer. Still another offers me a cigarette.

I have been warned more than once by people familiar with San'ya about the high incidence of tuberculosis in the area. And the danger of contracting a contagious disease, while probably exaggerated, is certainly real. Yet these men are kind enough to share, and I decide that this sort of sharing is worth the risk. I am not so sure that I would decide the same way now, for one of those who warned me, an employee in the Welfare Center, has since come down with a mild case of the disease.

Along with Iroha Arcade, Tamahime Park is at the center of things in San'ya. A forbidding rectangle about the size of a soccer field, the park is a gathering place for the Yama man, day or night. No one will disturb his sleep here, unless it be the occasional *mogaki.* The park's only amenities are a few short benches and two toilets, both usually in miserable condition. Often someone sleeps in the larger toilet on the park's north side, so that it is difficult to negotiate the urinals. The stalls are usually too filthy to want to negotiate at all. This is important information: in San'ya, it is useful to know the whereabouts of the best facilities for excretion. The larger taverns can be accommodating in the evenings. The preferred places are the coffee shops, for anyone sober enough to be let in. Some people of course do not worry about the niceties of location. Men urinating in the street, once a frequent practice throughout the city but discouraged in recent decades, is still a common sight in San'ya, day or night. The sight of a Yama man defecating in the street is also not that uncommon. I remember in particular a man squatting on the asphalt near Tamahime Park and catching his feces with a practiced hand on a sheet of folded newspaper. He was within sight of the toilet.

The park's half-dozen benches are a study in compromise, from the bureaucratic point of view at any rate, being large enough to accommodate the tired soul that would sit and rest for a few minutes but far too small to hold the exhausted body that would lie down and sleep—or so the designers no doubt thought. Comprising two metal slats each just three feet long and three inches wide and thus making for a seat barely half a foot deep, the bench would seem entirely inadequate as a piece of sleeping furniture; yet it does not daunt the Yama man. He can be found in a variety of postures, legs draped limply over the back of the bench or dragging on the ground like laundered clothes hanging on a low line.

Since 1977 Tamahime's most distinguishing feature has been the chain-link and wire-mesh cage that occupies more than half the park's total surface—a concession to local, and not-so-local, demands for a playing area immune to the intrusions of idle day laborers. It is used primarily for soft-ball games among boys from the middle school just across the street, and for "gateball" (croquet) by groups of elderly citizens living in the area. The ward official who informed me that the caged playing field became a popu-lar item in the 1970s and was to be found in many city parks had to admit that no other such facility was kept under constant lock and key, with reservations required well in advance. The space where a Yama man can actually rest in the park, therefore, has been severely curtailed for close to two decades. Most of the park has been paved over, and little dirt ground is still available. Would-be nappers must contend with dense shrubbery, on the north side, or rock piles, in the southeast corner. In either place you are likely to find several men camped out for the day or night, and sometimes for much longer. When space gets scarce, the turf battles begin. Once I encountered a whole village of tarpaulins and tents on the north side oc-cupied by men who paid their dues to an ex-con working his territory like a yakuza boss.

I have spent many an hour in Tamahime Park, often to eat, sometimes simply to rest. At various times I have been scowled at, smiled at, sere-naded, and occasionally fed. Munching on a rice-ball lunch one December afternoon in 1989, I enjoy the strains of a harmonica that is being passed around like a reefer among perhaps half a dozen men a few yards away. Their gig is eventually drowned out by a boom box, replete with CD player, lugged in by a solitary bloke who is entirely insensitive to the joys of live music. As I leave the park through the shrubbery on the north side, I make my way past several men napping for the afternoon. One man is slapping a fellow lounger vigorously about the head and shoulders. There may well be a reason for this expression of violence, but I am not privy to it.

Three or four months later I encounter a group of six, two of them women, camped out near the rock pile beneath a makeshift tent. I compli-ment the guitar playing of one of the men, whose music makes him obliv-ious, at least for the moment, to the elements. Another man ("M") intro-duces himself and one of the women, whom he identifies as his wife. They are here for the long haul: the ground beneath the tarpaulin is decked out in straw mats and futon, atop of which rests a propane gas burner and a ker-osene stove, an assortment of utensils with the foodstuffs to go with them, plus several musical instruments. A third man, a soft-spoken fellow with the fat knuckles of a karate expert, announces to me that the topic of discussion is prison, since one among them has just been released. They sit in a semicircle around a fourth man, the *oyabun* or "boss," who is reclining on his side, his left foot and leg badly burned up to the knee and wrapped in towels that are oozing with pus. The burn is two weeks old and he has yet to see a doctor. The kerosene stove fell on his leg while he was asleep. The soft-spoken man asks me for a contribution for bandages. I donate 500 yen plus an extra hundred—a sort of commission he requests by the bye. This is the largest donation I am to make on the street in all my visits to San'ya.

Two months after this incident I run into the "boss," whose leg has improved considerably, on Old Streetcar Boulevard. He is accompanied by M-san and his "wife." They are trying to flag down a cab back to M-san's apartment in Mukōjima across the river in Sumida Ward, where the "boss" occupies a three-mat room (six by nine feet; one mat is about three by six). M-san tells me he is also looking after another man who occupies a separate three-mat room in his apartment. While he is talking I take a closer look at his "wife," a well-preserved, long-haired woman in her forties wearing a tight-fitting sweater and stacked heels. I realize that I had seen her earlier that very day serving saké to a group of men sitting in a lazy circle just outside the east entrance of Iroha Arcade.

The Morning Labor Market

San'ya's most characteristic feature and its true center is not visible at all to the daytime observer: the yoseba itself, which is to say the actual gathering of workers offering their agility and muscle for a daily wage on or near Old Streetcar Boulevard just south of Namidabashi. Every morning of the year between the hours of five (or even earlier) and seven, including weekends and most holidays, several hundred to a thousand men stand about the boulevard hoping to get the nod from one of the area's several dozen—perhaps as many as a hundred—*tehaishi* (labor brokers), many of whom sport cellular phones and all of whom are connected, either directly or indirectly, with the yakuza—if not Kanamachi on the Kiyokawa side, then with Gijintō, Sumiyoshi Rengō, or some other group on the Nihonzutsumi side. The unsuspecting foreman who recruits on his own without first paying his respects (and his dues) to the *tehaishi* in charge of the territory will have a date with some bouncers, if he is lucky, or be the object of continual extortion, if he is not.

It being well before rush hour, the men pay little heed to the occasional car or truck that makes its way tentatively down the four-lane boulevard.

Many are engaged in animated conversation, for the yoseba is a sort of open-air club, where men can exchange information and opinions about the biggest construction projects going, the particularly miserable *hanba*, the hottest racing ticket, or the latest union activities. Some would warn you to be careful of what you say or whom you talk to; plainclothesmen dressed as day laborers do frequent the yoseba. There is no question that San'ya attracts the attention of the authorities. All movements are closely monitored by police officers at the Mammoth box, who are in turn supported on occasion by heavily armed riot units known as *kidōtai.*

The men who appear on the street on any given day represent only a small fraction of San'ya's total labor supply, which is estimated to be as high as nine or ten thousand. (This figure includes workers living outside the area who commute each morning to the yoseba.) Some men get work directly through their employers or from contacts other than the *tehaishi* on the street. Many jobs last several days, moreover, and other jobs take workers away from San'ya entirely, to work sites outside the city. Still other jobs can be had through want ads in the sports papers. Only a few men—the truly able-bodied or the truly dedicated—work every day, it should be added; many are too frail or too old to cope more than two or three workdays a week. Finally, there are almost never enough jobs to go around, and some men will not bother to present themselves on obviously slow days.

There is no little specialization among workers. Groups of men gravitate to various corners on or near the boulevard according to their skills: on one corner, the *tobi shoku*, men who put up scaffolding on buildings and who are generally the most colorfully dressed (as well as the highest paid); on other corners, masons, electricians, carpenters, and clean-up specialists; and finally the common, unskilled laborer sprinkled throughout. Specialization is tied to the business cycle, however. When work is scarce, skilled workers vie with common laborers for any job available.

Those who have work for the day board the minivans provided for them or take the train or subway to the *genba*, or work site. In the early 1990s, the daily wage (*dezura* in the yoseba argot) ranged from roughly fourteen thousand to twenty-five thousand yen and sometimes much higher, depending on the type of work. (Jobs like clean-up and digging paid at the lower end of the scale; plastering and scaffolding at the higher.) The actual wage allotted by the contractor supplying the job would always be higher, but the middleman inevitably took his cut. The practice of extracting a "commission" (*pinhane*) is illegal, but it is deeply entrenched—the grease that makes the whole system work. The San'ya-based day laborer may work at a job contracted out by a major firm, but he receives no job-related benefits. And because a great many men prefer to conceal their identity (sometimes to evade loan officers or parole officers, but primarily to relieve their families

Morning yoseba, from the front of the Palace House.

of any responsibility for them) and therefore have not established residency, they are ineligible for the national health-insurance program.

After the Oil Shock of 1973–74, when Japan entered a period of deep recession, the Tokyo Metropolitan Government instituted a system of "white cards" (*shiro techō*), which made it possible for men living in the yoseba to receive a kind of unemployment benefit. Until 1988, a man did not have to register with the ward to be eligible, only show that he was lodging in a doya. Now he must register. Someone who has worked a minimum of twenty-eight days in a two-calendar-month period is eligible for compensation, which is usually sixty-two hundred yen per day for thirteen days in a month. (An additional day of compensation is available for every four more days worked up to seventeen days.) To collect, a person turns in the card in the morning to the bureaucrats at the Tamahime Shokuan, the employment office run by Taitō Ward in Kiyokawa east of Tamahime Park, then lines up to receive cash during distribution hours (one to two-thirty) that same afternoon. Eligibility is demonstrated by the proper number of unemployment-insurance stamps (provided by employers), one for each day worked, affixed on the card.

Many do not work for the required number of days, however, because of lack of jobs or bad weather or ill health, and the ward has generally looked the other way when workers buy stamps on the black market to fill their cards. Gangsters control the market and make a nifty profit off the stamps (face value: ¥146), which sell at from six or seven hundred to upward of a thousand yen apiece, depending on demand. This income is added to profits made from other businesses designed to separate workers from their money as soon as they make it.

Failing to get work off the street, workers can try their luck on regular business days at two public agencies. The San'ya Labor Center, which recruits from six-thirty in the morning, is part of the Jōhoku Welfare Center and run by the Tokyo Metropolitan Government, and thus open to any Tokyo resident, regardless of address. The Tamahime Shokuan, which begins operations at six forty-five, is open to anyone registered with Taitō Ward, in which the Kiyokawa/Nihonzutsumi doyagai is located. (Day laborers living in Minami Senjū—in Arakawa Ward—may also register with the Tamahime Shokuan. Otherwise, they use the Senjū Kawara-chō Shokuan, located in Adachi Ward about a mile north of Namidabashi.)

Although these two agencies offer minimal *tehaishi* involvement (in the case of the Shokuan, none at all), and complaints about work can be forwarded directly to the city administration, they generate less than a quarter of the area's jobs. Wages are a good deal lower than what can be made off the street, a seemingly odd fact when you consider that the *tehaishi* are unable to take their cut (20 or 30 percent is not uncommon). The reason is that both agencies, in order to hire more people, accept jobs paying less money. For example, a construction firm offering what it would normally pay for two laborers may be asked to take on three or even four people for the same amount. The firm readily agrees, since it cannot be sure of the quality of manpower it is getting. The *tehaishi* hiring off the street may be costly, but they also weed out less able men. They have refusal rights over men selected by the Welfare Center and can therefore exercise some quality control, even though they are not involved directly in the hiring. They are shut out completely from the Shokuan, however, and the firms get their laborers without any sort of screening—which means the lowest pay rates of all.

The Welfare Center, a bureaucratic affair from top to bottom, is a forbidding-looking structure located just north of the Iroha Arcade in Nihonzutsumi. The fence and wall skirting it streetside are blackened with soot from countless bonfires set by men sleeping out to keep themselves warm. The Tamahime Shokuan, meanwhile, occupies the ground floor of a grim, early 1960s-vintage apartment building just north of the Asahi Street shopping district's east end, one of three apartments bunched together in the same block. These shabby affairs are home to families who have chosen to endure life in San'ya because of the lower rents until they have saved enough money for a down payment on a house elsewhere in the city. Unlike apartment dwellers in Kotobuki-chō, the yoseba in Yokohama, those living in San'ya have little incentive to remain in the neighborhood. The apartment complex, flanked on the north by the Parcel Post Distribution Center, is dwarfed by the massive NTT (Nippon Telephone and Telegraph) telecommunications building, located just to the west and surrounded on all sides by a high steel fence. The latter is built like a fortress, and atop it the vermilion-and-white control tower, an imposing pillar of antenna and satellite dishes (also used, it is rumored, by the Self Defense Forces and U.S. military), is visible from miles away. As with the Welfare Center, the wall opposite the Shokuan is blackened with soot from bonfires and cluttered with graffiti, typically epithets directed against Kanamachi Ikka.

Only when the men have gotten work for the day, whether off the streets or from one of the public employment agencies, do they go about other business: slurping down a bowl of *suiton* (flour dumplings in a broth), *tonjiru* (pork-flavored stew), or curried rice at one of the neighborhood's stand-up eateries; sorting through work clothes, new and used, sold at tiny stalls that are open along with the eateries for a few hours each morning; or surveying the lively flea market in Kiyokawa.

Located on the street that separates the neighborhood's only middle school from Tamahime Park and open from five to eight in the morning, the flea market is one of the area's best-known sights. Known to locals as the "morning market," it is sometimes dubbed the San'ya Thieves' Market. A good many of the items sold here are used, and no doubt a substantial number are fenced. Although nowhere near as large or as complete as the one in Kamagasaki, it is still worth a look. And that is just what many of the men do—come and browse. Window shopping, seemingly a lost art in other parts of the country (and in other parts of the world where Japanese customers have earned a bad name for themselves buying up expensive items sight-unseen), is performed with a practiced eye worthy of emulation. Here you will find, spread out on mats and tarps, nearly everything you might ever want or need in San'ya: alarm clocks, amulets, ashtrays, belts, bicycle pumps, blazers, blood-pressure kits, new and used boom boxes, used cameras, cassette tapes and CDs of everything from popular songs to *rakugo* (comic-monologue) recordings, cigarettes (by the pack or carton) and lighters, coat hangers, coffeepots and teakettles, old coins and coin purses, costume jewelry, dish sets, dolls, eyeglasses with both dark and prescription lenses, electric fans and electronic calculators, fishing gear, gas burners, *go, shōgi,* and other board-game sets, golf clubs and bags, hair dryers, handkerchiefs and *haramaki* (waistbands worn inside or outside the shirt), antique hibachis, ivory trinkets, *jikatabi* and socks to match (both split-toed and five-toed), *jinbei* and other traditional casual wear, *kan-pōyaku* (traditional Chinese herbal medicine), karaoke sets, knives and knife sharpeners (some deeply hollowed with use), leather goods, mirrors of all shapes and sizes, nude photo books, nuts and bolts, pendants, playing cards, a wide variety of pots and pans, a few quilts and blankets, rice cookers and old LP records, safety razors and safety belts, scissors and shavers, shoes and slippers, stuffed animals, suitcases, countless tools ranging from ratchets and planes to drills and power saws, transistor radios and televisions in all sizes, T-shirts and undershirts, not to mention a wide selection of work shirts and pants, umbrellas, videocassette tapes (most of them featuring soft porn), wallets, wrist watches, and, last (the list has hardly been exhausted) but not least, tickets to the public bath, normally costing (in 1991) ¥330 but selling for ¥200, the discount made possible because of recyling by senior citizens, who are allotted a certain number of free tickets every month.

Armed with any of these goods or simply having spent a few minutes sorting through them, the Yama man, invigorated by the sheer plenitude in his own back yard, is now ready to face the new day.

Edo, Tokyo, San'ya

San'ya's history is as new as the rise of Tokyo from the ashes of World War II and as old as the development of Edo, the shogunal capital that was to become Tokyo, into one of the world's major cities by the eighteenth century. In either case it has not been a happy one. The misery of surviving at or below subsistence level, the anger at having to live in a socially stigmatized quarter, and the disgruntled self-sufficiency necessitated by enforced isolation from the rest of society have left their mark on the area's residents. All of which is to say that San'ya's location did not come about by accident. To understand the area's history is to become aware not only of why Tokyo's major day-laborer population eventually settled where it did, but also of why so many Japanese feel compelled to conceal their nation's cultural and ethnic diversity.

The city of Edo, which the first Tokugawa shogun Ieyasu occupied in 1590, more than a decade before consolidating his rule over the entire country, was in the beginning little more than a small fishing village at the head of what is now called Tokyo Bay. Ieyasu fortified a castle where the Imperial Palace now stands, on a rise to the west of an inlet feeding the bay, and had his retainers and other feudal lords or daimyo settle on the hilly piedmont nearby: the Yamanote or "High City." For the merchants and artisans who would serve the samurai class he drained the marshy flatlands to the east: the Shitamachi or "Low City." The samurai occupied spacious estates generally to the west of the castle. The service classes, meanwhile, were crowded into tiny dwellings primarily in the city's much smaller eastern half. Only the peasants—the fourth group in this rigid Neo-Confucian caste system—lived outside the city. Two other groups, the outcastes (eta) and "nonpersons" (hinin), also lived in the city and formed an integral part of the economy. The outcastes, for example, had a monopoly on such trades as leather, used in making armor, and were thus indispensable to the samurai class. "Nonpersons" included such groups as prostitutes, actors, street entertainers, and executioners—all essential in their way to feudal society.

Despite their importance, the "nonpersons" and outcastes were social pariahs, and some were forcibly uprooted over the years as the city expanded and the execution grounds (near which a good many lived) were moved farther and farther to the periphery. When Ieyasu first occupied Edo, the estate of Danzaemon, hereditary leader of the eta, was relocated from Nihombashi to Torigoe, a mile or so north of Yoshiwara, Edo's principal licensed quarter. The subject over the centuries of countless woodblock prints, the original Yoshiwara was centrally located near the present-day Ningyō-chō—entirely too centrally, the Tokugawa regime (1603–1868) finally decided, from the standpoint of the samurai class's moral health. In 1657, the year of the Great Fire that leveled half of Edo, the quarter was moved to a section of thinly populated marshland a good half-day's journey on foot northeast from the castle, beyond Asakusa, a remote village with an ancient temple, and just shy of the Kozukappara execution ground (which had itself been relocated from central Edo only a few years earlier). Rice paddies were drained with the help of outcaste labor, brothels erected, a wall was thrown up around the entire quarter, and the area renamed Shin-Yoshiwara (New Yoshiwara). Ironically, the government edict had the effect of merely adding to the pleasure-seekers' exercise regimen (not to mention the wallets of boatmen who plied the Sumida River and up the San'ya Canal from Imado and deposited their passengers at Shin-Yoshiwara), and of turning Asakusa, which was on the overland route, into a bustling attraction with its hawkers, street entertainers, and unlicensed prostitutes. The Danzaemon estate, meanwhile, had been moved again in 1645 right onto the San'ya Canal (no longer extant) north of Asakusa.

The northeast is an unlucky direction in Chinese geomancy, and a temple or temples typically guarded a city against demons, evil spirits, and other unwelcome visitors prone to intrude from that quarter. Just as the great temple complex atop Mount Hiei protected the city of Kyoto, Kan'eiji in Ueno protected Edo. It needed a great deal of assistance, however, as the demons (most prominently the ghost of Taira no Masakado, the tenth-century Kantō rebel and would-be emperor) could cut a wide swath from the northeast. Many shrines and temples were either built within this space or rehabilitated to defend against or neutralize the intrusions. Asakusa was part of this space.

Although its temple, Sensōji, was the principal attraction, Asakusa was more than just a religious center. People went on pilgrimages bent as much on making merry as they were on expressing piety. Traffic to Asakusa increased considerably when Yoshiwara was moved to its new location, and soon markets, bazaars, teahouses, and later theaters sprang up near the temple.

Tokyo has changed enormously since this configuration of temple, entertainment zone, licensed quarter, and outcaste ghetto was first established in Asakusa some three centuries ago; yet traces of the configuration survive. Sensōji remains a mecca for worshipers, and the surrounding amusement center, while it no longer thrives, remains the premier location in Tokyo for seedy entertainments. Yoshiwara, although no longer a licensed quarter, is home to more than one hundred gaudy bathhouses (known as soaplands [sōpurando]) where sex can be had for a price. Hanakawado and Imado, located near the Sumida River just to the east and north of Asakusa, are the principal centers of Tokyo's shoe-making industry. Descendants of the outcastes still live in this area, and the neighborhoods have a run-down look.

With the Imado buraku just to the south and the Yoshiwara brothels just to the west, not to mention other buraku and Korean ghettos nearby, San'ya was one of the least desirable addresses in the city, although not as noto-

Construction in Tokyo: road being paved (Asakusa).

rious as what Yokoyama Gennosuke, at the turn of the century, called Tokyo's "three great slums" (Yotsuya Samegahashi, Shitaya Mannen-chō, Shiba Shin-Ami-chō) in his remarkable portrait of Japan's lower classes, *Nihon no kasō shakai* (1899). Nor was San'ya the city's largest yoseba earlier in this century. That distinction went to Tomikawa-chō, an area near the present Takabashi yoseba in what is now Kōtō Ward, until San'ya overtook it just before the war. All yoseba with doyagai were officially so designated in 1887. Cheap lodging houses not located in areas sanctioned by the authorities were prohibited from operation. Whether in the yoseba or in the licensed quarters, the state sought to centralize and wield control over the available labor for ready exploitation.

Before it became the city's most important day-laborer center, San'ya was known for its cheap lodging and unlicensed prostitutes, whose customers could not afford the costlier pleasures of nearby Yoshiwara. Adjacent to one of the main highways into the city from the northern provinces, it was a well-trodden district that even before the Restoration (1868) saw more than its share of itinerants, including pilgrims, merchants, and entertainers. As Tokyo industrialized in the Meiji and Taishō (1912–26) periods, seasonal workers looking for temporary lodging, as well as longer-term migrants looking for a toehold in the city, made San'ya their first stop. Koreans uprooted by colonialization of their country by Japan (1910–45) gravitated to neighborhoods like the present-day Mikawajima, west of San'ya, as well as to other depressed areas. For all its undesirableness, given its proximity to the nearby *buraku*, San'ya was heavily trafficked until the Yamanote Loop Line was completed in 1925, making Ueno Station the major terminus for migrants from the north and moving the city's center of gravity farther to the west.

San'ya's role as a yoseba, which began in the decades before World War II, was solidified during the Occupation following Japan's surrender to the Allied Forces. Like the rest of Shitamachi, San'ya burned almost completely to the ground in the disastrous fire bombings of March 1945. After the war's end, homelessness was the norm, starvation rampant, disease endemic, and the mood desperate. Nevertheless, recovery was surprisingly quick. People who had fled the city by the hundreds of thousands during the war began streaming back shortly thereafter in search of opportunity, and shelter was their first priority. San'ya was one of the seven original "barrack zones" designated throughout the city by Occupation authorities, and soon the area was dotted with temporary dwellings: tents at first; then ramshackle huts; and only later the somewhat more substantial wooden buildings of which there are a few still standing today. A night in one of these structures cost next to nothing, but occupants slept like sardines— sometimes two or three people per mat.

San'ya was the focal point not only of a building spree after the war but of new activity in the sex trade as well. The cabinet of Prince Higashikuni Naruhiko, which was formed immediately after the war to preside over Japan's surrender to the Allied Powers, secretly called on each prefectural governor through the Home Ministry's police agency to set up "comfort stations" that would accommodate the victors who were about to occupy Japan. San'ya was one of the areas affected by this mandate. The egregious tradition of "comfort women," which had stained Japan's wartime history abroad, thus continued even after the surrender, in service of both the native population and its occupiers. A decade or so later, in the years after prostitution had been banned and the neighboring Yoshiwara licensed quarter had folded up shop, streetwalkers (who were themselves sometimes called *tachinbo*, as were day laborers) could be seen plying their trade up and down Old Streetcar Boulevard, shopping baskets in hand, affecting the air of matronly housewives.

As part of a massive clean-up effort by the Tokyo Metropolitan Government during the first year or so after the war, thousands of homeless men living in the tunnels of Ueno Station (repatriated soldiers, air-raid victims, evacuees returned from the provinces, and others out of a job) were forcibly and repeatedly removed to one of several "relocation centers" that dotted the city. (Similar relocations were taking place in other cities; in Osaka, the homeless were removed from the tunnels of Umeda Station to Kamagasaki.) Some were sent to work in the coal mines of Hokkaido and Kyushu. The rest were carted off to San'ya in trucks and told that this would be their home, to share with an assortment of gamblers and gangsters, drug dealers and drug addicts, black marketeers and racketeers, ragpickers and pedicab drivers, prostitutes and pimps. These men would supply the initial pool of temporary labor that helped get the city, and the nation, back on its feet.

The use of a centralized labor pool for public-works projects has a precedent in Japanese history. Beginning in 1790, vagrants in Edo were rounded up, along with would-be exiles and other convicts, and detained at a camp on Ishikawajima, a small island at the mouth of the Sumida River east of the Ginza, where they labored at workshops pressing oil (a notoriously arduous task) or were dispatched to construction sites around the city. Today, although there is no place comparable to Ishikawajima, there do exist temporary barracks attached to construction sites known as *hanba* (which can also refer to the construction sites themselves), located throughout the city and the entire country, where men are occasionally escorted by force and where workers are housed—and in some cases virtually imprisoned—for the duration of a job.

Thus a supply of readily available temporary labor, centrally located, was in place by the late 1940s. Postwar reconstruction, followed by the boom years of Japan's "high-growth period," beginning in the late 1950s, created the demand. Japan's economy also benefited immensely, in the form of billions in military procurement orders, from the "small" wars in East and Southeast Asia following World War II: the Korean conflict in the early 1950s and the Vietnamese conflict in the late 1960s. It benefited as well from the 1964 Tokyo Olympics, which Japanese leaders used to showcase the nation's recovery from the war and to solidify its image as the preeminent non-Western industrial power. Indeed, the Olympics may have been the single most important generator of domestic demand after the war. Everything was done, it seemed in the early 1960s, "for the sake of the Olympics," which provided the pretext for building an infrastructure that changed the face of Tokyo and the nation. Not only dormitories and stadiums for the athletes were erected in its name, but expressways, the high-speed trains, and countless buildings and other structures as well.

The 1950s and 1960s marked a period of rapid social as well as economic transformation in Japan which went far beyond mere recovery from the war. Although a majority of citizens still lived in rural communities during the first half of this century, urbanization after the war soon made life in the country a distant memory for most Japanese. Farmers migrated to the cities during the slack seasons, looking for work in manufacturing and construction and living in *hanba* or in yoseba like San'ya. Coal miners, who saw one pit after another close down with the advent of cheaper energy from abroad in the form of oil, also came to the city looking for work. Not a few were single, but many were married; whole families lived in the doyagai until the 1960s. Doya residents were a much more varied group than they are today: office worker lived cheek by jowl with prostitute and casual laborer. Everyone was poor, but there was no great stigma to being poor then, since most of the city's residents, regardless of where they lived, were of limited means.

San'ya's day-laborer population reached its peak in the late 1950s and early 1960s, when as many as fifteen thousand made the yoseba their home. The increased demand for labor did not mean good times for all, however, because there were more and more workers competing for jobs. In the years before the Tokyo Olympics, it was not uncommon for Yama men to sell their blood (bloodmobiles would park near Namidabashi and lure men with a free meal), nor was it uncommon for ambulances to cart away men who had collapsed from too frequent donations. (Blood donations are now strictly limited, to four times a year, with a going rate in the early 1990s of four thousand yen for four hundred cubic centimeters, just under a pint.)

Inflation, rising expectations, and general frustration about barely livable conditions also accompanied the boom years. On New Year's Day in 1960, a scuffle at a *pachinko* parlor, ill handled by the police, sparked the first of more than a dozen uprisings, uprisings that continued through the decade. Some were major rebellions, lasting several days, involving several thousand day laborers, and resulting in the mobilization of up to ten thousand riot police. Dozens were arrested and dozens more were wounded. Amazingly, no one was killed in any of these disturbances. The workers' wrath was generally directed at the Mammoth box, which was built immediately after the first uprising. In one incident, however, workers tore apart the Asahi Shokudō, a restaurant on Old Streetcar Boulevard facing the Mammoth box, before attacking the police box itself. The cause: a crowd of Yama men took offense that the police would arrest a drunken day laborer, who had hurled his tea (or his soup, depending on the report) at a waitress from whom he claimed ill treatment, without arresting the male employees who beat him to a pulp afterward. The Asahi was owned by the late Kiyama Jinnosuke, a prominent San'ya businessman who was at the time chairman of the Doya Association and co-owner of the Palace House, among other doya.

Violence occurred on an even larger scale in Kamagasaki, in August of 1961, when word got out that police had left the body of a day laborer, the victim of a traffic accident, on the street for an unduly long time. A crowd of several thousand retaliated by burning a police box and stoning a railway line. (The largest of the yoseba, Kamagasaki has always been the most feared by authorities. More than a dozen surveillance cameras, perched atop intersections and at other key locations, monitor people's movements constantly to this day.) The violence in San'ya resulted directly in the establishment of two major bureaucracies: the Jōhoku Welfare Center (1965), built in Nihonzutsumi on the site of a dormitory for single men; and the San'ya Countermeasures Bureau (1968), housed in the Tokyo Metropolitan Government office—the former more to assist, the latter more to control, the day-laborer population.

Because it is not being replenished, the pool of men making a living today as day laborers in San'ya has dwindled considerably and the population is growing old. Whereas half or more were still in their thirties or younger in the 1960s, better than half were over fifty in 1990. More than two-fifths of the day-laborer population have lived in San'ya for at least ten years, and a substantial number have made it their home for decades. Those who migrated from the farms to San'ya in mid-century are sticking it out in the yoseba rather than returning to the provinces. The increase in average age has brought with it an increase in job-related injuries, illness, and the death rate. Yet signs that San'ya has passed its prime notwithstanding, no one is predicting that the yoseba will disappear completely.

There has been talk of moving the yoseba in San'ya to another part of Tokyo, the land-fill island Ariake (Kōtō Ward) in Tokyo Bay beyond the harbor, for example, being one of the more frequently mentioned sites. This will probably not happen for two reasons, however—at least not soon. One is a concern for image. The wards sometimes mentioned as sites for a day-laborer quarter (Chūō, Kōtō, and Ōta) would prefer that the problems of Taitō and Arakawa remain confined to those areas and not spread elsewhere. Ōta Ward is host to some fifteen hundred day laborers during an eight-day period around New Year's, Japan's biggest holiday and a time when virtually all work comes to a halt. But the temporary barracks put up for that purpose alone near Ōi Wharf, courtesy of the San'ya Countermeasures Bureau and at the cost of roughly four million dollars, are torn down after their use each year in the early spring, thus ensuring that the transient guests from Taitō and Arakawa never become permanent residents of Ōta. The other reason is a more practical one. Although socially segregated from the rest of the city, San'ya, situated within easy walking distance of both a major subway and train line, offers day laborers quick access to construction sites and other places of work. Relocating the yoseba to Tokyo Bay, while it would conceal an eyesore, would make life far less convenient for both worker and employer.

This is not to say, however, that yoseba like San'ya are immune to change. Indeed, San'ya's history during this century alone suggests otherwise. It is just that the changes are likely to occur more through economic circumstance than through administrative fiat, working incrementally to alter the residents' lives. An examination of the types of lodging available to the San'ya day laborer over the years makes this fact readily apparent. From "jumbo rooms" sleeping twenty and bunkhouses sleeping eight per room, to single-occupancy lodging houses and, more recently, to "business hotels" with more modern facilities, the trend is clear: San'ya, too, has been caught up in the wave of nuclearization and privatization of life which has swept Japan during the last few decades. It is the mark of increasing affluence, of course, but it comes at a price. Rather than provide cheap lodging to all, the San'ya doyagai caters more and more to those who can afford the luxury of a single room, leaving the rest to fend for themselves any way they can. For some that means sleeping under the stars.

The San'ya Doyagai

The majority of the area's nearly two hundred lodging houses are located to the south of Namidabashi in the northern part of Kiyokawa and the southern part of Nihonzutsumi. This is the heart of the doyagai. Given a day-laborer population of, say, eight thousand, simple arithmetic suggests that the average doya accommodates forty tenants; actual capacity varies from a dozen to several hundred. *Doya* is the preferred term for a lodging in the area; the common English rendering ("flophouse") does not do justice to the original. Not only do doya not look like flophouses, or single-room-occupancy hotels (although this is not to say that they are superior accommodations), but such a translation fails to suggest the doya occupant's role as a contributor to—as opposed to a parasite on—the economy. The bureaucratic term is *kan'i shuku(haku)sho*, or "simple overnight accommodation." Lodging actually comes in several varieties, of which three deserve special mention: the bunkhouse, the single-room apartment, and the business hotel.

In the years after the war, lodging houses with "jumbo rooms" (*ōbeya*) were the most common type of accommodation. Each room typically slept twenty people side by side on a floor of tatami mats. Another common accommodation was the *kaiko-dana*, named after the closely stacked shelves used for raising silkworm cocoons in rural farmhouses. The *kaiko-dana* were mere holes-in-the-wall, roughly the size of a single tatami mat and lined up in two rows, one on top of the other, with the ends facing a narrow corridor. The only advantage of these cubicles, which had minimal headroom and no amenities whatsoever, was that each slept just one person. They were no doubt the inspiration for a more recent invention known as the "capsule hotel," now found in many parts of the city, where men traveling on business or working late at the office can spend the night on the cheap, although at a tariff equal to or even higher than a three-mat business-hotel room in San'ya.

The jumbo rooms are a thing of the past, but cramped quarters are still very much the norm, whether a man sleeps alone or shares a room with others. Those who choose the latter course will be staying in what the Japanese call a "bed house" (*beddo hausu*, the postwar version of the *kaiko-dana*), and what I shall call a bunkhouse, after the actual piece of furniture used as accommodation: an upper or lower berth decked with a mattress and quilted bedding. Its dense-pack design makes for an efficient means of putting up a large number of people in a minimum amount of space. The bunkhouse is said to be the brain child of Kiyama Jinnosuke, the above-mentioned doya owner, and its mecca is the Palace House, facing Old Streetcar Boulevard next door to the Mammoth box in Kiyokawa. Built to its present size in 1962, it is a San'ya landmark and is known to every Yama man, regardless of whether he has ever spent the night there or not. Apart from a few six-by-six-foot rooms converted into singles—two-mat affairs costing sixteen hundred yen per night—most of the rooms sleep eight men on four double bunks. The tariff in the early 1990s was eight hundred yen, which sounds cheap until you realize that the proprietors are getting a total

Inside the Palace House. Two of the lower four berths in an eight-bunk room.

of ¥6400 per night for each nine-by-twelve-foot room when filled to capacity, which is usually the case. Still the low price per individual occupant is a powerful draw. Some men with a reasonably secure income stay for months and even years.

There are several other large bunkhouses in San'ya—modest inns such as the Akagi or Wakaba in Nihonzutsumi and the Nansen or Takashio in Minami Senjū, housing upward of a hundred men each. (Some of them have a few private rooms.) They, too, have their long-term tenants, as well as the more temporary dweller who moves up whenever he can to private quarters—or down, when money is scarce, to the street. Expect a steamy, sheet-sticks-to-the-skin night on a summer stay, for there is no air conditioning in these lodgings. And be wary of communicable diseases, such as TB, which are still prevalent in the doyagai.

The second principal variety of accommodation is the single-room apartment. The rents here are considerably higher, running around fourteen hundred to two thousand yen per night. The higher price—double that for a bunk at the Palace—means more space: a small room (typically six by nine feet) and often such amenities as a bath in the building and coin-operated washing machines. Cooking facilities are normally unavailable, however, and the men must bring in prepared food or eat out. Nor is there any air conditioning, although the rooms generally come with electric fans in summer and portable space heaters out in the hall in winter.

Higher prices also mean a more select clientele, but the rooms are nonetheless in great demand. Some of these lodgings are very well kept inside and contrast notably with their exteriors and immediate surroundings. A family atmosphere obtains in the smaller apartments, especially those in which both proprietors and tenants have enjoyed a long tenure. Tenants either have steady work or live on a fixed, if limited, income on welfare. (It should be noted that eligibility for welfare stipends is determined not so much by income level as by age, health, and availability of family support. The government will sometimes go to great lengths enlisting the last before releasing a welfare check. I learned that a day laborer was denied any benefits until the government's telephone request of support from a relative—living not in Japan but in the United States—was summarily rejected.) There is of course more space per person but less space per room than in a bunkhouse. At three mats in size, the apartment-style accommodation is smaller than what psychologists in Japan consider the minimum amount of space needed to prevent a variety of clinical depression caused by cramped quarters.

A third type of accommodation, which first made its appearance in the 1970s, is the so-called business hotel, a brick-, stucco-, or tile-covered, ferro-concrete structure that boasts certain amenities available in no other San'ya lodgings: central heating and air conditioning. A color TV in each room is also standard. A few offer minimal cooking facilities. The prices are predictably higher, ranging (in the early 1990s) from ¥2300 to ¥2700. The San'ya doyagai is fast becoming a district of business hotels, with about half the lodgings now of this type. Like the rest of Tokyo and much of Japan, San'ya was the site of a major construction boom in the mid- to late-1980s. Doya owners were encouraged to tear down their aging wooden structures and build anew by strict fire-prevention ordinances and by tax breaks (and perhaps by loans with lenient terms—it is probably no coincidence that the names of the major doya owners can be found among the board of directors of a local credit association). They were also encouraged by the higher rates that could be charged tenants. Such rates may merely just compensate for the reduced number of tenants that could be accommodated in the same space, but the owner receives the same income for far less work.

The high rates also mean, of course, that an increasing number of doya are affordable only to the young and able-bodied day laborers physically capable of working at least every other day. Their number is dwindling, however. As noted above, San'ya's population is aging rapidly along with the nation's as a whole, with one important difference. The day laborer's average age, in the early fifties as of 1990, is approaching his average life expectancy, which is in the mid-fifties and which compares very unfavorably to the national male average of over seventy-five. Men who worked regularly when they were younger and healthier now take sick more easily, and for them there is virtually no safety net. The final resting place for many of these men, who are too old to do hard labor but too young for welfare, is typically the street.

It is this most forbidding of landscapes that attracts the greatest attention, because it is the one to which outside observers have easiest access. But it should be remembered that there is far more to life in the San'ya doyagai than that seen on the streets. You must go indoors—not just into the Welfare Center or the San'yūkai or other facilities open during the day, but also into the taverns and shops and lodging houses, where workers spend their evenings and nights after a day on the job. To see the doyagai only in the daytime is inevitably to regard the stragglers who remain, and by extension the day-laborer population as a whole, as little more than castoffs. To view it both "before hours" and "after hours," on the other hand, is to grasp its economic raison d'être and the vital and mutually dependent relationship between marginal and mainstream society. Its rituals and codes of behavior, moreover, are most clearly revealed to those who have made it a point to visit in the early morning or, preferably, stay overnight. Those who choose the latter course can do no better than spend an evening in San'ya's largest bunkhouse, which is as good an observation perch of the yoseba as any.

An Evening at the Palace

On April 30, 1990, I reserve my room early at the Palace House, checking in at four-thirty in the afternoon. I know that the beds—all 530 of them— fill up quickly, having once tried to get in late at night and being denied entrance. This time I take no chances.

The clerk at the window pushes his glasses up the bridge of his nose when he sees me. Do I know that this is no ordinary hotel? he asks in a low voice. Yes, I do. Do I know that each room sleeps eight men, except for the private rooms, none of which is vacant? I do. Do I know that there are no amenities like a restaurant or private toilet or shower? I do indeed.

"Take this man to #104–8," the clerk orders his attendant. Shoes in hand and stepping into a pair of slippers I extract from a bin at the entranceway, I follow the latter straight back the main corridor to a room near the lavatory at the rear of the building. Bunk number eight is a lower berth by the door. Two heavy cotton futon lie folded one atop the other on a sheet-covered mattress, which itself lies atop a tatami mat—the Japanese version of a box spring. A small pillow adorns the head of the bed. It is the only unoccupied berth, and it has set me back eight hundred yen.

The four bunks on either side of the room are separated by a slender walkway barely two feet wide. This is the room's only public space. The rest is private property. The occupants actually refer to their individual bunks as "rooms" (heya) and indeed they function as such. Men have entire wardrobes draped about their bunks, some items stretched out to dry on hangers and on makeshift clotheslines, the rest in bags tied to the bedposts. Each "room" has its assortment of personal belongings and victuals. I note a cassette-tape library at the head of one bunk, a small boom box at the foot of another. I also note books, snacks, canned goods and condiments, remnants of cooked food, thermoses, umbrellas (one bunk has three), and knick-knacks. Everyone's shoes fit underneath the lower bunks. Each bunk has an ashtray and a tiny closet, which fits like a medicine cabinet into the wall.

The Palace's rooms are built around a courtyard. Through the window I see bicycles lined up in a row, clothes hanging out to dry, and a forlorn azalea patch dwarfed by the building's drab, concrete walls. I explore the common room upstairs. Three or four coin-operated gas burners, along with a water-boiling unit, sit on a long wooden table in the back of the room. Two dozen lockers, perhaps half of them filled with cooking utensils, line the far wall. On the near wall are three massive vending machines: one for soft drinks, one for beer, one for saké. In the middle of the room several rows of old wooden benches are arranged pewlike before the altar of a large-screen, late-model stereo TV.

After getting a bite to eat outside and working my occasional shift at Maria, a small restaurant run by a Christian missionary, I return to the Palace after dark and make for the bath, which is open from four to ten o'clock. It is all that it has been chalked up to be. The only brightly lit room in the building, it is also the biggest. Whereas the Palace as a whole projects miserliness, its bathroom effuses sumptuous luxury. A spacious, stainless-steel tub divided into two sections with separate temperature settings is the centerpiece. In the manner of a public bath or spa, the room's walls are lined with shower heads and spigots offering all the hot water I could want. The changing room is equipped with a weighing scale, color TV, and several washing machines and dryers. Men enter the bathroom with one-hundred-yen coins in their ears—change for the washing machine (two hundred yen per load) or dryer. I am treated to a sight rarely seen nowadays in public baths outside the yoseba: a man, no doubt a member (or former member) of a yakuza gang, with joints missing on both pinkies and sporting a colorful tattoo of peonies on his shoulders and chest.

I enjoy my bath, not caring that I am being given the once-over.

"Having a nice soak?" A smart-looking forty-year-old man with a thin mustache finally breaks the silence. He also wears a tattoo: a monochrome filigree adorns his shoulders as if draped over them like a finely crocheted shawl. He has been sizing me up for some time.

"You bet."

"Feels mighty good, doesn't it? Nothing like it after a hard day."

"You bet," I say, as I exit the tub and settle down to the business of washing.

The man gets out and follows me to my spigot. "Hey, want to feel even better?" He lowers his voice. "Do you know what a *shaka* ['Buddhist savior'] is?"

"Yes."

"Interested? Say, for this much?"

He flashes five fingers. If he means fifty thousand yen, she is quite expensive. If he means five thousand yen, she is a suspicious bargain. I decide that he may in fact mean the latter, but reply as if I believe it is the former. I have other business to attend to this evening, regardless.

"Thanks, but I don't have that kind of money."

"Don't worry, I'll take care of it for now. You can pay me back later."

"I wouldn't think of putting you to that kind of trouble. Anyway, I didn't come here for that today." I continue to scrub myself.

A few minutes later, my tattooed acquaintance is flashing fingers to another bather.

Lights are out by ten o'clock. Nearly all doya in San'ya have a curfew, unlike those in Kotobuki-chō in the port city of Yokohama, where some workers are up at all hours to handle shipments on the docks. Tonight the lights go out early, at nine-fifty, and one man rushes down to the front desk, where I have come to pick up the bag I left while bathing, to complain. "What the hell are you doing?" he grumbles. "I was eating dinner and now I can't even see my food." He loses the argument. The soft-spoken clerk who admitted me earlier makes short work of him by reverting to language and a tone of voice which would do any yakuza proud.

I am still wide awake and decide to bide my time at a tiny alcove filled with vending machines (the saké goes for ¥190, the beer for ¥320) and a bill changer, striking up an occasional conversation with other like-minded occupants. I chat at length with one man who has the prim manner and trim apparel of the country businessman he claims he used to be.

I continue to linger. The businessman eventually leaves and soon another man appears in his place. The newcomer, who is dressed much more shabbily, has been here twice before. He regards the men buying spirits from the vending machines with a show of undisguised disdain, even as he tipples from his own One Cup saké jar. As soon as the alcove becomes vacant he turns to me.

"Just look at that. All these fellows do is drink themselves into a stupor. It's a crying shame. They're plastered from morning to night. . . . Me? I don't touch the stuff in the morning. I have one or two little jars in the evening and that's it."

I venture the observation that he has already had a cup on each of his two previous visits.

"That's right, and this is my third. I'm splurging because I've had the chance to talk to you."

His slurred speech suggests that he has actually had much more. He then takes it upon himself to inform me, with no little animation, of the presence of thieves who will take anything that is not tied down. I thank him and excuse myself, retreating to a wash basin in the hallway to brush my teeth.

It is past eleven o'clock. I am the last man in my room to bed down and am serenaded by a chorus of light snoring from all quarters. Other than that, the room is quiet. In fact, the whole doya, filled with five hundred tired souls, is surprisingly quiet, undisturbed by any rowdy drunks, who I understand are routinely turned away at the door. Here, sleep is sacred. Only the bill changer, spewing out coins throughout the night, occasionally breaks the silence.

4:45 a.m.   I am awakened by the sound of flushing toilets and shuffling slippers—dozens of pairs of them. The dim spring light is just beginning to show through the window. The order of morning activity is the reverse of what I am used to. Here the men get up and immediately take to the streets. Only after they have secured employment, or have resigned themselves to no work, do they think about breakfast and otherwise prepare for the rest of the day.

8:00 a.m.   After spending a couple of hours watching negotiations between day laborers and *tehaishi* on the streets around Namidabashi, I breakfast at a local eatery with an acquaintance living in San'ya and then head back to my apartment in south Tokyo.

Revealing though the evening at the Palace was, this introduction to the San'ya lodging house only scratched the surface of day-laborer life. As the following chapters show, it took many more days and nights in the doyagai, countless conversations with day laborers and other San'ya residents, and, most important, some time on the job myself before the neighborhood lost its exoticism and began speaking to me in a vital, personal way.

❃

CHAPTER 2

LIVES

The following conversations with people who either live or work in/out of San'ya, presented here in the form of monologues and in roughly chronological order by group, took place from the fall of 1989 to the summer of 1991. The speakers are generally identified only by their place of birth or upbringing (prefecture, city, town, or village, in the case of those from the provinces; ward or district, in the case of those from Tokyo), or, when such information is unavailable, simply by the place of meeting or other metonymical device. Descriptions are kept brief in the interest of anonymity, giving only the speaker's age, occupation, place of meeting, and the occasion, if notable. Additional information is presented when deemed crucial to understanding the conversation. For an explanation of the interviewing method, see Interviewing.

Day Laborers

NAGANO. MID-THIRTIES. DAY LABORER. TAMAHIME PARK. FALL FESTIVAL. NOVEMBER 1989.

The 1989 Fall Festival is my most serious introduction to San'ya to date, because I am able to chat with a large number of day laborers for the first time. Some of the conversations are recorded here. The soft-spoken

Nagano is oddly pensive as he observes the festivities from his perch on a makeshift stage, which is not now in use.

I've lived in San'ya for thirteen years now, but I'm originally from Nagano. If you've been there, you know what good *soba* noodles taste like. In Tokyo they dilute the buckwheat with too much flour. Sure, you've got to mix in some flour to stretch the batter. But they really overdo it here.

I do roadwork, mostly, and I've done it all over—Tokyo, Kanagawa, Yamanashi, Saitama, Chiba. Sometimes as far away as my home prefecture. If the job is close by I get there by train or subway, or by one of the minivans that the *tehaishi* arrange for us right out of Namidabashi. For jobs farther out I live in a *hanba*.

The *hanba* jobs I've had usually run for about a ten-day stretch. The work can be sheer torture. The pay's decent, though. I don't mean that you make a killing, because you never know where the next job's coming from. Right now I'm in between jobs and down to my last bill. I'm sleeping in the park for the time being—right over there behind the rocks. It's not too cold yet, so I make out all right. It's no fun sleeping out during winter or the monsoon season, though. No fun at all.

Things really aren't all that bad now. I mean, I still have December to look forward to, and December is boomtime for construction workers. I'll make a bundle then. You've got to make a bundle or you'll never make it through the New Year's holiday, because business stops cold. Things are hard then. But I've always made it through before. And I don't see why I won't make it through again.

Cheers. Let's drink to good times.

UTSUKUSHIGAHARA. MID-FIFTIES. DAY LABORER. TAMAHIME PARK. FALL FESTIVAL. NOVEMBER 1989.

In his dress, manner, dialect, and delivery, this native of central Japan has taken on the patina of a Tokyo Shitamachi resident.

I guess you could say I'm an old-timer, but I'm not from around here. I come from Nagano. No, not the city. It's a place in the mountains called Utsukushigahara. It's just like the name says. Beautiful meadow.

I first came to San'ya in 1952. Why? The reason's simple. There wasn't a job to be had in the provinces. So I came to the city to help the family back home make ends meet. I'm the first-born son, and they were my responsibility. I took any work I could get.

I hate to admit it, but I'm slowing down a bit. I just got out of the hospital awhile ago after a three-month lay-up. I had a run-in with the police and got my shoulder smashed for my trouble. I still like to get out and support a good cause, and I'm not afraid of a fight if things come to that. Thanks to my enthusiasm, I've done time in Abashiri [the Hokkaido prison]. With a record like mine, San'ya's about the only place for a fellow like me to get by.

My wife's forty-six. She's a nurse and lives here in Tokyo. I've had two girls by her. They're in their twenties now. I've asked her a hundred times for a divorce, but she always refuses. Says it's for the girls' sake. She's worried about their marriage prospects. Finding them husbands with an ex-con for a father in the wings is a real headache, she tells me, but apparently things'd be worse if I were to vanish from the scene altogether.

I guess I should be honest and tell you I had a third child by another woman. That caused problems. Ended up giving my brother all the money I had and told him to take care of the kid. I admit I've done my share of foolish things. But I still manage to keep going.

So, you're from America. You know, I can remember the Occupation like it was yesterday. Being in the countryside saved us from getting bombed out, but after the defeat, we were in for a shock. Suddenly our village was overrun with GIs!

If you want to know the truth, I'm glad Japan lost the war. It was rough going those first years after 1945, but we were sure better off in the long run, no doubt about that. If Japan had won and the military had its way, we'd have become a police state, and there'd be hell to pay. So you see, things could be worse. That's right, a lot, lot worse.

TORIGOE. LATE FIFTIES. DAY LABORER. TAMAHIME PARK. FALL FESTIVAL. NOVEMBER 1989.

Hi there. How're you doing? Glad you could make it today. So, what do you think of San'ya? Yeah, it's a bit dreary, I'll admit, but it's home. It's been home to me for thirty-five years now. I know just about everybody. It's like one big happy family here. Not that it's an easy life. But the union [Santōrō] has been good to us. And it shows in the men's faces. Just take a look around you. We're really enjoying ourselves.

Say, do you have gatherings like this in America? I mean where the day laborers and street bums pitch in with their own money and elbow grease to make the event a success? We don't rely a bit on help from the outside. And we're proud of that.

Here, drink up. [Torigoe hands me a can of High Sour," a *shōchū*-based cocktail.] That's the nice thing about this union. They don't care if you drink. They even make it a point to serve alcohol at functions like this. I myself really shouldn't be touching the stuff. I'm a member of Alcoholics Anonymous. Been a member twice, in fact. Never been able to kick the habit, though. You've got AA in the States, too, don't you? They've got a good thing going, I'll admit, but I could sure do without the religion. I don't know how it is in your country, but here you have to put up with a lot of preaching before you can get with the program.

The union's much more low-key. They don't make a fuss about lushes like me. I like that. They understand. Like I said, we're just one big happy family here. I don't know how much longer that'll last, though. We hear rumors all the time now about us getting moved clean out of San'ya to someplace like Harumi in Tokyo Bay—or Ariake, which is even farther out. Well, they're forgetting one thing. This is home for us. I was born and raised in Torigoe right here in Taitō Ward. Others come from as far as Hokkaido and Okinawa. But this is our only home now.

The park here didn't used to have a cage, but look what they've done to it. Now I hear they want to fence in the whole business and lock us out altogether. Well, we're not going to let them get away with it. After all, where else can we take a load off our feet and relax? Where else can we spend the night when we're out of dough? San'ya wouldn't be the same without this park. No, the bureaucrats won't get it without a fight, I can tell you. They'll have to take it away from us over my dead—— Hey, Ume-chan [the nickname of a union officer]! Here's my contribution [he hands Ume-chan two hundred yen]. Sorry I can't give you more, but it's all I can afford right now. Now let me have a swig from that saké bottle you were lugging around. What, you're out already? Damn!

YAMAGATA. EARLY FORTIES. DAY LABORER. TAMAHIME PARK AND SAN'YA TAVERN. NOVEMBER 1989.

Among the many laborers I meet at the Fall Festival is a stocky, ruddy-faced man in a baseball cap who has overheard several of my chats with other men. After we talk in the park, he invites me to have a drink with him elsewhere. We walk to a tavern nearby, which is closed, and then to another near Minami Senjū Station, which is open and filled to capacity. At least two of the waitresses are Chinese; they are part of a rapidly growing population of migrant workers in Japan earning hard currency to send home. The two of us run up the tab, going through beer after beer and several entrees. Yamagata insists on footing the bill.

They call me "Tiger Spade" and let me tell you, I can wield a mean shovel. Once some drunkard was throwing his weight around and trying to pick a fight. And so I gave him a look that could kill and told him, off the top of my head, "Hey, do you know who you're messin' with? Tiger Spade, that's who." He backed off in a hurry. [Laughs.] Anyway, the name stuck.

You know, those union leaders made some flashy speeches and the audience cheered them on, but who do they think they're kidding? They're not doing anyone a bit of good. Not in the long run, at any rate. Okay, I admit they've improved the day laborer's wages and working conditions. But their failings are inexcusable. And their biggest failing, if you ask me, is their inability to lift these men up spiritually.

I say "inability," but maybe it's just plain refusal. I mean, the union doesn't even seem interested in making the workers' think seriously about the future. It won't help anybody to play the mother hen trying to keep all the chicks under its wing. The workers will never get a better life if they don't learn how to fend for themselves. They'll just keep on living like dogs. The only way you're going to change the system is to deal with it head on. You've got to pay your taxes. You've got to vote. Do you think any of the men here do that? Do you think the union tells them to? Or to join the national health-care or retirement programs? I doubt it.

You can probably tell that I'm a new face in San'ya. I wonder if you can tell that I've had an education. I'll bet there aren't too many around here who can boast a university degree, let alone one from a national university like Tōhoku in Sendai. I've been working here and there ever since getting booted from my first job. Don't ask where I worked—you'd recognize the name. The job took me all over the world. Places like Saudi Arabia. Your country as well. A couple of times, in fact. The first trip was eighteen years ago. The next trip was about three years after the first. My second son was born there. My third was born six years after that. He's nine already. My oldest boy'd be seventeen if he were still alive. The time really flies, doesn't it?

I came to San'ya only about a month or so ago, and I don't plan to stay here long. But in the meantime, the money's good. I make sixteen thousand yen a day, and I'm going to be working all but two days this month. Figure it out. Not a bad wage, is it? And I save it, too. I spend only ¥320 a day on the train fare to and from the *genba* (construction site) in Komagome. Another eight hundred goes for my bed at the Palace House. A little more goes for meals, and some more for the rent I pay for a tiny room out in Higashi Jūjō where I was staying before. I hold onto it because I need space for my belongings. There's no place to put anything in the bunk they give you at the Palace. The rest I send home. Every last penny of it.

Home is in Yamagata Prefecture. The wife and kids are there. I tell you, there's no one who loves his wife more than I do. We've known each other since we were in middle school. I guess you can say it's a puppy love that went all the way. I've been living away from her about four years now. We see each other maybe ten times a year—every couple of months, plus the Obon and New Year's holidays, plus any other time something comes up.

And things do come up. So it's not that bad, really. The separation, I mean. I couldn't get time off like that to be with the family if I were working in a regular job, that's for sure.

My wife and I toughed it out in Tokyo for about ten years after I got fired. Things just didn't work out, though, and so she went back to Yamagata with the kids. She supports herself teaching the tea ceremony and flower arrangement. She's a licensed instructor. She could probably support both of us, in fact. What does she make, now—something like two hundred thousand yen a month? But I have my pride, you know. I'm the kind of guy who has to be making his own living. I can't just lie around. Maybe that's my problem—this feeling of pride.

It's what made me lose my job. My boss said something that made me mad and I hit him. I regretted it later, but he deserved it. I mean, how could I just stand around while he was chewing out a friend at work, right in front of me, and all over nothing? So I belted him one in the mouth. I got my walking papers the next day. Fired for conduct unbecoming an employee. A dismissal notice plus a ¥1,500,000 "retirement bonus." Maybe you could call it consolation money or silencing money. Whatever.

I've had my share of jobs since then. A trading company here. An automotive firm there. Let's just say I've made the rounds. Not just in Tokyo, either. I've done my time in the provinces, too. The memories aren't all good. One night I slept out on the grounds of a village shrine. That was a mistake. I let my pride get the better of me again. I really shouldn't have kidded around with the cop who woke me up. He dragged me to the police station and I spent the rest of the night in jail. They released me after they called my home in Yamagata and checked out my I.D. I wish I could say it was the only time something like that happened. Fortunately, my wife knows how to handle a phone call like that when it comes.

You know what my problem is? I'm just not a very good organization man. I'm working my tail off now so that I can become independent in a few years. Start my own business, maybe. I've got a realtor's license. It'd be nice to get into real estate as a consultant, or maybe into investing. You've got to have money to make money, though. That's why I'm saving now for all I'm worth. And putting up with this separation. I don't know how many times I've thought of going back to Yamagata. After all, my wife's family lives there and so does mine. My mother's still alive and well, and I'm sure she misses me, even if the rest of the family doesn't. But life in Yamagata is just too provincial for my tastes. And my life's too prodigal for theirs. They regard me as the family failure. I don't know, maybe I am. I've got a brother who works in the Ministry of Finance. Just think, the most prestigious agency in the whole national bureaucracy. You can't do any better than that. Now *there's* a success story if there ever was one. But Mom still loves me the most. And my brothers know it. Well, the fact is, I fuss over her more than any of the others. I never forget to bring her presents when I go back to Yamagata.

At this point we move away from the park, chatting all the way, in the direction of Old Streetcar Boulevard, where we hope to find a tavern open for a drink.

Looks like Tokiwa is closed. Oh well, maybe it's for the better. Let's take the hike up to Senryō. We could drop in any one of these little dives on the way, but we might as well go to Minami Senjū's finest. It's up the street from Namidabashi, just shy of the station. So you'll be that much closer to home. You'll be taking the train out of here, right?

Don't kid yourself. Senryō is no great place. But then, there isn't a decent spot in all of San'ya. The food everywhere is mediocre, and the prices are outrageous for what you get. The merchants here really stick it to the day laborer. Not just at the diners, but the clothiers as well. The store owners know damn' well that these men aren't going to do their shopping anywhere else, so they serve up poor merchandise at inflated prices. Look at the work shirt in this shop window here—¥6800. See what I mean? Tell me now, would *you* pay that much for this rag?

Anyway, don't expect great food at Senryō. But at least it's not too noisy there, and we'll be able to hear ourselves talk. They've got a couple of Chinese girls working there who speak Japanese with a cute accent. They give the place some atmosphere, some charm. That's hard to find in a neighborhood like this. I like the Chinese. I've got a lot of Chinese friends. I like China. You know, China was Japan's original teacher. We owe a huge debt to that country. Now, for the first time, it's our turn to be the teacher. And the Chinese accept that openly. Their government says that it has much to learn from Japan and they make no bones about studying our business and technology. All up front. The Koreans are different. All *their* government does is remind us of how badly we treated them during the war while trying to get to our technology on the sly.

Not that we Japanese are any better. We've relied on the United States to protect us from outside threats for over four decades now, and so all we've had to do is concentrate on our economy. But have any government officials ever made a public declaration of thanks? Not on your life! It's disgusting when you think about it.

We arrive at Senryō, sit down at the counter, and order some beer. A man in his thirties wearing a heavy sweater is sitting next to us; he interrupts our conversation and starts chatting with me. He is one of the few I have met

*in San'ya who is visibly surprised by the fact that I am speaking Japanese.
Yamagata intervenes.*

Hey, why should this guy's language impress you? We're in Japan, after
all. Is that such a big thing to ask the people who come here—speak Japanese? I mean, the Chinese girls working here speak it, don't they? That
doesn't seem to impress you one bit. Now, how come? They're both new
arrivals, yet they're already holding down a job. Why should we give Americans a free ride? My friend here says he's been studying the language for
years. Well, he'd *better* be able to make himself understood, or there's really
something wrong with him. You must be new to San'ya. That's right, I can
tell. Just look at your hands. They're soft as gloves. Oh, no wonder, you
were *wearing* gloves—as a taxi driver! Well, let me tell you something.
You'll never get far around here until you put some calluses on those hands.
. . . Okay, so you're interested in a job? Yeah, I think I can help out. Just
show up tomorrow morning at five-thirty in front of the Palace. That's
where I'm staying. I'll give you a few pointers then. That's right, five-thirty.
I'll be there. [The former taxi driver leaves.]

He'll never show up. You can bet your last yen on it. Did you hear him
complain when I said the time? But that's when things happen here in
San'ya. If you want to be in the game, then you've got to play it by the rules.
He doesn't have it in him, I can tell. Just a piece of trash. I hope he's not the
wave of the future. That'd mean Japan's new generation of day laborers will
really lose out to the migrant workers. They're coming here in droves now,
aren't they, from all over.

San'ya's one hell of an interesting place, isn't it? Still, I'll be glad when I
get out of here. Get set up in some business. Be back home with the family. I
only wish that all my family were still around. My oldest boy—I told you
about him, didn't I? He'd be seventeen now if he were still alive. He got run
over by a truck soon after we returned from my second trip to the United
States. He wasn't used to having cars drive on the wrong side of the road. I
mean, it was the wrong side of the road to him, in Japan. You drive on the
right side in the States. We drive on the left side here. Just think. Seventeen.
But there's no bringing him back, is there? No bringing him back.

IROHA. LATE FORTIES. DAY LABORER. SAN'YA WORKERS' HALL, IN IROHA
ARCADE. APRIL 1990.

*I do not know where this man is from, and so he shall be named after the
arcade where I first meet him. There is something of the patrician about
Iroha. His speech, demeanor, and clean, unmarked face give him an air of
distinction. Other men speak to him deferentially, using his given name*

rather than a nickname, as is common in the yoseba. Iroha is one of a half-dozen men who have volunteered their labor for the day at the San'ya Workers' Hall construction site. I have ventured inside the building and happen to catch the group during a break. The air is lively, and Iroha is in a mood to talk.

Well, this *is* a surprise. You're from the United States and teach Japanese literature! I should tell you that I'm not entirely ignorant of your field. I know the name of Donald Keene. He's published a lot in Japanese, hasn't he? He has good taste in literature. Or should I say he likes the kind of literature I do.

I've read a fair amount in my day. My candidate for the best tale ever written is *Arabian Nights. Journey to the West* comes a close second. As for Japanese authors, I like Natsume Sōseki. He was a superb writer. You probably know that he was influenced by *rakugo* [comic monologue]. *Rakugo* was one of the great traditional arts in Japan. It was the best literature of protest we had. Thanks to *rakugo* the common people could voice their resistance to authority.

My interest in *rakugo* goes way back. I was an officer of my middle-school *rakugo* club. All of us members were taken with *rakugo* and its spirit of resistance. We wanted to live that spirit. We began by swearing that we'd boycott the national universities, since they are the institutions that turn out the bureaucrats. They're generally more prestigious than the private universities, but we didn't want to be tarnished by establishment values. Maybe that's why I like this place. The spirit of resistance still lives here. You're not going to find many supporters of the regime in this neighborhood!

You know what? None of my cohorts ever did go to a national university. We all entered private schools, myself included. Yes, those really were the days! I didn't go on with my studies, though. Something just snapped. . . . Enough said.

That's right, I speak of *rakugo* in the past tense. That's because there are no good comic artists performing nowadays. You have to know what it means to be poor. You have to live the poverty you talk about in order to generate the kind of humor that made *rakugo* so great—the kind that cuts to the quick.

Drop by again sometime. If I'm off work, I'll give you my rendition of a traditional ghost story. I tell a pretty good one, if I do say so myself.

FUKUOKA. MID-SIXTIES. FORMER DAY LABORER. BUNKMATE AT PALACE HOUSE. MAY 1990.

Unlike my fellow occupants, I am not in the market for a job this morning, a day between holidays during Golden Week, when the construction business tails off. One other man lingers in the room, and we eventually strike up a conversation.

I've lived here at the Palace for four years. This is my home. What you see here is all I've got. A few clothes in these bags. The coats hanging above my bunk. My transistor radio. A couple of pots for cooking noodles on the gas burners upstairs. That's about it. I don't need anything more.

I worked for years as a day laborer. Nothing complicated or specialized. I didn't have the skills for that. I did clean-up and loading jobs. You know, the simple stuff.

Simple—but the work wears you out. And when you work hard day in and day out, drink is about the only consolation. So I drank. Drank way too much, in fact. Ruined my health. The alcohol eventually went to my head and—well, it's never been the same since. [Laughs.] Ended up in the hospital. Then here at the Palace. I'm on welfare for disability. It isn't much, but it's enough to get by on. After all, the bunks here are only eight hundred yen a night.

I was able to get on welfare without having to register as a resident. I don't think you can do that now. I had no other means of support. My parents in Fukuoka got fed up with me long ago and finally disowned me. I've still kept in touch with some of the folks back home, and bless them, they even urge me to come back. But the rest—well, let's just say I'm going to stick it out right here.

I don't have to work, and I spend my time resting and reading. Can't do too much reading, though, since it hurts my eyes. It all goes back to the alcohol. I also take walks. I really enjoy the area around Sakurabashi—you know, the pedestrian bridge that spans the Sumida River above Asakusa. Yeah, it's a pretty sight. Well, not exactly pretty. That's the wrong word to use about Tokyo. But it's heaven compared to this neighborhood. And of course I spend time talking to friends. I mean, the people right around here. After all, they're the only friends I've got.

The men in this room are all old-timers. The one in the bunk you slept in was here for five years until he moved into another doya. His boss wanted everybody together in the same place so that he could keep tabs on them. The man who just left is a *tobi*. He's still young and he's built like a rock. He'll do fine, as long as he keeps his health. That's the big problem, of course. Anyway, he sure has it good now. [Earlier the *tobi* had flashed his wallet to anyone who would look, counting out fourteen ten thousand-yen bills—or well over a thousand dollars—which represented the earnings from his recent job at a *hanba*.] The foremen take care of guys like him. He even gets an allowance for his bunk here at the Palace when he's working at a *hanba*—something like a thousand yen a night, I think he said. He puts

Construction in Tokyo: *tobi* working on a highrise (Hongō, near Tokyo University).

down an advance just to have the same bed to come back to when the job is over. I wouldn't trade places with him, though. That high-rise work is *dangerous*, I tell you.

It's going to be tough getting a job today, because business is slow during Golden Week. There'll be a big crowd on the street waiting for work, and a lot of the men'll come up empty-handed. I know. I've been there.

YAMANASHI. FIFTY. DAY LABORER. TAMAHIME PARK. JUNE 1990.

Yamanashi is one of four or five men I see on this particular day, hands clutched to the park's locked cage and gazing wistfully at a group of children playing softball inside. I have just finished eating lunch in the park. He notices me as he moves away from the cage and starts the conversation, assuming that I am a priest. (A small number of foreign missionaries do work in San'ya.) Round-faced and donning a baseball cap, Yamanashi is one of the very few day laborers I have met who looks younger than his years.

Life is really the pits, isn't it? I'm fed up with the whole business. I can't work or do anything. I went to see a doctor the other day and told him I was feeling awful. But he said there was nothing wrong with me. Just a case of depression. Hell, I could have told him that. Depression isn't the word for it. It's absolutely unbearable. I don't like to be with anybody anymore. I just want to be alone. I don't have any reason to live. I think of dying all the time.

This place is so depressing. Nothing at all like home. I'm from Yamanashi. A town called Enzan. Beautiful spot. Mount Fuji towers over everything. That's where I grew up. Haven't been back in twenty years, though. I got laid off from the job I had in town. Then I got booted out of the family. I suppose I could have found another job, but I just said to hell with it and came to Tokyo. I spent most of my time working out of Takabashi [a small yoseba in Kōtō Ward] before coming here to San'ya.

I really can't stand it here. But there's nowhere else to go. You're kind to say that parents who disown their children will forgive and forget. But it's too late in my case. Mine are gone now—both of them. And I don't have any kids of my own. There's nothing tying me to life. I'm fifty years old and I'm at the end of my rope. This really is the end. I can feel it—the bitter end.

TSUCHIURA. EARLY FORTIES. DAY LABORER (*TOBI*). WELFARE CENTER. JUNE 1990.

I encounter Tsuchiura drinking with a circle of men in front of the Welfare Center, now closed for the day. A burly, thick-set man, he speaks with an Osaka accent that is not quite that of a native Japanese. Although it is hard to tell for sure, his features suggest a person of Korean descent.

Hey, who are you, a missionary? No? A professor? Like hell you are—don't pull my leg! Where are you from, anyway? The United States? You mean you've come all the way from America to see this slum? Sure it's a slum, can't you tell? It's the pit of Tokyo.

Well, what do you think of the place? Just like New York, I'll bet. A slum's a slum, wherever it is. Once you get trapped you can never climb out of it again. Well, maybe a few people can. Like Mike Tyson. Now there's a man to watch. He boxed his way right out of the ghetto. [Tsuchiura starts shadow boxing while still sitting down.] Pow, pow! One in a million. He got out, but the rest never do.

Look at me. I'm stuck here. But it wasn't always this way. I was even married once, to a girl in Tsuchiura. She worked in a department store. That's where I met her. I took to her right away and decided to make my move then and there. Invited her out to dance. She said yes. And before you knew it, we were love birds!

Things didn't work out, though. I got hooked on drugs. It got to the point where I was taking speed every day, and she finally ran out on me. Well, I can't say I blame her. Anyway, I'm off drugs now. Sure, I like my liquor, but you've gotta have something to keep you going, don't you? Okay, so what do you expect? I'm just a bum. Sure, I work. I do good work. I'm a *tobi*. You know, one of those guys who climbs way up to the tops of buildings and prances about the girders. But I'm a bum, too. I admit it.

Okay, go ahead and take my picture if you want. But you're not going to find out much about this place by wandering around with a camera on your shoulder. Why don't you let me walk with you? I'll show you the real San'ya. Of course, you're gonna have to pay tuition, if you know what I mean!

MUKŌJIMA. LATE FORTIES. DAY LABORER (*TOBI*). STREET NEAR WELFARE CENTER. JUNE 1990.

This heavy-set, robust-looking man is dressed in impeccable tobi-shoku *garb: navy-blue turtleneck sweater, tan* shichibu, *and prussian-blue jika-tabi. He has been tailing me ever since I left a circle of drinkers (including Tsuchiura) from the Welfare Center to a spot close to Maria Restaurant. There he accosts me.*

Hey, don't run away. I just want to talk. I don't know why you're here, maybe you're some journalist, but I want to set you straight about a few things before you start broadcasting to the rest of the world what you've seen today.

Now take that group you were with a minute ago. I hope you realize they're nothing but a bunch of tramps who're drinking their money and lives away. Don't believe a word they say about hard times. If you work regularly here you can make plenty, and when you can't get work you can collect from the Shokuan. I've been doing this kind of work for more than twenty years, so I ought to know. I've worked out of San'ya and Senjū Kawara-chō. Got my own apartment in Mukōjima now. I couldn't stand to live like them—right there on the street. Don't let them fool you. They're here because they want to be.

I guess the same goes for me, too, doesn't it? But I'm proud of my work. And I can tell you this. It's a carefree life. Nobody gets on your back here, and that's worth a lot. In fact, there's no better way to live, if you're a lone wolf like me. I'm a bachelor and I swear by it. What's so good about getting married? People are making a lot of fuss these days about the royal wedding [of Akishinonomiya, the emperor's second son, and Princess Kiko]. What a bunch of hogwash! And what a rip-off, too! Hundreds of millions in tax-payers' money for that farce. The whole imperial family's a laugh.

I don't need anyone to take care of me when I get old. If you get sick, then you just have to put an end to things yourself. Slit your gut. We Japanese have got to maintain our spirit. We're samurai, after all. We know what to do with a sword. Remember Mishima [Yukio, the writer]? Swish, swish! [He waves his arms through the air.] The same way you Americans know what to do with a six-shooter, right? Bam, bam! Like Billy the Kid. Now there's a cowboy for you. Lightning draw. Like our samurai swordsmen. Swish, swish! Bam, bam!

RINGO. EARLY THIRTIES. DAY LABORER. ON THE STREET IN THE KIYOKAWA DOYAGAI. JUNE 1990.

I have crossed paths several times with this baby-faced man, who is never out of his day-laborer garb of jikatabi *and* shichibu, *and we sometimes exchange a few words. This is the closest thing to a conversation we have. He invariably assumes that I am a missionary, and I invariably deny it.*

"Hey, Beatles! Boom chika boom, chika boom. *Michelle, ma belle . . .* Oh, hell, I don't know the words. Ringo's my favorite. He's got rhythm. Boom chika boom. I first heard the Beatles when I was in grade school. They were my life. How about you? Well, here I am, up against the wall. Boom. It's the end of the line here. I know what you're thinking, but it's not true.

There aren't any bad people in San'ya. We're here because . . . we're all lonely. I'm going to make it, though, I swear! Well, what do you think? Boom! [He literally bangs his forehead against a cinder-block wall next to a lodging house, and then staggers off.]

WADA. LATE FORTIES. DAY LABORER. SAN'YŪKAI. JULY 1990.

Wada, a gaunt, wide-eyed man with a shaved head, is seated with several other men in the clinic waiting room that opens onto the street. He is talking excitedly to a San'yūkai volunteer, a foreigner, who is having difficulty grasping the thick northern accent. At this point I speak up: "I've been to Akita. I can follow you. Tell me what's on your mind." He immediately rushes to my side, eyes even wider, and starts chatting, the alcohol heavy on his breath. The woman he refers to is someone in her early forties whom I have seen three or four different times in the company of the men drinking in circles just outside the Iroha Arcade's eastern entrance. I have also seen her with a man (the "stud" mentioned below) who just a few weeks earlier introduced her to me as his "wife" and who also befriended the "boss" with the burned leg I encountered in a tent in Tamahime Park.

That's amazing—you've been to my home town in Akita. Well, have you ever tried the special stew we eat in wintertime with rice molded into tubes and cooked right in the broth? That's right, *kiritampo*. Well, how about the fish called *hatahata*? It's a real delicacy and you can get it only in Akita. Oh, you've tried that, too? Okay, have you ever seen the ice huts called *kamakura* they put up every February for the kids in Ōmagari? What? In Yokote, you say, not Ōmagari? Hell, I'd forgotten, it's been so long since I've been back.

Well, I bet I can still tell you something about the Philippines. I worked for a merchant-marine company and spent some time there. Marcos was still running the show then. I was up to no good—just screwing around for the longest time. I mean that literally. Getting laid there is the easiest thing in the world. I was screwing some new chick every day. Ended up with five kids. I don't know where they all are. Just hope they don't come to Japan and pester me when they grow up! I know I don't look like much with my head shaved this way, but you should have seen me with my hair long and all slicked back. I was a rake. You couldn't find a hornier man anywhere.

I'm here for a check-up today. You know, drinking problem. I work like a dog when I'm sober. Nobody works harder than me. But when I drink, it takes two or three days to sleep it off. So I never get ahead.

I get calls from my mother in Wada. She worries her head off about me. Thinks I'm still hanging out with a bunch of yakuza. Yeah, I've been that route, too. But that's another story. . . . [Whispering.] Hey, see the chick sitting over there on the sofa who came in with that stud? What do you think? You like her? She's an easy lay. Look, I'll fix you up if you want. No? Well pardon me for asking. I mean, I get horny just looking at her. Will you get a load of that ass!

KŌCHI. EARLY FORTIES. DAY LABORER. IROHA ARCADE. SAN'YA WORKERS' HALL RIDGE-RAISING CEREMONY. JULY 1990.

The air is festive at the ridge-raising ceremony of the San'ya Workers' Hall, now nearing completion at the eastern end of the Iroha Arcade. I happen to be standing next to Kōchi during the speech-making in the multipurpose room, and we begin to chat afterward, enjoying the spread laid out in front of us.

Cheers! *Shōchū*'s my drink. What's yours? We put away a lot of this stuff where I come from. Kōchi. That's in Shikoku. The home of Sakamoto Ryōma, the Bakumatsu [end of Edo period] hero. Ever heard of him? There were some fine samurai around in those days, but those days are gone. Now you can make a living there only two ways—from the sea or from the land. I can't say anything about the farming life, but I can tell you something about life at sea. That was my father's life, and he pounded it into me at an early age. If you're not a fisherman, you're not a man. That's what he told me. He drove it home day in and day out because I was the first-born son.

But I couldn't face a life like my father's! I just wasn't cut out for it. I had to get out. A friend from my schooldays living in Tokyo invited me to try my luck in the big city and got me a job in a sushi shop. I got fired after about a year, though. Too much drinking. I bounced around after that—Takadanobaba, Kotobuki, Kamagasaki, and then here. I worked when I could, and mooched off family and friends when I couldn't.

Things really fell apart eight or nine years ago. I visited my kid brother in Nerima Ward and asked him for some money, but he turned me down flat. "Come on, now, can't you take care of yourself?" he said. How about that— my own kid brother telling me off! I couldn't argue with him, though. I really wasn't doing a good job of taking care of myself. I still don't. I like my *shōchū* too much.

I can't afford to stay in a doya, so I'm spending my nights at Tamahime Shrine. I've been there for a while now. Just the other night I had a real scare. The guy sleeping next to me kicked the bucket. Just like that. Here I am minding my own business when suddenly there are all these sirens. Here come the police. Here comes the ambulance. But all the help in the world can't bring a dead man back to life. There he is lying face up, with his arms curled up tight like this. Dead as a doornail. The shrine priest said he'd asked the man a few days earlier if he should call an ambulance. The guy was obviously sick. But he refused! He probably wasn't up to the hassle they give us Yama men at the hospital.

Anyway, I didn't get a wink of sleep after that. I couldn't get him out of my mind. I'd been lying right next to the guy. Was it my turn next? That's what I was thinking. What would happen then? I mean, we all want to go to heaven, don't we? That's what we all think when we're alive. But what do people think when they're dead? Maybe they're not worried about hell. Maybe there isn't any hell worse than the one here on earth.

I guess I'm sounding pretty morose. Well, enough! Today we celebrate. A couple more months and the Workers' Hall will be open for business. You won't be able to make it? I'm sorry to hear that. Let's see, now. How about giving me your address in the States? No, I'm not going to call on you. It's just that I buy a lottery ticket every now and then, and if I ever strike it rich, I'll send you a ticket and you can come visit *me*, how's that? No, I'm serious. If I win you can come and take in the Grand Opening yourself.

Wish me luck. Now, let's drink to my success!

NUMAZU. MID-FIFTIES. DAY LABORER (*TOBI*). SAN'YA TAVERN. JULY 1990.

Numazu is among the crowd that gathers outside the San'ya Workers' Hall following the ridge-raising ceremony. Dressed for work in his flared shichibu *and* jikatabi *and wearing a baseball cap, he strikes up a conversation with me on the street and invites me to continue it at a tavern.*

I come from Shizuoka Prefecture, just down from Numazu on the Izu Peninsula. I was raised on a farm, so I know a thing or two about growing rice. The irrigation water has to be cold and the soil not too fertile. That's why the northern prefectures actually produce a better crop, even though they have a cooler climate.

I was the last of twelve children. My father was in his early fifties and my mother in her middle forties when they had me. I used to kid Dad about it. Where would I have been, I'd tell him, if you hadn't gotten drunk that night and fallen on Mom before you passed out?

With that many kids in the family, you'd think I'd get lost in the shuffle. But that wasn't the case at all. People paid attention. Not because I was the baby of the family. And not because I was such a good boy, either. It was simply because I *was* a boy. There were only three of us. The other nine were girls. There'd been a long string of girls before I came along, and so everyone made a big fuss over me when I arrived. All because I was a boy. Nobody noticed when a girl was born. She would be just another mouth to feed. Just another burden to get married off. That's how things were then in my village.

The women, strange to say, saw things the same way as the men did. I still have memories of my grandmother constantly trying to feed me. I must have been around five or six at the time, and only just starting to understand the ways of the world. This would be the late Shōwa teens [early 1940s]. The war was in high gear, and things were tight, even in the countryside. But at least there was enough food to go around—or so I thought. Grandmother would insist that I get the best and most of everything. Then she'd turn around and snap at my sister—the one who was closest to me in age—whenever she tried to get her fair share. "You're just a girl," she'd tell her. "You don't deserve what a boy gets." That's the way it was in those days. Of course, Grandmother and the rest of my family were under pressure from the government. It took a dim view of a house that brought only girls into the world. "What, another girl?" they'd say down at the village office. "See what you can do to get rid of her. We don't need any more girls. Make sure it's a boy next time." Anyway, you get the picture.

Well, Grandmother's policy of fattening brother and starving sister finally took its toll. My sister died of malnutrition. She was only seven or eight. Can you believe it? So here I am, nearly fifty years later, happy and healthy and grateful for it. But sometimes I feel like a vampire. It's as though I've been living off someone else's blood.

Life got pretty frantic toward the end of the war. U.S. bombers made nightly sorties directly over our village. We were right smack on the route to an aircraft factory in western Shizuoka, and the bombers would drop a load on us every once in a while just for good measure. It scared me to death and yet it was dazzling, like a gigantic fireworks display.

After the war ended, the Americans charged in again, this time in their Jeeps. The GIs would hand out chocolate and gum right and left. That made a big hit with us kids. I'd play hooky from school, grab my share, and then show it off later to my classmates, making like I was a big shot. After all, not every kid had the guts to walk right up to the enemy.

Not that I was friendly with the Americans. I lost my eldest brother in the war. He got killed in Borneo by the GIs, and now they were here in my own village. Once General Ridgeway paid the village a visit. I don't have the faintest idea why. All us kids lined the street with flags in our fists. This was on school orders. When the general and his wife arrived on the train, we started waving the Stars and Stripes like mad. It gave me the creeps. But I still waved my flag. Nearly half a century has gone by since then, and it still bothers me. I guess I can't look at an American, or someone who looks like an American, without thinking, "They killed my brother!"

I was only about ten or so when my dad died. By the time I got to middle school I was getting restless. I was thinking of something wild to do, and then hit upon it—a bicycle ride from Numazu to Tokyo to see my aunt. She was Dad's younger sister and lived in Minami Senjū, in an apartment not too far from here. It was a long haul from Numazu, about a hundred kilometers [sixty-two miles] or so, I think. Still, it took me only about eight hours. I'd grab onto the back end of a truck on the uphill stretches and then let go on the downhill stretches. Cars went a lot slower then, so it wasn't as dangerous as you might think.

I left home without saying a word to anyone and arrived in Tokyo with only about four or five hundred yen in my pocket. My aunt let me stay until my money ran out, though, and then sent me back to Numazu. So you see, my habit of doing things on the spur of the moment, like taking you to this tavern after meeting you back there on the street—it goes way back.

I came to Tokyo for good when I was in my early twenties. I had a job at the local city office, but the pay was lousy—about a hundred yen a day. So when someone told me I could make five times that much in the construction business, I said count me in. I made San'ya my home base, because my aunt was close by in Minami Senjū. I've done all kinds of work. Not just in construction, either. I've tried my hand at taxi driving and truck driving, too. I've got a half-dozen vehicle licenses on me. You name it, I can drive it. From a fork lift to a ten-wheeler. I got those licenses on the advice of my foreman at Shimizu Construction. I worked with them in the late fifties. Thanks to them I've got Tokyo Tower among my credits. All 333 meters [1093 feet] of it. I'd go way the hell up those girders and risk my goddamn' neck. I'd do anything in those days. I was young and a little crazy.

Crazy, but not stupid. Shimizu Construction kept making me do all this shit work they'd never foist on anyone else. I guess they were just trying to keep a country boy in his place, but I finally said enough is enough and told them I was getting out. My foreman, though—now he was all right—he told me to make sure I had the means to earn a living on my own before I quit, if that's what I was really aiming to do.

I took his advice seriously. Now there's always something I can do. I'm never hard up for work, and I've never had to lean on the family back home. Actually, I don't go home at all anymore, now that both my parents are dead. My one brother who's still alive left the farm long ago and took a desk job in the city. My eldest sister married a man who was adopted into the family and took over the farm.

I'm still going strong, thank you. I'm not the man I used to be, but I can still handle any job. Here, shake my hand. See what I mean? Still got a good grip, don't I? You work with your head, I can tell. Who knows, maybe you've got a good one. But that won't help in this business. It's your arms and legs that put rice on your table. Me? I make enough for the rent and then some. I pay fifteen hundred yen a night for a room at the Wakaba Inn. That's a private room. I wouldn't dream of being cooped up in the bunk rooms they have there. That sort of accommodation really gets on my nerves. It's bad enough as it is with this Chinese fellow living next door. I guess he came over on a tourist visa, but I'm sure he's overstayed it by now. Anyway, he has this irksome habit of stomping on the floor suddenly to quiet people down. The problem is, he makes a lot more noise than the men he's trying to hush up!

Still, things are better than they were at the last place I lived in—the Akagi Inn across the street. Someone was up at three o'clock every morning cleaning the toilets. Newcomers like me of course were put up in the rooms right next to them. It was unbearable.

Things are going pretty good right now. I've managed to stash away about eight hundred thousand yen in the Welfare Center credit union. That'd buy me a plane ticket to the States and then some, wouldn't it? I'd really love to go some time. I've never been out of the country, and I've always wanted to learn more English. When I drove a taxi I always made it a point to pick up foreigners and try what little English I had on them. I had this fantasy about laying some beautiful blonde. So I prepared for the big day by practicing for all I was worth. The big day never came. But a guy's got to dream, right?

KOSHIGAYA. MID-FIFTIES. DAY LABORER. SHINDEN, IN SAITAMA PREFECTURE. EXPRESSWAY CONSTRUCTION SITE. JULY 1991.

Koshigaya and I are part of a four-man crew scraping splattered cement off a row of girders that support a section of elevated highway. He chats with me during the morning break while the others listen on, as if for their own enjoyment.

So, you're here in Japan by yourself? I suppose you've got one of these by now [flashes his pinkie, indicating girl friend]? Okay, suit yourself. You don't have to tell me. It's just that you give the impression you're in the market for a nice chick. Well, maybe I can fix you up.

I know what a horny lot you foreigners can be. I remember this one stud who came around to the public bath near where I was living a couple of years back. I swear he had the biggest cock I'd ever seen. I couldn't take my eyes off it. He'd be sitting on his little stool soaping himself down like the rest of us and it would be dragging on the floor tiles. I'm not kidding. His prick was touching the floor!

Not that I'm ashamed of what I've got. I'm pretty well endowed in that department, thank you. And I still have occasion to use it, too. No, I'm not as young as you think. I'm fifty-five. See, it's right here on my white card. But I haven't slowed down too much yet. I just got back from a tour of Thailand last month. Just for sex. I went with this guy from Koshigaya. We happened to meet at a *pachinko* parlor there. I was sitting right next to him playing the machines. We got to talking and hit it off, and the next thing you know he's inviting me to come along with him to Bangkok! He's the son of one of those nouveau-riche farmers who made a bundle by selling off some land, and he has money to burn. We made ourselves home at some swanky hotel and blew the wad. The poor guy's so ugly he couldn't snag a Japanese girl if his life depended on it. So he makes it with foreign meat. All you need is money. That's why the Thai girls swarmed all over him. The girls there love the Japanese. After all, we're loaded.

Your money still goes a long way in Bangkok. You can get laid there for real cheap. Just three thousand to five thousand yen for the whole night. Don't you worry about the girls. That's good money for them. Most workers get paid next to nothing. A man there earns maybe twenty thousand yen a month, and a woman only about twelve thousand. That's what I heard, anyway. Heck, we make that much in a single day on the job here in Japan!

This farmer friend of mine is a real character. He's all puffed up because one of the girls he met there writes him a letter! In English, of course. Needless to say, he can't read a word, and so where do you think he goes to get it translated? A church! You know, one of those places that offers English-conversation classes to parishioners. Of course the letter doesn't say anything profound. Just the usual fare. "I love you." "Please come back and see me." That kind of crap. But he sure likes to show it off. You know damn' well why she wants him back. To spend more money on her, of course!

Anyway, we had quite a time with the best that money could buy and we went through two million yen in a month. Had a new girl in every other day. He's still in his early thirties and I had a hard time keeping up with him. I mean, I'm old enough to qualify for pension benefits in some countries. Like Sweden, for instance. They really take good care of the old folks there. Sure I know about it. I keep tabs on what's happening in the world. I watch TV. I read magazines. If you lose your curiosity about things, your life's as good as finished. That's right, over and done with.

Shiga Kōgen. Early sixties. Day laborer. Shinden. Expressway construction site. July 1991.

I overlap with Shiga Kōgen for four days at the Shinden work site. A diminutive man with stooped shoulders and receding gums, he works silently for the first two days I am with him. On the third day, under the girders, he strikes up a conversation.

My name is Kawagishi Shōji. You won't find too many of us. There're only about five hundred with the same characters as mine in the whole country. I know. I looked it up. You'd be surprised how many of us are famous.

I'm looking forward to my moment of glory. I've led a pretty ordinary life so far. No, I'm not talking about my work as a day laborer. I've been doing this for less than a year. Before that I was a truck driver. I spent better than twenty years behind the wheel. I had my own four-ton rig. At one time I had two. When times were good back in the 1970s I took home up to ten million yen a year. That's when ten million was really worth something. Not that it was all profit. I spent two million of it on gasoline alone. I've driven through every corner of this country. Up and down every highway and byway. I slept on the road more than I did at home. But I tell you, I never would have guessed that someday I'd be crawling about the girders on a job *underneath* a highway! Never in a million years!

I lived with my wife and son. Just the three of us. Sometimes my boy would help with the driving when he was younger. But he's in another business now. My wife died eight years ago, and I live alone now just outside of Tokyo. I come to Namidabashi every morning and pick up my work off the street.

I didn't bother to renew my license the last time it came due, because my eyes are getting bad. I could go ahead and drive anyway without a license, I suppose. In fact, I did that at the beginning. And when I got caught, I'd bluff my way out of a jam. I'd tell the cop, "So go ahead and arrest me. Nothing could suit me more. I've got no place to sleep and if I'm not bringing in an income I'm a burden to my family. Lock me up and feed me well!"

I work maybe twenty days out of the month. The other ten days I spend on my hobby. Song writing. I think I've got a good thing going. Listen to this. It's a song I'm working on right now. Here's how it starts: *Kimama ni ikiru . . .* [He croons a stanza with a weak but practiced voice.] The words reflect my way of life. "Live the way you like." *Kimama ni*—freely. Doing things your own way. That means a lot to a man like me. I don't have a title for the song yet, and I still have to come up with a flip-side melody. But once I do—gangbusters! I'm sure it'll be a hit. I already have a pen name. Hoshino Masaharu. The "Hoshi" is after a famous songwriter's name. The "no" is after the "no" in Nagano, the prefecture where I come from. My home is Shiga Kōgen. You know, the ski resort. The "Masaharu" is an alternate reading of the characters of my given name. I can't wait to see it on a record label.

ARAKAWA. LATE FORTIES. DAY LABORER. IROHA ARCADE. JULY 1991.

Arakawa is a short but powerfully built man with better-than-average looks and knots of gristle on both shoulders that bespeak years of load bearing. A contemplative soul who sports a mustache and wears glasses when not working, he is a steady drinker. Our paths cross frequently. We work for a few days at the same construction site in Shinden. We see each other often on the street in San'ya, and we sometimes squat down on our haunches (as is the custom in Japan when chairs are not available) for a chat. The following is an early conversation.

I was born in Tokyo. I'm no country boy. I'm an Edokko. And a good-looking one at that. The best of the lot here, don't you think? What do you say to that, Kagawa [his companion; see below]?

So, you're an American. I was too young to remember much about the war, but there's one thing that sticks in my mind—the bunch of unexploded napalm bombs I once saw strewn about the ground near my home. This must have been a few years after the war. It was an eerie sight, I tell you.

Tokyo was a mess in those days. But I don't have a chip on my shoulder about what happened. You were the enemy then, but things changed fast after that. After all, when we were hurting, the Americans really helped by buying Japanese goods. That much I know.

I also know that Japan was up to no good during the war, regardless of the propaganda you hear then or now. We did some terrible things on the Asian continent, and I hope that we can do something now to help the Chinese. I'll be frank with you. I'm no fan of the Soviet Union, but I do like China, and I think we owe the Chinese something. And we're in a position to help out.

I'm not much of a traveler, but when I do take a trip, I always go to China. Or Taiwan, I should say. I've been there three times. You know, the usual sex tour. One of the women I ran into spoke with the most beautiful accent. I found out that she was from Beijing and I decided then and there that I'd learn the language myself. I began watching the Mandarin-language study program on the NHK educational channel as soon as I got back to Tokyo. I kept it up for a good long while, too. [He reels off a few phrases in very passable Chinese.]

I want to visit the mainland some day. I'm saving up for it at the Welfare Center Credit Union. They make you hold on to your money there. You can't withdraw more than ten thousand yen a day without a legitimate excuse. But I show them my passport and visa and away I go. [Looking about at a party of drunks lying on the street a few yards away] I'll tell you, though, it gets harder and harder to come back to this shit hole. That's the only word for it. A shit hole. It's no place to live out your life. The only thing to think about here is getting out. I mean, getting out for good. But it's not that easy, is it. Not easy at all.

KAGAWA. MID-FORTIES. DAY LABORER. IROHA ARCADE. JULY 1991.

A strapping six-footer with a high, gentle voice, Kagawa is the constant companion of Arakawa and is forever cajoling the latter to go easy on the alcohol, which he claims (with some justification) to hold better than his friend. My path crosses with Kagawa nearly as frequently as it does with Arakawa. I first met him at the Shinden construction site. His uniform is his trademark: navy-blue pants with the legs rolled up, a bright-red shirt with white horizontal stripes, and a pink towel twisted around his bushy head. An attractive man, he is missing several front teeth. This, too, is one of the early conversations, during my first period of "unemployment," over beer and shōchū.

I come from Shikoku originally—Kagawa Prefecture. I've been in San'ya only about six months, but I've lived in Tokyo for a good while now and know it like the back of my hand. I've got a driver's license and I swear I've been up and down every street in this city.

I used to work in Hachiōji [a suburb in west Tokyo] until someone lifted my tools. That's right, the whole set. One and a half million yen worth. No, they sure *don't* come cheap. A good plane alone'll cost you forty or fifty thousand yen. You see, I was a carpenter. That was my trade. I've been at it for a long time now. I went through an apprenticeship after middle school. The whole bit. Anyway, I was working in Hachiōji, like I said. Had my own place and everything. In fact, I'm still keeping my apartment. The rent's fifty-five thousand yen a month, plus utilities. You may think it's a waste of money. But if you let it go, think of what it costs to take out a new contract, what with several months' worth of rent in key money, a deposit, the realtor's fee, and all the rest.

I'm in a holding pattern now. I've still got some savings left. About five or six hundred thousand yen. Enough to make it through for the time being, but not nearly enough to buy another set of tools. When you're in my kind of business, you've got to have the whole set. So I've got a long way to go. Today I was lucky. I got work as a *tobi*. The pay is good. But other days I make less. Then there are the days when I don't get work at all. So you see, it's going to be a while before I can save another million yen.

Listen, don't feel obligated to drink with me can for can. Even my friend Arakawa here can't keep up. I've had lots of training and I know how to hold it. I was raised on *shōchū* since my apprentice days. *Shōchū's* the best. Your body absorbs it easily, and you don't get hung over the next day.

No, I insist, this is my treat. You're not going to push any money on me. You know I'm stronger than you are. I'll stuff those coins down your throat!

AKITA. LATE FORTIES. DAY LABORER AND UNION MEMBER. NEAR TAMAHIME PARK. JULY 1991.

I know Akita from several previous meetings. He was one of the organizers of the Santōrō Year-Forgetting Party I attended in 1989. I run into him this evening on the street while guiding an acquaintance through San'ya. To make conversation, but also out of concern for my current unemployment, I ask him if he knows of any job possibilities. The following is his response.

Sure you can get work. You can start right now if you want. I'm serious. They're looking for someone at a job right close by for the night shift. It's easy work. And you'll get twenty-one thousand yen. What, not interested? Spare me your excuses. What do I care if you're taking somebody around and showing him the sights? You say you wanted work and I tell you there's a job going begging, and now you turn it down. I'm not talking about tomorrow. I'm talking about right now. You've got to deal with the present. Don't be so choosy.

That's the problem with you educated types. You're all the same. Just like Tottori and Kobe and Osaka [Santōrō officers]. Look, I only got as far as ninth grade, and then I left school. I'm not like those university types that run our union. I don't have their smarts. But I know how to run machinery. I've got a license to operate a forklift. If you're really serious about looking for work, don't waste your time with any of them.

Listen, I just remembered another job at a *hanba* in Chiba. It goes for about a month, I think. How about it? You can start right away. It pays fifteen thousand yen. That's damn good for *hanba* work. Of course, they don't pay you all at once. They give you five thousand yen a day and fork over the rest when you leave. What? You say you'll think about it? Fine, suit yourself. But don't ask me for another favor again. I don't want to hear about it.

EBISU. LATE THIRTIES. DAY LABORER. OFFICE-BUILDING CONSTRUCTION SITE. SHIBA, IN MINATO WARD. AUGUST 1991.

A boyish-faced man volunteers to look after me the morning I am picked out of a crowd to work at a genba in Shiba, near Tokyo Tower. He seems curious about this foreigner in their midst, but he ends up doing most of the talking. Small but well-built, he is rather less energetic than the other laborers I have worked with. The conversation begins early morning on the commute to the work site, continues throughout the job itself, and ends late that afternoon after a visit to the office of his friend.

This must be my lucky day. I was hoping to team up with you the moment I saw you in the group this morning. I mean, how many chances do you get to talk to an American in this line of work? I've seen you before on the platform at Minami Senjū Station. You were probably on your way to work on some other job. You're easy to spot in a crowd, you know.

So you grew up in Southern California! I've been there myself. That was nearly twenty years ago and I was just nineteen. I was fresh out of high school and working in a big company. I won't tell you the name, because I'm sure you'd recognize it, and it's just as well you didn't know. It wasn't all that big when I was first starting out, but it's grown into a worldwide operation. They hire a hundred people every year from the best universities now—places like Keiō and Waseda.

Anyway, this company sent me on an overseas assignment. That's how I ended up in California. I spent a year there. The company's sales office was in Compton, but I lived in downtown L.A., in a one-bedroom apartment near Olympic Boulevard. The rent was just $120 a month. I wonder what it goes for now.

Life was great in the United States. I got to hobnob with all the company bigwigs who came over on business. It was always the bigwigs who came— the division managers and company vice presidents. Of course, I didn't know at the time that they were VIPs. At least it didn't register. Here I'd be cracking jokes with men who are my father's age, and then when I get back to Japan I find out that Mr. A. is the company's managing director and that Mr. B. is the executive director, and so on. And I start acting like a dummy in front of them. That shows you what an ignorant fool I was.

I traveled a lot when I was in the States. Phoenix. Las Vegas. The Grand Canyon. And along the East Coast as far south as Key West. Chicago, too. That's where company headquarters were located. They're in New York now. The Chicago office is still going strong, though. My friends who had the inside track in that company usually got assigned there.

I could've had the inside track, myself, if only I'd gotten the right education. It would have been easy enough to get into a university, because the high school I went to was affiliated to one, and it always allows a certain number of its own students in automatically without taking the entrance exam. It works that way at a lot of private schools, you know, including Keiō and Waseda. That way students coming up through the system don't even have to worry about studying for exams. It was the only possible way for someone like me, since I always got such poor grades!

Well, none of that panned out. You see, my old man got sick and died just as I finished high school. I'm the first-born son and I was responsible for taking care of the family. So I got a job in the technical division of this company that's now very famous, and worked there for twelve years. That's right, twelve long years. You probably don't believe it seeing me working here like this, but let me tell you, I've got staying power when I put my mind to it!

The problem was that I wasn't getting anywhere in that job. My friends and colleagues who'd gotten a university education were advancing steadily in the trading division, but I was just treading water as a technician. Then the company asked me to accept a transfer to one of their provincial branches. That was adding insult to injury! I was born and bred in Tokyo and I wasn't about to live in the country. So I told them thanks, but no thanks, and got out.

Of course, once you leave a place like that, it's almost impossible to get a job at another company of the same caliber. So you've got to set your sights lower. Sometimes a lot lower. What I mean is a place that'll take just about any warm body that walks in.

Well, to make a long story short, I decided that the corporate life wasn't for me. And so I tried my hand working in a *hanba*. It wasn't all that bad. The pay wasn't too good, but you could still make out all right because there were no big expenses. You got free food and lodging, and there was no place to spend your money off hours, since you had to stay cooped up right there on the premises.

I'd work long stretches at each *hanba*. Some of the big jobs last a couple of years. I've helped put up some really good-sized buildings. My specialty is the finishing work on the exterior. I've managed to pick up my share of skills in this business.

Between jobs I'd just cut loose and hit the road. I like to travel. I'd spend all my money and then start over again at another *hanba*. I must have carried on like that for five or six years.

I'm pretty new to the day-labor scene. I started getting work out of San'ya just a couple of months ago. I don't live there—no way! I've got a room over in Ebisu [one stop below Shibuya on the Yamanote Loop Line]. It's a plain old doya in everything but name, though. The place sleeps eight men to a room, and it sets me back thirteen hundred yen a night. I know that's expensive, but Ebisu's in the high-rent district, so it can't be helped. I found out about the place from the Welfare Center. I was new and I didn't know where to turn and I wasn't very keen on having San'ya as my home address.

My mom lives here in Tokyo and she's still going strong. We don't have much to do with each other right now, though. You can guess why. She's not too pleased with my present career, and so I rarely keep in touch. I've called home exactly once since starting work as a day laborer. When I told her what I was doing, she just said, "Oh, no!" and that was the end of it. People think a *dokata* is the lowest of the low, and my mother is no exception. I'm sure that the idea of her son living like a tramp is eating her away inside, but what's a guy to do? I've got to earn a living, don't I, and the job offers aren't exactly dropping in my lap.

Don't get me wrong. It's not that I haven't got connections. There's this friend I have from high-school days working in a trading company. You probably haven't heard of it, but it's on the up and up, and who knows, someday it might be in the same class as the firm I worked at before. I interviewed there for a job myself four years ago between stints at a *hanba*. It's a grueling experience. You go in the morning and take two written exams—the standard exam you get wherever you go and another one prepared by the company, followed by some sort of memory test. The interview itself takes place in the afternoon. That's where I fell down. I flunked it, pure and simple. And flunked it again when I tried a couple of years later. So it looks like I'm never going to get that inside track.

I still like to pay an occasional visit to my friend, though. I saw him just a couple of weeks ago, in fact. The company's not too far away from where we are now. Maybe you should pay a visit yourself sometime. I'll supply the introduction. I'm sure they could use somebody who can speak both Japanese and English.

You know, the more I think of it, the better I like the idea. I mean, you were surely meant for better than this. You say you've tried teaching English and that you got fed up with the routine. I can understand that. But you've got to admit that you're in a dead-end job now and that your linguistic talents are just going to waste. And don't go telling me that the money's good. You sound as if you're happy to be making fifteen thousand yen a day, but that's near the bottom of the scale. I took this job because it was close to home. A fifteen-minute train ride from Tamachi Station takes me back to Ebisu.

We change into our street clothes and leave the genba *to visit the friend's office. The walk advertised as fifteen minutes turns out to be closer to thirty. Ebisu plants me in a waiting-room sofa, marches up to the receptionist (with whom he is obviously on familiar terms), and exchanges greetings. He directs an occasional comment to me in passable English— the first he has spoken in my presence. The receptionist rings the friend in question, but he is out of the office for the day. We do not tarry, and head immediately for Tamachi Station. Ebisu is visibly upset by this turn of events, but I tell him I am not the least bit disappointed. The pace of our walk has slackened noticeably.*

Listen, I'm really sorry things turned out the way they did. I never dreamed he'd be away. I guess I should've checked first, but I never call before I go. It's just too awkward. Oh well, there'll be other times. At least you saw the place. Now you know where it is and you know I wasn't lying. I'll tell you what. I'll call him up and arrange things so that you can drop by yourself sometime.

I guess I've used up my reasons for paying courtesy calls there for the time being. Somebody who flunked his job interview twice can't be playing the hanger-on forever! Ha! Here I am laughing about how I blew my chance at a second start. But it doesn't do any good to cry now. If only my old man didn't croak when he did and if only I'd made it to college, I'd probably have a cushy job by now in a nice, fat company and be settled down like everyone else and making my mother happy. But you never know what life will bring, do you? You just never know.

NARITA. EARLY FORTIES. DAY LABORER (*TOBI*). SUMMER FESTIVAL, TAMAHIME PARK. AUGUST 1991.

Narita is a large, powerfully built man whose only apparent blemish is a few missing teeth. He is standing just outside the park with several others, eyeing the festivities. My query about where he comes from gets the conversation going.

My home isn't far from here. I come from a landowner's family in Narita, near the airport. My family's well educated. Even my mother went to school. That wasn't too common before the war. We live in the same neighborhood as the mayor. I know him myself. I haven't been back for a while, though. I'm living in San'ya because I did something once that I shouldn't have. No more to say about it. At least I've got marketable skills and I make good money at what I do. Like scaffolding. I can get twenty-five thousand yen a day for that.

History sure has a way of repeating itself. I don't know how else to put it. Just take a look at the book everybody's talking about these days—*The Coming War with Japan*. It's going to be Pearl Harbor all over again. And Japan is going to lose. I mean, how can we possibly win a war against the United States? Your country is awfully big. Flabby, but still big.

We may have become an economic giant, but we sure have a long way to go on the political front. We don't have any leaders worthy of the name. My candidate for the world's greatest leader is Joseph Stalin. You had to hand it to him. He knew what he wanted and he knew how to get it. Dulles was a hard bargainer, too. But my hero is MacArthur. That sonofagun said "I shall return" when he left the Philippines, and I'll be damned if he didn't do just that. Then he became Japan's godfather. He got this country out of desperate straits. Can you imagine what would have happened if the Soviet Union had taken over Japan? Thanks to MacArthur, Japan got strong and rich. And thanks to that, your country and mine are headed for another war. Like I said, history has a way of repeating itself.

CHITOSE. EARLY SIXTIES. DAY LABORER. SUMMER FESTIVAL, TAMAHIME PARK. AUGUST 1991.

Chitose, like Narita, is viewing the festivities in the caged area from outside the gate. Of average height and build and with very baggy eyes, he is a robust but weathered man who looks a full decade older than his age. I notice him eyeing me from time to time during my chat with Narita. Once he has claimed me as his partner in conversation, he occasionally shouts down would-be participants.

Hey, you're not Japanese, are you? No, I didn't think so. It's just that, I mean, look at you, wearing those *geta* and everything. I was thinking to myself, "Well, maybe the guy's half-Japanese. He doesn't *look* it, but you never know." So I just had to ask.

So where *are* you from, anyway? The United States? Well, then, I'll have to try out a few rusty phrases on you that I picked up when I worked at an American military base in Hokkaido. You know the airport at Chitose? That's where it was. This was just after the war. I was seventeen and out of school, and I'd hang around the base and try to get work. I got to know a sergeant who took me under his wing. He'd call me "my boy" and arrange to get me an odd job now and then. The others wouldn't give me the time of day. Some of the GIs would pull some cute stunts on me. You know, like stomping on my foot and then turning the other way as if nothing had happened. Oh well, at least I absorbed some of the language. Not that I became fluent or anything. I picked up a lot of vocabulary but never could string sentences together. Learned my share of cuss words, though. "Goddamnsonofabitch." Every other word they used was a cuss word.

I came to Tokyo five years before the Olympics. There was a construction boom going on and this place was humming. Since then I've worked at all sorts of jobs. And I've met all sorts of people, too. One of the oddest was an American journalist I met just a month or so ago. I was walking around right here in the park minding my own business, when all of a sudden this foreigner walks up to me with an interpreter who asks me if I'd mind answering a few questions. I say no, go ahead, and this guy starts asking me about everything under the sun. So I give him my two bits. After all, I don't have anything to hide. I tell him that I don't see why Japan spends billions on aid to Southeast Asia or to countries in the Gulf War when it doesn't even keep an eye on its own back yard. Anyway, we'll never get a return on our investment from those places. Then he asks me what I think about the Pacific War and MacArthur, and so I tell him. MacArthur was the unlucky general, I say, because he had to fight us Japanese. We were really dug in and making life difficult for the Americans. Meanwhile, Eisenhower and Patton were having an easy time of it on the European front. It obviously made a difference after the war. Look at how far Eisenhower got. The reporter seemed downright impressed with what I was telling him. He scribbled down about ten pages of notes and said that this was really interesting stuff and that he was so happy to meet such a unique individual. On and on like that.

Now look, here these others are butting in on us. They think you're really something just because you're wearing *geta*. Big deal! [Chitose is wearing *jikatabi*.] Well, I think it's about time for me to split. See you later.

NAGOYA. LATE THIRTIES. DAY LABORER. SUMMER FESTIVAL, TAMAHIME PARK. AUGUST 1991.

When I first ran into Nagoya earlier that day on the street, he began talking to me as if we already knew each other. Tonight at the festival I chance to sit next to him outside the caged area. Once again he addresses me as if I were a good acquaintance, beginning the conversation practically in mid-sentence. As he talks he very deliberately consumes two boxes of sushi while nursing cans of Oolong tea and lemon soda pop. There is no alcohol on his breath, but he does not look well and has a persistent cough. Our conversation is ended by a cloudburst that douses the festival shortly before its scheduled conclusion and sends everyone running.

The main thing is patience. Basically, that's what it's all about. If you can't be patient and really study the horses, then frankly you have no business betting. I ought to know. I've been doing this since I was twenty-nine. That's almost ten years. No, I haven't been in San'ya all that time. Only about eight years. I worked in Nagoya a couple of years before that. That's where I come from.

I still lose my cool sometimes and bet on just any old horse with a nice-sounding name. Names like Classic Dancer. Or Happy Guinness. I always regret it. You really have to be up on the horse and the condition it's in. The horse is 70 percent of the race. The jockey's just 30 percent. So you've got to know the horse. I make it a point of going to the racetrack whenever possible. Betting off-track is convenient, but then you can't see the goods. Be-

Summer Festival: men relaxing.

sides, those places are filled with yakuza and police. I don't want to mess with either, frankly.

I had a big day earlier this year. The kind you always dream about. You probably won't believe this, but I walked into the track with ¥40,000 in my wallet and walked away with ¥257,000. A pretty good day's work, don't you think? I placed several small bets and scored every time. Then I put everything I'd won on this one horse. I kept only what I'd started out with. The horse was a winner and—boom!—I was more than ¥200,000 richer.

That doesn't happen every day, of course. I've had my share of bad luck. But you've got to keep with your strategy. That and reading the sports papers. And spreading your bets around. And not losing patience.

No, I couldn't make a living off the track. I work regularly as a day laborer. At least regularly enough to get unemployment compensation on my off days. Frankly, I don't think much of the bums who just lie on the street killing time. The benefits at the Shokuan are there for the asking. You can make out just fine, basically, if you play by the rules.

Hey, the rain's really starting to come down, isn't it? You'll have to excuse me. Time to head back to my doya. It's next door to the Palace. Just eight hundred yen a night. Might as well go study the horses a little more. Even after ten years at this game, I've just scratched the surface. I'm a perfectionist, you see. This is my life's work. That much I know for sure.

TOYAMA. LATE FORTIES. DAY LABORER. WELFARE CENTER. AUGUST 1991.

At four on a very warm afternoon I am about to enter the Jōhoku Welfare Center on an errand when I am approached by a man with thinning hair and bleary eyes and wearing typical laborer's garb: navy-blue pants with side pockets, a gray, long-sleeve cotton sweater with the sleeves rolled up, and a small towel draped about his neck. In one hand he holds a small bag of rations. A dark tan does not hide his jaundiced complexion. Two finger tips on his right hand are mashed from what I later learn to be years of working at a metal press. His rapid, slurred speech is difficult to comprehend. For some reason he assumes that I am a doctor or someone in a position of authority and insists on calling me Sensei. At first I tell him otherwise, but find it impossible to alter his preconception. Thrust into the role of public servant, I yield to the demands of that role.

Sensei, can you help me out? I feel lousy and I don't know what to do about it. A doctor examined me in Ueno awhile back and said I had a shadow on my lung. Then I come here today and they won't even take a look at me. They say there's nothing wrong. Well, how do *they* know? *I* can tell things aren't right. All I have to do is walk up a couple flights of stairs and I'm gasping for breath. And this medicine the doctor at the Ueno clinic gave me—it's awfully powerful stuff. I can't think straight when I'm on it. I can't speak straight, either. One dose leaves me absolutely tongue-tied.

There's no way I can work when I'm like this. And it's too hot out even if I could. To make things worse, I'm down to my last bill. I've been sleeping for a week now in the arcade. That's how long it's been since my last job.

Life's not much better in a doya, though. The last time I tried sleeping in one I gave it up after a single night. Everyone coughing and snoring and getting up in the middle of night. It really got on my nerves. I'll never get used to bedding down with a roomful of other people. It was better when I had my own apartment. I worked for seven or eight years at a factory in Kyōdō [Setagaya Ward, in west Tokyo], stamping out license plates at a metal press. Nothing special, but it was a job. I got laid off a couple of years ago, though. That's when I came to San'ya. I had other jobs in Tokyo before that. Haven't been back home in Toyama for thirty years. I left right after I got out of high school. Tokyo wasn't much fun at first, but once I got used to it I could never go back. It was just too quiet at home. Dead, is what I mean.

I got this loaf of bread and some underwear from the Center. This'll tide me over for a while, but what I really need is some medical attention. Just look at me. I'm a wreck. My eyes are all gummy. My stomach's protruding. And I can't keep my mind on anything. It's all because of my illness. I had this one job out in Kunitachi [suburb west of Tokyo], thanks to the Center. The pay wasn't bad—about twelve thousand yen. But I just couldn't keep up. Then I lost the permission slip you need to continue. The job before that was at a *hanba* in Chiba Prefecture. The work was awful, and it paid just nine thousand yen a day. I don't know who was making money off the job, but it sure wasn't me. I tell you, I'm just not cut out for this kind of work.

Listen, isn't there anything you can do to get the folks upstairs to look me over? I've just come from there and I can't very well go back by myself. Can you put in a good word for me?

We ascend the stairs to the third floor. It is now four-thirty and the consultation rooms are closed. I excuse myself momentarily and disappear into the back office to confer with Nerima (see p. 110), a bureaucrat I know at the Center, who tells me that I really need to return when the consultation rooms are open. Toyama and I agree to rendezvous in front of the Center at nine next morning. He is there, sitting at the Sōgidan desk.

Thanks for coming, Sensei. I was out on the street again last night. This time it was in front of a shop past the Yamagataya [a well-known eatery north of the arcade] under the awning. And you know what I got for my trouble? My bag stolen, that's what. It had my bread and underwear in it.

My new job slip, too. So now I'm back to nothing. Ugh, what a way to start the day!

We tramp up to the third floor. Four or five men are already there, most of them horizontal, on rows of straight benches in the waiting area. Toyama's name is called at 9:10. He asks me to accompany him. We slip into the second of nine tiny consultation booths, each barely thirty inches wide. There is just enough room for me to stand behind the seated Toyama. Nerima awaits us with an assistant. Informal yet never patronizing, she is utterly professional. She has a file on Toyama which apparently goes back several years—longer than Toyama says he has been in San'ya. She reviews a history of medical problems: alcoholism, liver disease, mental illness. The record shows that he has stayed in two of the city-run shelters located in various sections of Tokyo, caused a number of alcohol-related disturbances (which he denies with the only emotion he shows during the interview), and was subsequently refused all future admittance. He was admitted to a private clinic in Ueno, where the senior physician prescribed sedatives and urged him to continue working if at all possible. After offering a litany of physical complaints, Toyama is asked what he wishes to do.

I don't know what I want. I just want to get out of this mess. Nobody treats me with any respect. I can't do any heavy labor. I can't talk straight. I slur my words and people make fun of me. I get tired easily. Even the foreign laborers run circles around me. It's humiliating. I've fallen pretty low. I know I've got to work. But what can I do?"

Nerima's assistant arranges a job for Toyama through the San'ya Labor Center downstairs. After a short wait, he reports on his successful negotiation, and we all descend to the ground floor. Toyama picks up his permission slip, job description, and directions to the genba. *It is a fifteen-day job at a* hanba *in Saitama Prefecture at ten thousand yen a day, or two thousand less than the Kunitachi job. We then tramp back upstairs to the consultation booth where Toyama collects from Nerima's assistant the five hundred yen made available to workers for transportation. He receives the money plus a new supply of bread, beverages, and underwear. He signs a receipt for the five hundred yen. If he does not pay it back within a given period of time he forfeits any future Welfare Center benefits. Back on the street, Toyama and I chat for a moment before parting.*

You know, Sensei, my mother's from Asakusa. She's a Tokyo native. But she went to Toyama to marry my dad. They're cousins. That's the problem. They're too closely related. I have three brothers and sisters. Two of them are normal. The third isn't quite right in the head. And then there's me. A basket case. And I'm the eldest son, too. My dad—he's eighty now—he wrote a letter to me way back when saying he wanted to kill me and then die himself. No, I don't have the letter now. He ordered me to tear it up. . . . I'm all torn up inside, too. Ripped to shreds. Can you understand what I'm saying? I mean, even with the way I talk? I really appreciate your being here with me today, Sensei. I just hope you don't become schizoid yourself listening to me talk. You don't think it's catching, do you?

Union Members and Sympathizers

OSAKA. LATE THIRTIES. SANTŌRŌ OFFICER. BŌNENKAI (YEAR-FORGETTING PARTY). IN A RENTED ROOM IN MINAMI SENJŪ. DECEMBER 1989.

Boyish good looks and full cheeks make Osaka appear at first glance much younger than his years. Deep crow's feet and practiced speech, however, lend an air of experience; decaying teeth and casual attire make him blend in well with his compatriots. A sociable man, he has a ready greeting for everyone he encounters when working his constituency, whether at a festival gathering or on the street. His is one of the more recognizable faces in San'ya.

Sure, call me Gon-chan. Everybody else does. It's a nickname I gave myself many years ago. I don't need it now, but it's stuck. You see, when I was a new arrival here people told me I ought to be using an alias. They warned me not to give my real name to the doya managers. The idea was to keep a low profile. You never knew who the police were checking up on. And so I hit upon the name of a Korean friend of mine back in Osaka—that's where I come from. His surname is Gondō. And that's what I started calling myself. Meanwhile, everybody else called me Gon-chan, using the diminutive. I suppose it went better with my baby face.

I did pretty well in school when I was a kid and made it into college, but I ended up dropping out. I was going with this girl I met at the same school and made her pregnant. Marriage was out of the question. My parents wouldn't hear of it. I decided I'd better make myself scarce. As far as I was concerned, there wasn't any place to go except San'ya. Kamagasaki was too close to home. I've been here now for fifteen years.

I started this union when I was twenty-six. I did it for two reasons. First, I thought it was important to nurture a sense of community here. Yama men typically think of themselves as transients, but a lot of them were putting down roots here even then, and they needed the support of an organization that could help them address some long-standing issues: dealing with the yakuza, coping with medical problems—things like that. Second, I was baptized as a Christian and raised with a sense of obligation to my community. I'm not a paragon of the faith, but the Christian sense of obligation to one's community is something I take seriously. My community just happens to be the yoseba, that's all.

I've run twice for the Taitō Ward Assembly, and got trounced both times. I picked up 304 votes in the last election—yes, I can still recall the exact number. You need to clear about eleven hundred votes to win a seat in the Assembly. It's not all that many, but I didn't even come close. I'd say there are about eight thousand day laborers here in San'ya. You'd think it'd be a cinch getting elected with a ready-made constituency like that. But very few of them are eligible to vote, because they don't register with the ward.

Why? I guess it has to do with the sense of transience I was talking about earlier. It also has to do with the fact that a lot of men are trying to get away from someone—a relative or creditor or whomever. Registering their address with the city would blow their cover, and you have to register to vote. There's a lot of apathy, too. Many are cynical about my getting involved in politics. They think I'd cut my roots in San'ya once I got elected and go on to a career of money-grubbing like so many other politicians.

But politics doesn't have to be all bad, you know. Sometimes political clout can make a real difference. I realized this four or five years ago when the police were giving us a bad time during the Winter Survival Struggle (*Ettō tōsō*). We asked the one politician we knew to get the police off our backs so that we could get on with our business in Tamahime Park. He's a member of the National Diet. Well, it worked like a charm. The hassling suddenly stopped. It made a believer out of me. That's when I started wanting more of the power out there to be working for us instead of against us all the time.

Oh, yes, about my girl friend. She's still around. Right here in Tokyo, in fact. But I'm not with her any more. And my kid—he's fourteen years old now and going to middle school. He lives in Tokyo, too. I don't see much of him, but I keep in touch by phone.

TOTTORI. EARLY THIRTIES. SANTŌRŌ OFFICER. SPRING FESTIVAL, TAMAHIME PARK. APRIL 1990.

Soft-spoken and heavy-set, Tottori lacks the rough edges of many Yama men. He is an accomplished lobbyist and knows how to work the phone on behalf of union causes.

I'm from a farming village in Tottori Prefecture. That's way to the west of here. My father didn't work the fields, though. He worked in the Ministry of Posts and Communications until he retired.

I wouldn't call myself an intellectual, but I guess you could say I have a naturally curious bent. I was brought up in a very provincial environment. For example, people told me I shouldn't associate with *eta* [outcastes] or with Koreans. They didn't tell me why. They just said I shouldn't. It was only when I got into college here in Tokyo that I started questioning things. I took to reading philosophy, particularly the Taishō-period stuff. Nishida Kitarō, Miki Kiyoshi. Those sorts of writers.

But I also got to thinking, here I am reading all this philosophy and yet most men make their living by the sweat of their brows. Some are sweating pretty hard. I heard about San'ya just before I got out of school. It was still winter, and I was reading about men freezing and starving to death somewhere right here in Tokyo. I decided to go have a look. I got to talking with someone on the street, and before you knew it I was working as a day laborer for a lark.

I'm not an old-timer like some members of our union. I've been here just seven years, but I consider the place home. I often think about my final resting place. Maybe it has to do with my philosophical bent. Or maybe I'm just a typical Japanese obsessed with the grave—I mean in the sense that a tombstone so graphically symbolizes the family and all it represents. Well, I've come to think of San'ya as a place you can tap roots into, and I'd like to get the men here to think of it in that way.

People talk a lot about ill feelings between shopkeepers and day laborers, and there are rumors about the workers getting moved out of San'ya. But I don't think that's going to happen. Why not? It's very simple, really. When the chips are down, the shopkeepers would oppose any relocation of the yoseba. I'm sure of it. Yeah, I've heard all their complaints about the workers. They are a blot on the neighborhood. They loiter in the arcade. They get drunk. They piss in the street. The list goes on. But they also bring in business. And that's what the shopkeepers want. That's the bottom line.

My elder brother lives and works right here in Tokyo. He's five years older than me and he should be the one to worry about heading up the family back in Tottori. But he has no intention of returning. And so my father is pressing me to assume responsibility for the household. I've resisted up to now. I don't want to sink back into the mire of provincialism. And the longer I stay, the deeper my commitment to the life here becomes. But it's not that easy to say no to my parents. I'm not sure what will happen.

KOBE. FORTY. SANTŌRŌ OFFICER. UNION HEADQUARTERS. APRIL 1990.

Kobe is a sturdily built man with shortly cropped hair that is thinning on top. He is one of the few younger men here who wears glasses. The place names referred to in his home town suggest that he grew up near one of the largest buraku *in Japan.*

That's right, people call me Ume-chan. I named myself after Sakamoto Ryōma, the great samurai activist from Tosa during the years before the Meiji Restoration. He was a man of action, and he went by the name of Saitani Umetarō when he lived in Tokyo. It has a nice ring to it, don't you think?

I've been in San'ya for close to twenty years now, ever since leaving college. I grew up in Kobe, in a district called Banchō. My high school was right next to the Minato River. I know what life is like at the bottom of society.

I went to school on the Japan Sea coast. Shimane University. It's not a first-rate institution, but it is a public university and so it has something of a reputation. Not that I made the most of it. I got involved in the student movement there, which was in high gear at the time, and took part in many demonstrations protesting the American bases in Japan and the U.S.-Japan Security Treaty, which was up for renewal in 1970. The movement ended in a dismal failure, though, and since I was in way too deep to salvage my academic career, I dropped out of school. I worked here and there and lived from day to day, until I finally ended up in Tokyo.

Once in San'ya I got my jobs off the street like anybody else. I worked regularly when I first started out. But after a while I got involved in the labor movement. The Work Site Struggle Committee [Gentōi] was the biggest thing going at the time. There was a lot of in-fighting, though, and the organization eventually broke up. Our union formed out of one of the splinter groups. I've been with it ever since it began.

When you've been here as long as I have, you meet all kinds. I know men who've been in professional baseball and boxing, not to mention some in show business and even the circus. I know several former actors. I swear we could put together a repertory theater with the material we've got here. I knew one fellow who could sing an aria from *Madama Butterfly* and another who reads *Pravda* in Russian! I can't say I believe every last one of the stories the men tell me, but I can tell you for sure that I've heard them all.

I've reached a turning point in my own life. I've been living alone for years and yet I'm still legally married. I've got a son who's going into sixth grade. My wife and I would've been separated long ago if it weren't for him. The problem was simple. We got married way too early. We were classmates in college. She's a school teacher now and it wouldn't look good for her to be divorced, but I think it's about time to cut the knot. My official family register is in the city where my wife and son live. But I've established residency in San'ya, because I really am here for the long haul.

But so are all the others, whether they realize it or not. Here's an example. Have you noticed how many bicycles there are around here? That's because more and more Yama men are putting down roots. I see a common ground for them and the merchants here. In fact, the way I see it, the street people could be the start of a new consciousness. The merchants don't like vagrants sleeping in front of their shops, and I can't say I blame them, but they've got to remember that Yama men aren't too fond of sleeping out themselves. Braving the elements takes a lot out of you. So both sides have a stake in doing something about the problem. It seems to me that building a shelter right here in San'ya is an idea whose time has come. When a Yama man goes to the Welfare Center and asks about a place to stay, they ship him way off to a shelter in some other ward! There's talk about converting the Parcel Post Distribution Center into a shelter, and I really hope it happens.

What with all the union activities, I work as a day laborer only a few days out of the month. I can still qualify for unemployment compensation, though, because I buy the rest of the insurance stamps I need for my white card on the black market. That's what a lot of men do. It's how you get by here.

Himeji. Early forties. Writer, publisher, and activist. At a printing press in Shinjuku Ward. June 1990.

I have met with Himeji, friend of Kobe and supporter of San'tōrō, on numerous occasions. After promising each other for months to have a good long talk, we finally rendezvous at a press where the political commentary magazine he edits is printed. We continue the conversation at a coffee shop and then move to a restaurant where we can drink with our meal. He is a tall, broad-shouldered man with a boyish face. Only the crow's feet around his eyes betray his age.

I grew up just outside Himeji [west of Kobe]. My father is a farmer, although he works at other jobs during the off-season. Most farmers have to do something else. He used to work as a guard at the local prison. My sister and two brothers all live near home.

I'm the black sheep of the family. Not that I willfully foiled family expectations. It's just that one thing led to another, and before I knew it I was here in Tokyo, and here for keeps. I still maintain contact with my family. I guess you can say I'm lucky, because I know I can go back home anytime I want.

Actually, I'm under a lot of pressure to do just that. But in a way, the pressure is precisely what steels my resolve to stay in Tokyo. I do think of home. I think of the family grave plot and imagine the spot reserved for my ashes. I think of my parents, who want me close by. But then I get to thinking about the system of ancestor worship on which Japan's family system is based. And I think about the emperor system and how it has taken such cruel advantage of people by exploiting the institutions of family and ancestor worship. And then I make up my mind each time to stick it out for a little longer and continue my work here, for whatever it's worth.

I first came to Tokyo when I was still a student at Shimane University. That's right, the same university that Kobe went to. I was two years ahead of him. I majored in philosophy and religion and at one point considered a career as a scholar. Anyway, Kobe and I were both active in the student movement. He supplied the brains and I supplied the brawn. At least that's how he likes to tell it. I think he told you he had a student wedding. Did you know that it was my sister he married? They didn't tell anybody. But one day we noticed her using Kobe's family name. No ceremony. No family gathering. Nothing. Everybody was shocked.

But back to the student movement. We were both very active—especially during the protests against the U.S.-Japan Security Treaty. I was reading my share of Marx. It was my senior year, although my academic standing there was only as a sophomore. I'd fallen behind because the school had closed down for a year, and even after it reopened I was attending more demonstrations than classes.

I first came here soon after that. You see, I'd read in the newspaper that a man had starved to death in a Tokyo neighborhood called San'ya. I couldn't believe the words on the page. This wasn't after the war, when everyone was in desperate straits. This was post-Olympic, high-growth Japan, and the country was already getting rich! I just had to see the place with my own eyes. I didn't know the first thing about doodly, and so I just wandered about. Before I knew what was happening, some yakuza types picked me up and hauled me off to a *hanba.* That was my introduction to life in San'ya: forced labor in a construction camp!

I'd known of course that not everyone in Japan was getting a fair shake. I joined a *buraku*-awareness club in high school after becoming acquainted with a *burakumin* in my class. Himeji has many *burakumin.* You probably know the city as a picturesque castle town. But did you know that the famous Shirasagi keep is surrounded by what are called the "seven hamlets" around its base? In premodern times the samurai needed *eta* craftsmen to produce their armor because the outcastes had a monopoly on the leather trade, and so they had the *eta* live in these hamlets in the shadow of the castle.

Anyway, I worked on and off as a day laborer in San'ya for about ten years. All the while I took part in workers' demonstrations. The pattern was always the same. We'd confront the yakuza that control the area. Then the police would come in, round us all up, and let the yakuza go free. I've been in the slammer at least a dozen times.

You ask about the overwhelming predominance of men in San'ya. I can see how you'd think there's a carefree attitude toward women here. On occasions when women are around, such as festival time, the men often affect indifference or show guarded respect. But this is only for show. The libido is always there, just under the surface. How do the men get by? Many ways. There's Yoshiwara, of course, right down the street. Sure, it's expensive, but the men who return from the *hanba* have money in their pockets and sometimes they'll blow the wad in a soapland. Then there are the woman working the food stalls right here in San'ya. They all sell their bodies on the side. You wouldn't know by looking. They're not a pretty sight and they're all past their prime. But they're cheap. Actually, there aren't many of them around any more. The police have cleaned up the area. It's funny, though. The clean-up had more to do with politics than sex. During the years of all those uprisings, what do you think those savvy little ladies did? They'd supply the men with stones to throw. How's that for moral support!

So there are ways for the men to get sex. At least the men who can afford it. The rest just grin and bear it. I should add, though, that the area has a large gay population. That's no accident, either. It's just a fact of life here.

Let me set you straight about one other thing. You suggested that a festival in San'ya seems to be pretty much a copy of the kind you see in mainstream society, and that by adopting a traditional cultural form, the day laborers were in danger of being co-opted by the establishment. In a superficial sense that's true. I mean, we'd all like to have our place in the mainstream, wouldn't we? But the men here know damn' well that that's an impossible dream. And that's why there's such a great let-down after festival time. Some men border on the suicidal. But they still dream. They're intimately acquainted with the spirit of *kudoki*. I don't mean the word as it's used to denote courtship—man loves woman. I mean it in the other sense used in traditional music like *nō* chanting or *jōruri*—a lament. The men want to leave the yoseba, but they're stuck here. And they want you to understand their feelings, even though they know you can't. That's why *enka* [popular song] singers like Misora Hibari and Yashiro Aki have such a following here. A song like "Tsugaru Kaikyō fuyu-geshiki [A Wintry Scene on the Straits of Tsugaru]," for example, is steeped in the *kudoki* spirit.

It's getting late. Time to head back. Home is in Kawaguchi now. All you have to do is cross the river out of Tokyo and the rents go way down. A lot of foreign migrant workers live there. I'm single now, and it didn't matter where I went. You see, I broke up with my wife a ways back. She was a girl friend in my university days. That's right—a student wedding. I suppose it was doomed from the start. No, she isn't Kobe's sister!

KODAIRA. EARLY FORTIES. ENGINEER AND FORMER RADICAL ACTIVIST.
SŌGIDAN SUMMER FESTIVAL. TAMAHIME PARK. AUGUST 1991.

Kodaira mans one of the food stalls that line the festival area inside the Tamahime Park cage. He is here to lend his support to Sōgidan. He is also passing out fliers advocating prisoners' rights.

Let me tell you first of all that I was once what you'd call an extremist. In 1975 I took part in a plot to bomb a police box in Akabane [in north Tokyo]. Maybe you heard about it. Well, the plot fizzled. The police got wind of it and we were nabbed. I was put on trial, sent to prison, and released in 1981. A while later I got married, settled down in Kodaira [a Tokyo suburb], and started a business.

I don't deny my crime, but I paid for it with time behind bars. It was a high price to pay. I experienced firsthand the conditions in prison—really, really horrid. Not just the living conditions but the way people treat you. Prisoners lose all their rights once they get put away. After I got out, I wanted to see what I could do to change things. One of the improvements my group has lobbied for is unrestricted visiting privileges for the minor children of inmates. That's why I'm passing out these fliers. Many argue that prison inmates shouldn't be allowed to visit even with their own kids, because it would be a harmful influence on them. But that argument completely overlooks the benefit of maintaining a familial bond, not to mention the moral support it provides an incarcerated parent.

When I left prison I helped start a group dedicated to the rights of prisoners. We joined forces with another group to form our present association. There are eleven of us in it, including a member of Sōgidan. That's how I got involved supporting various activities they sponsor, such as the Summer Festival. We like to help each other out whenever we can.

The police monitor our comings and goings very carefully. You can see them right now, just outside the park. There's no question why they're here. They want to keep tabs on activists coming from the outside with a mind to stirring things up. As for me, I'm just a water-works engineer in a distant Tokyo suburb minding my own business and trying to raise a family. But I'm still pushing to give the men who are doing time a fairer shake.

MIYAZAKI. LATE THIRTIES. DAY LABORER AND UNION LEADER. SUMMER
FESTIVAL. KOTOBUKI-CHŌ, YOKOHAMA. AUGUST 1991.

I spy Miyazaki on the street in front of the eight-story public-housing complex that towers over the Kotobuki-chō yoseba. His long, bushy hair and granny glasses bespeak the fashion of another era. He wears a festive happi *on this, the first day of the Kotobuki Summer Festival. I know him*

from a previous visit, when I attended a meeting of the Carabao Society, a
support group for foreign migrant workers in Japan. Although not part of
the San'ya scene, this conversation is included for comparison and for the
light it sheds on the yoseba in general.

Hi! It's good to see you again. Thanks for coming down. Here, let me give
you one of my cards. I think I told you I go by the name Miyazaki, but it's
actually a kind of nickname. I was born and raised in Miyazaki Prefecture,
and when I first got here people called me by the place I came from. That's
not unusual. In fact, most of the men living here go by some sort of alias
rather than their real name. They might simply use a shortened version of
their surname or given name, or name themselves after the province they
come from, as I do, or use some descriptive term. The only time I use my
real name is for official purposes, like when signing a document. Or getting
married. Yeah, I'm married. My wife's right over there, in the dark-colored
dress. Got two kids. They grew up right here in Kotobuki. We used to live in
a doya. Now we're in an apartment nearby.

My case isn't that uncommon. There are a lot of day laborers and former
day laborers with families here. That's what sets Kotobuki apart from
San'ya and Kamagasaki. It didn't happen by chance, either. Public housing
went up here just as it did in the other yoseba. The difference is that the
Yokohama government gave first priority to families living right here in the
doya. That's why Kotobuki didn't witness the big flight away from the area
which took place elsewhere. In San'ya and Kamagasaki, families not only
moved out of the doya but out of the neighborhood, and the families moving
into public housing came from all over. Since the people who moved into
the apartments in Kotobuki were locals to begin with, the feeling of community with the single male day laborers has remained. There's a much
warmer atmosphere here, I think, than in either San'ya or Kamagasaki.

When you've lived here as long as I have you get a really good sense of
what Japanese society is about, because you come into contact with so
many different people. Many of them are the victims of severe discrimination. Ainu, Okinawans, *burakumin, hibakusha.* You'll also see a lot of
foreign workers, probably because Yokohama is a port city. That's another
thing that gives Kotobuki its special flavor. Maybe eight hundred Koreans
and a couple hundred Filipinos live here. That means about a thousand out
of a total day-laborer population of six thousand or so.

I started out working here with children. I ran a day-care center with my
wife for something like ten years. I'm not an educator by profession,
though. I'm a photographer. I left Miyazaki to go to college in Tokyo and
started taking pictures as a hobby. I eventually got so involved in it that I
quit school and started a company for photojournalists. There were about

twenty of us, all committed to documenting specific issues, like the *hi-bakusha*, or the people of Okinawa, or the yoseba. The company itself eventually folded, but I kept up my interest in these issues. I took my camera with me to Kotobuki and began taking a closer look. It's a place I knew from before.

That was sixteen years ago. I got involved in the labor movement and helped start up what's now called Junichirō. It's the Yokohama chapter of the Hiyatoi Zenkyō [National Organization of Day-Labor Unions]. That's also when I began that day-care center with my wife. She was working as a nurse and I got acquainted with her through some church-sponsored medical activities we were both involved in.

Our day-care center finally came to an end, and my wife's back in nursing. In fact, she earns the money in our home right now. I can't cut it as a day laborer with all the other projects I'm involved in—the union, the medical activities, and more recently a support group for foreign workers. It's called Carabao, after the Tagalog for water buffalo, because it's known as a sturdy animal that works hard for other people. The organization is in its fifth year. It started up not too long after the nursery closed. Our chief focus has been Filipinos, because of the community here in Kotobuki. But we aim to help any foreign worker who runs into difficulties while living in Japan. We don't care if they don't have the proper credentials, and the fact is, most of them don't. They're here to work. And believe me, there's work to be had. The influx of Asians is one of the major changes in Kotobuki—that and the aging of the domestic population. You've got to wonder what this neighborhood will be like in twenty or thirty years. Who knows, there might not be a yoseba here anymore. Or if there is, it may have turned into a foreign ghetto.

I wonder what I'll be doing that far down the road myself. I guess I'm getting old enough to start reflecting on life. Just last year I went to my twentieth high-school reunion. A couple of us tracked down all the graduates in our class now living in the greater Tokyo-Yokohama metropolitan area and sent out a hundred invitations. About forty showed up. Not a bad turnout, actually. It was good to see my classmates after all those years. The majority wore business suits and were working predictably enough in some office job. My classmates seemed to have different expectations of me, though. One of them took a look at me and said, "You know, you were always the oddball in high school. So I'm not at all surprised to hear that you're doing the kind of work you do." Not that I could explain what I was doing all that well. It's just too bizarre to them. They didn't have the foggiest idea about life in the yoseba.

I mean, it's hard enough to explain things to my wife, let alone anyone else. How about your wife? You say she's Japanese. Does she understand

ng to do here? Does she approve? Here you are living in the
.nderbelly and working yourself as a day laborer. Now can you
.me that she likes the idea, even for the sake of research, or that
.feel abandoned? These are the kinds of questions I ask myself. I
.ven't made things easy for my family. I've thrown myself into my
.1ost to the exclusion of everything else. If I have any time left over I
spe.   . with the kids. My wife complains that she comes in last. I suppose
it's true. I'd be lying if I said she's pleased with the situation. We've come to
blows about it and we've almost gone our separate ways. But we've stuck it
out. Lord knows I'm grateful.

I'm planning something a little different in the near future. A trip to the
Philippines. It'd be my first trip abroad. I'd like to take the whole family. I
want to see what life is like in a country that exports labor all over the
world, including workers to the yoseba here and to factories all over Japan.
But I also want to show the kids some of the world beyond Japan. I think
that's really important.

I guess the thing that keeps me here is the chance to meet all kinds of
human beings. I think that on the whole you'll find the people here far more
interesting than the ones you meet up with in mainstream society. And
goodness knows they're sure easier to talk to. But maybe that's because I'm
an oddball, as my classmate said at the reunion. I read somewhere that
about one percent of all adult males in Japan work at one time or another in
a yoseba like this. So in our class of one hundred, I guess that I was the one.
I'm that odd man out, and not minding it a bit.

Proprietors and Shopkeepers

HAKUBA. LATE SIXTIES. DOYA MANAGER. AT THE DOYA. MAY 1990.

*Hakuba manages a fairly typical doya of the apartment type: a two-story
wood-and-mortar building with about three dozen rooms, all of them
three-mat singles. I enjoy his zest for life and rarely pay a visit to an
acquaintance in the doya without also having a chat with Hakuba. This is
an early conversation.*

I seem to have a destiny, and its name is charcoal. It sent me here to
San'ya forty years ago. Now it's sending me to Indonesia!

I come from a farm in Hakuba, up in the mountains of Nagano Prefecture.
You may have heard of it. It's a famous ski resort now. So famous that it
became a candidate for the Winter Olympics awhile back. It really is a
beautiful place. The Japan Alps rise straight up from the valley floor. Here,
let me get out the photo album. See what I mean? Look at the snow! I went

back last month for a big reunion. That's when I took all these pictures. Met some people I haven't seen in thirty years. The town's really changed. Everybody worked the farms when I grew up there. Today about half are doing something else. Look here. The roofs are made of tile now. The thatched roofs have all disappeared. They were so picturesque.

Anyway, the people there gave me the royal treatment during my visit. It's a good thing, because I was entirely at their mercy. You need a car to get around in the country now, but I don't even drive. There are cars everywhere in Hakuba. A lot of families have two cars. Unbelievable!

Nobody did any skiing when I was growing up. We had our hands full just trying to earn a living. Farming alone didn't bring in enough money, and so we took on other jobs to make ends meet. That's the way things still are. My kid brother runs a gasoline stand there now. You'd think that'd bring in a terrific income with all the cars you see on the road. But not so. The population is going down. Like I said, every household has at least one car now, but there are fewer households overall. And that means a lot fewer people in farming to buy fuel for their machinery, too. My brother makes a go of it by selling all sorts of other products at the gasoline stand.

Since I'm the elder son, you're probably wondering why I left the village while my kid brother stayed behind. Well, it's like I told you—charcoal! After the fall harvest, we villagers would work on all sorts of winter projects. For example, we'd gather wood in the forests before the snow locked us in. The hardwood there's perfect for charcoal making. There's still nothing better for cooking, if you ask me. Just the thought of it makes my mouth water. Anyway, we'd gather it into thirty-kilogram [sixty-six-pound] bundles and send it down the mountain on a cable relay. There were two of us working this contraption. We were in a hurry to get our load off the mountain. The cable got stuck in the pulley for some reason, and I tried to pry it loose with a metal pipe. That was a mistake. Once the cable was freed, the weight of the bundle made the pipe spring back. Caught me right on the temple. I remember my partner calling out my name faintly in the distance. He was standing right on top of me, of course, but I was virtually out cold.

The next thing I knew I was in the hospital. People were making a big fuss over me, but I couldn't utter a sound in reply. I'd suddenly turned into a mute! The accident didn't affect my hearing, though. The doctors were talking right there in front of me about operating. On my head, mind you! I wanted none of that! I gestured for a piece of paper and pen and started writing furiously. "Dear Doctor: I have my eyes. I can see fine. I've got my ears. I can hear fine. I don't feel at all inconvenienced. So please don't touch my head!" Well, you know what happened? A couple of days later a nurse came in and started shaving my right temple. That shows you how much doctors listen to their patients!

———

It wasn't long after the operation that the chance to run a doya in San'ya came up. Some relatives in Tokyo wrote and asked me to give the "hotel business" a try. Some hotel! I took them up on it anyway. After all, I sure wasn't helping the family business. And so my kid brother took over the farm.

I didn't know what to expect when I moved here. That was in 1950. It was only five years after the war, but the way of life here had been pretty well established. Even the Doya Association had already been set up. I'm a long-standing member myself now. My aunt and uncle managed three doya, and they put me in charge of this one.

Lodging was a lot cheaper then, but space was awfully cramped. Each room slept twenty people. That sort of accommodation cost you fifty yen a night. People slept side by side on a long row of tatami mats. It's funny, though. The men would sleep in those big rooms and put up with a crowd, but they were very fussy about their bedding. We'd take great pains to stack each futon in the proper order when we cleaned up during the day so that the men would get the same one night after night. There was hell to pay if you didn't.

A three-mat single was a luxury then, and cost ¥250. That was all you could make in a day if you got work through the Shokuan. The daily wage was fixed at ¥240. You could get up to ¥600 for work off the street, though.

San'ya has a very different look to it nowadays. The buildings here fall apart quickly, because most managers don't take proper care of them. So they get torn down and business hotels—little three- and four-story jobs— go up in their place. Some doya owners are on the lookout for more property and will buy anything that comes up for sale. I know an owner here who must own twenty doya if he owns one. He's able to buy because other owners who manage their own doya can't find anyone to succeed them and they end up selling out.

I don't have anyone to succeed me. My children are grown and have their own careers. So my wife and I still keep at it. I don't know what'll happen to the place when we finally leave. I'm just the manager. The owners are in Shinjuku and they have their hands full with other real estate. Their San'ya property is on the back burner, which suits me just fine, because this way I can call my own shots. We renewed our twenty-year contract just five years ago. The fee was ten million yen. That plus ¥220,000 per month in rent. It's not bad, really. You can pay that much for a tiny one-room office in a swankier part of town. Just figure it out. With a full house we can gross better than a million and a half yen per month. No reason at all to rebuild.

Even as it is, we're filled to near capacity all the time. We're cheaper than the business hotels but we offer virtually the same facilities, minus the air conditioning. Of course, we charge a good deal more than what you'll pay at a bunkhouse, but our regulars appreciate the advantage of keeping the same address. If you miss a single day's payment at a bunkhouse, you're out on your ear, but I'm willing to wait a day or two with tenants I know. I just tell them, "All right, pay up the next time you get work." I'm sure it's the same with other managers as well. Anyway, that's why we have a good many long-time tenants. Three or four of them have been here at least a decade. You get to know a lot about a person who's been living under the same roof with you for ten years. It's more than just a landlord-tenant relationship. It's family.

Oh yes, forty years after the accident that brought me here, I've become involved in charcoal making again. Can you believe it? I'm a member of a group based in Hino, out in the west end of Tokyo Prefecture, where trees still grow in abundance. I use my old training to help young people learn an ancient craft. I really enjoy it. I feel as though I'm in my element again.

You can't beat the flavor charcoal gives to food. Unfortunately, the demand for it has declined drastically over the years, because everyone is cooking with propane or natural gas, even out in the country. And since so little charcoal is made here in Japan these days, the price has gone way up. An oil company is trying to work around that problem, though. It's started a joint venture with a firm in Indonesia, where labor and materials are still cheap. The oil company asked me to draw up plans for a large kiln to test their product. They built it and tried it out, but apparently it's not burning right. So I'm going down there myself to have a look. From Hakuba to San'ya to Jakarta. You just can't predict what life has in store for you, can you?

NIHONZUTSUMI. MID-FORTIES. COFFEE-SHOP PROPRIETOR. AT THE SHOP. JULY 1991.

Nihonzutsumi is a spry, intense woman whose passionate speech reveals an uncommon commitment to her profession. When she is not in the kitchen upstairs baking cakes or sorting coffee beans, she works the tables along with two or three assistants—trainees at a cooking school where her husband teaches part-time. The shop is immaculate, the service impeccable, and the greetings spirited and cordial. A sign near the entrance, to be seen in many San'ya coffee shops, reads: "No one under the influence of alcohol allowed on the premises."

I'm sorry to hear that you have a weak stomach and that coffee doesn't agree with you. But please don't let it stop you from trying one of our blends. I think you'll be pleasantly surprised.

Most of what's bad about coffee has to do with how it's prepared. You shouldn't let the beans sit around for very long after you roast them. They keep well when they're still green, but they spoil very quickly once they're roasted. They start to oxidize and turn acidic within a week or so. And that's what causes stomach problems.

My husband and I began our business here in 1968. He's from Hokkaido, but we met at the university we both attended in Tokyo. He decided to remain in Tokyo and we've been living here ever since.

I was raised right here in San'ya. My parents ran a restaurant on this very property. I was one of five children, and none of us was happy about the place we grew up in. We were all itching to leave. All my brothers and sisters did leave, in fact. I'm the only one who stayed. Looking back, I know I made the right decision, although I wasn't so sure of it at first. The reason is simple. My husband and I wanted to offer the finest product possible to a clientele that appreciates the best. And after working here for more than twenty years I can assure you that San'ya customers are true connoisseurs. You can't tell by looking at them, but they really know their coffee.

Our shop wasn't much more than a hole in the wall before we remodeled about fifteen years ago. Before that it used to be dark and dingy and there was never enough room for everyone. But it had its own special charm that our customers seemed to like. Since it was so tiny, a lot of men would drink their coffee out on the sidewalk. The place had the look of a café terrace. And it had the feel of a vaudeville hall. That's because we entertained our guests with broadcasts and recordings of *rakugo* artists. The men loved it.

We've found that the best way to do business here is to meet any problem head on and to let people know from the first where we stand. Take our alcohol policy, for example. We don't allow people under the influence on the premises. You can see our sign there by the door. We had to fight a few battles in the beginning to make people understand that we were serious. My husband wrestled several rowdies out the door in the early years. They'd kick and scream, but they'd finally get the message.

Men who are rowdy when they're drunk can be gentle as lambs any other time. I remember a man who began causing trouble the moment he set foot in the door one evening. We finally made him leave. The next morning he arrived with bouquet in hand and a sheepish grin on his face and said he'd heard that my husband was a flower lover and wanted to offer something by way of apology for the previous evening.

So you see, the men here aren't a bad lot. They're honest, hard-working, and very neat as a rule. They're careful with the china, I'm happy to say, and a lot of our coffee cups have been in use for twenty years. The men are considerate, too. They'll volunteer to double up in order to make room for other customers. And they'll even tell us if they're going to be away for a while—say, out on a job in the provinces. That's important for us because we roast only enough of each kind of bean to satisfy our customers' needs. Any more we'd just have to throw away, since they won't keep, as I told you.

Most of our customers are day laborers, but others come as well. Local middle-class residents, of course, and a few from outside. The worst customers by far are the outsiders. Especially intellectuals. I wouldn't trade a single day laborer for a whole shopful of professors. They're so arrogant! They walk in here as if they own the place and elbow their way to a table without a thought about the people who are already sitting down. When one of them comes in, our other customers will start trickling out without even finishing their coffee. When we see this happening we expressly detain them and tell them to take their time.

I'm the only member of my family left in San'ya. My parents have passed on and my brothers and sisters all have moved out. But I'm hoping that our business won't die with us. We have no children, but we do have one young employee who's taken a keen interest in the shop. So I think that the problem of a successor has been resolved. Anyway, I'm keeping my fingers crossed.

KANAZAWA. LATE FORTIES. SUSHI-BAR CHEF. AT THE SUSHI BAR. AUGUST 1991.

This tiny shop—a mere hole in the wall eight feet wide and five feet deep—is one of the few left in the San'ya doyagai. It is located near my doya. Kanazawa and I have exchanged greetings regularly and engaged in brief conversations when he has no customers. Late one evening I become a customer myself. During my half-hour there two men order the combination take-out, which is 600 yen. My portion of tuna, eel, and two varieties of shrimp also comes to 600 yen. Our conversation takes place between visits by a couple of other sit-down customers.

No, I'm not from where the sign says. I was born in Kanazawa [on the Japan Sea coast]. By the time I was eighteen, though, I was in here in Tokyo. I gave this stall the name I did as a novelty. I checked the phone book and couldn't find one shop with that name. You can find hundreds named "Edo-zushi" or "Edomae-zushi." That wasn't for me. I wanted something different, and this filled the bill. I set up shop here more than twenty years ago. Before that I worked for a few years at a stall just around the corner. So I've been around awhile. I don't mean to give you the old-timer spiel. I've just piled up the years here, that's all. This place is nothing to shout about. I know that. I mean, look at this place. Definitely not the big time.

Sure, the neighborhood's changed in the years I've known it. It's changed a lot. People used to be more concerned about each other's welfare, for one thing. They'd go out of their way to help each other out. Now everybody's on his own. There used to be a lot of seasonal workers, and they had their families to worry about. And there used to be a lot of women around. But not anymore. Anyway, everybody's on his own now and fending for himself. I guess we're becoming more like you Americans! Everything cut and dried. In the old days feelings always had the upper hand over cold calculations. You thought of the other guy, not yourself.

Sorry—I'm closing up. [These words are directed at a would-be customer.] No more rice. That's all she wrote. I'm not going to cook any more now. It takes forty minutes to prepare. No, it *won't* help to bring your own rice. I'm not kidding, I'm through for the day. Finished!

MINOWA. EARLY FIFTIES. PROPRIETOR OF MEN'S CLOTHIER. AT THE SHOP IN IROHA ARCADE. AUGUST 1991.

Minowa, a bespectacled, round-faced man who models the casual look he sells in his store, works with his wife in a closely packed space that is barely twenty feet wide and fifteen feet deep. His shop markets clothes that have the middle-class patron in mind and are priced beyond the means of most day laborers. Vagrants are commonly seen loitering on the street in front of the shop.

I suppose you know that San'ya was burned to the ground during the war. There was absolutely nothing left. This whole area was a bed of ashes with nothing to obstruct the view. I wasn't around myself—my family had evacuated to the country—but people tell me that you could see the Matsuya Department Store way down in Asakusa. That's almost two kilometers [1.25 miles] from here. It was one of the few ferro-concrete buildings around at the time and it survived the bombings. It must have been an eerie sight.

I grew up in Minowa, just a few minutes' walk from here. It was a different world when I was a kid. I walked to school in *geta*. My feet were bare. I didn't take to wearing shoes and socks regularly until I was twenty. We all wore the same drab uniforms, no matter what school we went to. None of us dressed up the way the kids do today. At home we cooked rice in a cauldron over a wood fire. I remember arranging the kindling and carefully fanning the flames by blowing through a bamboo pipe. Nobody had flush toilets back then. People would carry their waste to the San'ya Canal [connecting Yoshiwara to Imado] and pole down to the Sumida River where they'd dump it.

San'ya was a much livelier place when I first started doing business here. First of all, there were several cinemas right close by. They were small affairs compared to movie theaters in other parts of the city, and so the owners would entice residents to patronize them by offering a little some-thing extra. They might put on a live skit along with the movie, for exam-ple. We had our own stage theater, too, the Yoshikagekan. It was located about halfway down the arcade, where the supermarket is now. Troupes from all over the country would perform there. After a performance, the actors would come out of the theater still in costume and greet their fans on the street. You just don't see those troupes around anymore. Nowadays everything is on TV. Anyway, the Yoshikagekan burned down in November 1964. I remember when, because it happened right after the Tokyo Olym-pics. News of the fire made the front page, because three people died. The actors would spend the night right in the theater, and apparently one of them was smoking in bed. That's all it took.

Since you're going to be around for a while, we'll have to get together on one of my days off. I'll be happy to show you around. We can take a look at what little is left of the old city. There are still some sights worth seeing.

DOYAGAI. SEVENTY. DOYA MANAGER. MANAGER'S ROOM. AUGUST 1991.

Built just after the war and located in the heart of the Kiyokawa doyagai, the lodging house run by this manager is a relatively old structure. It has only single rooms.

This doya is virtually unchanged since it first went up, except that there were no singles then. Each three-mat room slept two or more. One room actually slept five, if you can believe it. A man and his wife and their two small children, plus the man's mother. It was insane. And it was noisy. The two little ones bounced up and down the hallway all day. Kids are kids. There's a limit to how quiet you can keep them. They finally had to leave.

In the early years there wasn't much construction work going on. You wonder how people got by. A lot of men made their living shining shoes. They'd live in a doya and set up shop in front of one of the big commuter stations like Ueno or Tokyo. Another common occupation was recycling cigarette butts. You'd see men spiking butts on the street with steel-tipped bamboo rods and sticking them into their backpacks. After they made their rounds, they'd take the butts home, remove the good tobacco, and dry it out. Then they'd reroll the tobacco with new paper and sell the cigarettes in threes and fives for a few yen.

If you've been here as long as I have you really do meet all kinds. Years ago a woman gave birth to a baby in the doya next door. My wife raced over to help out. She took the mother and baby to a hospital after giving emergency care. A week later the woman left the hospital—without the baby. Nobody had the faintest idea where she went. The baby had to be put up for adop-tion. Let's see, how old would she be now? Over thirty, I guess.

I remember a strange coincidence. This also happened at the doya next door. An officer from the Mammoth box was called in to arrest a man for gambling on the premises. It turns out that they knew each other. They'd been classmates at the same school! It's hard to imagine a more graphic example of two lives going different ways.

This place is full of hard-luck stories, of course, but every once in a while you'll hear a story about someone who's managed to turn his life around. I recall a long-time resident of our doya who'd left his family and a good job in a truck-manufacturing company. He had been married to the president's daughter. I don't know if he'd been adopted into the family or what, but maybe the weight of his position was just too much for him. He wasn't a lazy fellow. In fact, he was such a hard worker that he got noticed by a Hitachi subcontractor and ended up with a regular job. He even remarried. What's really amazing is that he married the woman on the condition that the children from her previous marriage approved of him—which they did!

The police kept a lot closer watch on the men in the early days. They ordered all us doya managers to take our registers to the station every morning for inspection, and they'd copy down our guest list for the previous night. The registers included a physical description of each tenant as well as his name. We were told to keep notes on everyone staying here.

Not too long ago the police did something a bit unusual. All the doya managers in San'ya were called to a meeting at the station headquarters in Asakusa. This was just after the riots in Kamagasaki last October. The chief of police himself led the meeting. That gives you an idea of its significance. He told us that the dust may have settled in Osaka, but there were rumors about certain elements starting something in San'ya. They were worried about Sōgidan, which has connections with the Osaka union. He said there was no way that the police and the *kidōtai* [riot police] could stop trouble by themselves. They wanted us to help keep an eye out for suspicious-looking characters.

Sōgidan has been quiet these days. Last year they were marching through the streets just about every morning to demonstrate against various yakuza misdeeds, and the *kidōtai* were out in force trying to keep the parade route hemmed in so as to avoid a clash with Kanamachi Ikka. Kanamachi doesn't have a lot of supporters, especially after they resorted to violence and knocked off a couple of Sōgidan people a few years back. But whatever points Sōgidan may have scored on the sympathy front it squandered on the front of common decency. Just think of the noise factor. I complained about it at a recent meeting of the Doya Association, which happens to be located right next to the Sōgidan headquarters. The marches always start up right at seven o'clock, just when we're trying to watch the NHK Morning News on TV. Sure, I understand how the union must feel about the yakuza, but they're certainly not going to win any friends among the established community by carrying on as they do. If they want the community's support, there going to have to present themselves in a more palatable way. It's as simple as that, if you ask me.

SENZOKU. EARLY FORTIES. PHOTO-SHOP PROPRIETOR. AT THE SHOP. AUGUST 1991.

I visit the shop, which I had visited once before on a walk with Minowa, to buy film. It is located near the Iroha Arcade's west entrance.

I've lived here all my life. This is where I grew up. It's home. But I'll be the first to admit that it's hardly the ideal business location. Just take a look around you—here I am sandwiched between the San'ya doyagai and the Yoshiwara soaplands! I get clients from both neighborhoods. They're a very different breed from my regular clients, and they sure have their quirks. Sometimes a San'ya man will come in with film to develop and never come back to pick up the prints. Who knows what happens to him. Maybe he gets sick and ends up in some hospital. Or maybe he leaves the area for Kamagasaki, say, and forgets all about the pictures he took. I don't know.

The clients I get from Yoshiwara are usually bathhouse managers who want to buy a Polaroid. They like to take their own pictures of the girls to show their customers. The customers are choosy, you know. They want to see the goods beforehand. So the manager'll take snapshots and show his girls' features to best advantage. If the girl's got big breasts he'll take a frontal shot close up—and so on. The customer checks out the pictures, points to the girl he wants, and then in he goes.

I don't much like it in the arcade. It's awfully sleazy. If I have any business in San'ya I sail right through it on my bicycle and don't stop for anything. I make my deliveries to clients and get the hell out.

The arcade's been around for a good long while. The roof is a relatively recent addition, although you sure couldn't tell by looking at it. It went up only about twenty years ago, and it's already in need of repair. They never should have put it up. It's meant to protect shoppers from the elements, but it ended up attracting all the bums in the area instead. They sleep in the arcade when it rains, and the roof keeps that awful stench of urine trapped inside. Your friend who runs the men's clothier down on the far end of the arcade really has his hands full, doesn't he? He's got to clean up after them every morning. It's bad enough when they piss on the street, but sometimes they do their big business there, too.

In the old days the laborers never came farther toward this end of the arcade than the street that bisects it in the middle. Now they come all the way to the greengrocer right on the corner there. They sit in circles drinking and then pass out right in front of the shops. A lot more men flop in the arcade than before. Some of the drunks make trouble for the residents. They tug at women's skirts as they go by. Make lewd remarks. That sort of thing. Makes it really unpleasant going through there. They say they want freedom of movement. But if you ask me, that kind of freedom ends up causing trouble for everybody else.

I frankly don't think things have changed all that much here, at least in my day. And I don't think they will, either. This place'll never turn into a Shibuya or Shinjuku or Ikebukuro. It'll always be a backwater. A step behind the times.

Thanks for your patronage. I hope I'll have the chance to develop your film for you.

MINAMI SENJŪ. EARLY FORTIES. TOFU-SHOP PROPRIETOR. AT THE SHOP. AUGUST 1991.

I visit the shop at the suggestion of a friend, and am rewarded with the following story, told as the shopkeeper waits on patrons.

You can say that I've grown up with San'ya. Our business certainly has. It peaked during the years when San'ya was liveliest. That was about three decades ago. It's a very different place now.

My mother's home was right in the middle of San'ya, just a few doors down from the Mammoth box. Her family ran a tofu shop, too. I used to visit their house on my own from as early as I can remember. I couldn't have been more than about five when I first started going. When it was still early in the morning I'd run down to the railroad crossing and dash across it. There was no pedestrian bridge in those days. Then I'd race past Namidabashi and on to my mother's house. The area around Namidabashi was an unforgettable sight. The street was packed solid with day laborers in their working garb, and the *tehaishi* were busy sizing them up. There wasn't any room for automobile traffic, and the trolley cars could just barely make their way through the crowd. I couldn't believe all the people.

I went to elementary school close by but commuted to a middle school in Suidōbashi. Of course nobody there knew a thing about San'ya except its reputation for being a tough neighborhood. Needless to say, I saw the place differently, and I'd take advantage of my own familiarity in several ways. One thing I used to do was buy up U.S. army surplus that you could find in San'ya shops for real cheap and then turn around and sell it to my classmates at a nifty profit. It was in great demand at my school. Some of the surplus was clothing actually owned by GIs, and it bore the touches of the men who wore it. An ordinary jacket might bring in a hundred yen or less, but I'd go out of my way to collect ones with names or designs embroidered on them. I could get two hundred yen for those.

That's not all. Once in a while I'd invite a classmate for a visit and then casually show him around as if it were the most natural thing in the world to do. After all, I'd grown up here and played on the streets and hardly gave the place a second thought. But my friends were overwhelmed. They'd flinch at the sight of a man wearing a headband. I got a big kick out of their reactions.

My family built its business around San'ya. In addition to my mother's store there were several other stores owned by relatives in the surrounding area—Senzoku, Asakusa, and of course here in Minami Senjū. The family had four branches in all and each one supplied tofu to at least twenty clients—mostly eating and drinking establishments. There were over a hundred clients in all. But one by one my relatives have quit the business because of age or illness.

The shop in the doyagai is still there, but it stopped selling tofu after it was converted into a convenience store awhile back. But it's a store with a difference. They set up a small kitchen in the back room and started serving breakfast. Then they decided to add a hot dish to the usual fare of *onigiri* [a type of rice ball] and they hit upon *kenchinjiru* [a stew of vegetables and pork]. You'll see a long line of men at the serving window every morning.

San'ya isn't the lively place it was when I was a kid thirty years ago, and at the rate things are going, I wouldn't be surprised if the doyagai disappears altogether. Then all my childhood memories of walking through those crowded streets in the morning will be nothing but a dream.

Bureaucrats

Jōhoku. Late forties. Director of Welfare Desk, Jōhoku Welfare Center. At the Center. December 1989.

I pay an unannounced call one day to the Welfare Center and am courteously received by Jōhoku, who provides me with pamphlets, brochures, and a few observations of his own on the yoseba.

I've worked at the Center for three years now. Like every civil servant here, I'm under the employ of the Tokyo Metropolitan Government. I don't know how many more years I'll be on the job, but I'm sure it won't be many. All employees on the permanent staff are rotated every three to five years. There's no question that the Center is unique among the city's administrative facilities. University students majoring in social welfare tour the place all the time.

Several changes during my tenure here have affected the workers. Until recently, they didn't need proof of residency to get a job through a public agency like the Center or the Shokuan. All they needed was to show that they were living in the area, and the seal of the doya they were staying at would do just fine. But starting a year ago, the law has required them to file for residency with the ward they're living in. If they don't, they can't receive a white card and with it the privilege of unemployment compensation.

The law was enacted to prevent fraud, but it's made life more difficult for those who just barely find enough work to keep them going or who are sick or injured and can't work at all. It's had the effect of widening the gap between those who can work regularly and those who can't. It really doesn't matter what I personally think. I don't have a say in policy, and neither do my colleagues. We just carry it out. And so we often find ourselves caught in the middle.

Another thing having an effect on workers is the recent influx of cheap foreign labor. The Japanese day-laborer population is getting older, and there are fewer and fewer able-bodied men around to handle the really strenuous jobs. The foreigners who come in are in their twenties and thirties. They work without any benefits and with no complaints. They can't afford to complain, because they're generally here illegally. You won't find them in the doyagai—it's very expensive here for the space you get. They live elsewhere in the city on a shoe-string budget and share three or four to a room.

You often hear about how strenuous the day laborer's work is, but that's not necessarily true. I'm told that a lot of *hanba* work is relatively easy. But let's face it—most of the men who come here can't afford to be picky about their jobs. They're here for other reasons. And that's what it all boils down to—why they're here. There's no one reason, of course, but I guess it comes down to this: they've lost their family ties. If they were on good terms with their families, they'd have stayed where they were. But something's gone awry, and so they end up here. It's not a happy situation, and I can't say I condone it, but that's what happens. Time and time again.

NERIMA. MID-FIFTIES. JŌHOKU WELFARE CENTER EMPLOYEE. SAN'YA COFFEE SHOP. AUGUST 1991.

Employed as a "temporary" worker eighteen days a month, Nerima has been on the job for nearly two decades—far longer than any of her full-time colleagues, who are routinely transferred. The author of several books on San'ya and known for her efforts to draw attention to health problems among day laborers, she speaks with the deliberate, confident tone of one who has seen and heard a great deal.

This job has never gotten easy, even after eighteen years. I constantly feel as though I'm caught between a rock and a hard place. I have to look at things not just from the day laborer's point of view but also from the city's point of view and finally from my supervisors' point of view. In the end, though, I guess I'd have to say that I feel closest to the day laborer.

Maybe it's because my own position isn't all that different from theirs. After all my years here, I still hold just a temporary job. Not that I'm in any financial straits. I am married to a man who holds a respectable position at a university here in Tokyo. I live in a nice home in Nerima. My children are grown and making it on their own. In fact, I became a grandmother recently. But I never feel far removed from the men I work with at the Center, even when I'm away from San'ya. I'll run into them when I'm out on the town shopping in places like Ikebukuro or Shinjuku. My daughter lives near the park in West Shinjuku, and I'll often see a familiar face there. In that sense I never leave my job.

I've always had an interest in society and its problems, but my public consciousness was totally misguided at first. I used to be a school teacher, and my field was social studies. I was quick to point out the problems that plagued the world. Your country was an easy target at the time, what with the civil-rights demonstrations and the war in Vietnam. Everything seemed so black and white. But what did I know about my own country? Very little, I'm ashamed to say. I wonder now how I was able to teach my students anything.

I had to quit teaching and return to life as a housewife for a while. I won't go into detail about why, but once things settled down on the home front, I began to get restless and ended up enrolling in a community college to major in social welfare. The curriculum required that we make field trips to various welfare facilities around the city. One of those facilities was the Center here in San'ya. It's strange. The moment I set foot in the building something clicked inside. I was overcome with this feeling of, "Yes, this is the place." And so I took a job that was being offered there.

I'm sure you know that San'ya's heyday began only after the war. But the history of the yoseba itself is a long one. And the more you delve into that history, the more you realize how little things have changed since the days of the Edo-period *ninsoku yoseba.* The purpose remains the same—to generate a supply of temporary labor, to keep it centralized and under strict control, and to cut off sustenance to workers who've become expendable.

It doesn't take any rigorous analysis to figure this out. All you have to do is listen to the men who come and visit me during consultation hours. Their problems follow a depressingly similar pattern. They revolve around housing, health, and jobs. The very basic things, really. I hear variations of the same story from morning to night, and the situation is getting worse, not better. The men are getting older, and more and more of them are sick or are too weak to work for long stretches. That means they're making less money and are more likely to be sleeping on the street. Even the healthier ones gravitate of necessity toward the less strenuous jobs, which of course pay less well. Experience doesn't count much in this business, and the pay goes down with age. Instead of getting fifteen thousand yen for a job, they might get only twelve thousand or even nine thousand. That means the labor brokers' cut for these jobs is huge. They really feast off older men.

City officials like to tout the figures on Tokyo. We have fewer homeless citizens than any other major city in the world. So why make a fuss about such a small population? they ask. But I take a different view. It's precisely because there are relatively few homeless here that the government is in a position to make a real impact. But what few measures it has instituted thus far have been generally geared toward control, not welfare. There is talk about building a shelter or inexpensive lodging facility for homeless workers right here in San'ya. The place most often mentioned is the site of the Parcel Post Distribution Center on Meiji Boulevard. If the government does go ahead and build a facility, well, that's fine, of course. But it's also got to plan for the long term—I'm talking about medical care along with shelter—and not just in terms of a cosmetic face-lift to keep an eyesore under wraps.

Nearly everyone living in this area is familiar with the drunks lying about the street at all hours, for instance, or the morning yoseba with men standing around Namidabashi waiting for a job. But there is a lot going on that very few people notice. The *tehaishi* working the streets, for example. Each one is connected with a gang and each gang has its own turf. They never stray from it. The balance of power is delicate, and it's invisible to a passerby.

Another aspect of life here people usually don't notice is the hierarchy within the so-called lumpen-proletariat. To outsiders the workers may all look alike, but in fact there are at least three distinct groups. The *tobi* and other *shokunin* are at the top of the heap. They make the big money. They swagger around and lord it over the rest. They can be extravagant, and they're not afraid to empty their wallets at the drop of a hat on food or clothes or anything else. Below them are the *dokata*. These are the ordinary, unskilled laborers and they get paid much less. And below them are the *aokansha*—the men who for any number of reasons can't or don't work and who are forced to live on the street. The others treat them like dirt. I keep telling the men who work as *tobi* or *dokata* that they shouldn't waste their time looking down their noses at others less fortunate. But the feeling of superiority of one group over another is very strong.

If anything, this sense of class-consciousness has intensified because of the recent building boom. Some men really do make good money. I remember one *tobi shoku* who visited the Center about some physical problem.

He didn't have health insurance, but he did have something like two or three million yen in his pocket!

San'ya has changed a lot since I first started working at the Center. The bunkhouses are disappearing, and business hotels are going up in their place practically by the month. The cost of a room keeps going up, and more and more men are sleeping on the street. This could be a very different place in twenty or thirty years, especially if the Doya Association has its way. It has a lot of power, and its power is concentrated among a handful of landlords who own over half the beds among them. There's no doubt that they're pushing for a different clientele than the one they've got now.

That doesn't mean the yoseba here will disappear entirely. It's too convenient for everyone involved. Yet with each passing day more men need help. And everything I do—the books I write, the surveys on workers' health, the mandala for workers who have died in San'ya—all that is my way of drawing attention to this need. Progress is painfully slow. But I have gotten a few things going and I have developed a network. I know there will be improvement over time. I just hope I'm around long enough to see it.

MAMMOTH. LATE FORTIES. CHIEF OF THE MAMMOTH POLICE BOX. AT THE POLICE BOX. NO DATE.

I have walked past the Mammoth box more times than I can count during all my days in San'ya. But I have yet to talk to, let alone glance at or exchange greetings with, any policeman. The less contact, I have always felt, the better, given my purpose here. The police function is too critical to ignore altogether, however. I have wanted to talk, yet know that without the proper introduction I would have difficulty obtaining any useful information.

I get that introduction through a contact at the Welfare Center, who gives me the name of someone working in the San'ya Countermeasures Bureau, who in turn promises to inform the Mammoth box that a visitor will be making an appearance. I wait several days so as to be certain that the message has been delivered. It has: the chief is expecting a "Mr. Haura." Although surprised at first to see a foreign face, he recovers his aplomb and telephones the San'ya Countermeasures Bureau in my presence to confirm the visitor's identity. "How much should I tell him?" he asks. "The standard briefing? Like I'd give to journalists? Very well."

Mammoth wears the typical plainclothesman's garb: navy-blue pants, long-sleeved shirt, and sleeveless gray vest. He escorts me to the small anteroom directly behind the recessed front that faces the street. The anteroom has its own view of the street through a tiny, shoe-box size peephole protected by thick wire grating. The interview is more lecture than conver-

*sation. It is clear that Mammoth has a prepared speech and that I am to
listen, not talk.*

I've been on the job here for a year and a half now, which means that my
assignment is at least half over. The term is two to three years. My association with San'ya goes back a lot further than that, though. I worked for three
years in the Security Division of the Metropolitan Police Board (Keishichō),
and another three years before that in Public Safety at the Asakusa Station,
which has jurisdiction over this area. So all in all I've got close to a decade's
worth of experience under my belt monitoring activities in San'ya.

The men who work for me are a select group. I picked them with great
care. The first thing you'll notice about them is their size. I like them big
and burly. If you have to use force, it helps to have some weight to throw
around. They've all had training in the martial arts, and everyone here holds
at least a second-degree ranking in *kendō*. A couple of the men upstairs hold
a sixth-degree ranking.

The second thing you'll notice is the uniform—or should I say lack of
one. We don't want to stick out like sore thumbs and cause trouble by our
mere presence. So we dress in mufti in order to blend in better with the rest
of the population. That doesn't mean we don't take precautions. Everyone
here wears protective equipment, because you never know when trouble
might start. [He taps on his shirt and produces a hard metallic sound from
the armored vest he wears underneath.]

Special protection alone won't keep you out of trouble. That's why I made
it a point to bring in older officers. We value experience. The youngest man
here is twenty-six. He's a special case, and even he's way above the minimum enlistment age of nineteen. All the rest are in their thirties and up. I
have no use for the paper-pushing desk cop who's more interested in job
security and family than in the rigors of police work. Not that the men here
shouldn't be family men. It's just that police officers who let personal concerns interfere with their work are courting danger, pure and simple. The
one split second you let down your guard could be your last.

I'm not talking in the abstract. A police officer was stabbed to death right
here by a radical activist named Isoe Yōichi in 1979. He's doing time now in
a Hokkaido prison. He would've gotten the chair in your country. You don't
get on death row by killing a single police officer in Japan, though. The labor
unions in San'ya know this and try and take advantage of the law.

There are two unions working out of San'ya, and they're committed to
revolution. That's what makes our job different from one in any other part
of the city. You see, there are actually two communities living in San'ya—
the ordinary citizens and the day laborers. To go with the two communities
we have essentially two lines of work. One consists of community relations

[handwritten margin note: 2 citizens. ordinary + day labor]

and regular criminal work, such as going after petty thieves and the like. In this respect we're just like any other police box in Tokyo. We give directions to pedestrians and respond to emergency calls. The second line of work consists of surveillance, suppression, and any other measures necessary to contain the revolutionary activities of the unions.

Sōgidan in particular. They are an ultraleftist group steeped in Marxist-Leninism. Some of the members used to belong to the Red Army, and they don't believe in compromise. They use the laborers as pawns and foment violence by exploiting their grievances and channeling their energies into revolutionary activity.

I guess I don't have to tell you that there are a lot of grievances to exploit. The men who come to San'ya are at the bottom of society. They've lost their families and their jobs and they're here all alone. They take whatever work they can get, and believe me, the work isn't pleasant. The *tehaishi* take their cut, of course, and so the workers never even see part of their wages. Yes, we here in the police force know all about capitalist exploitation. We read Marx, too, you see. After all, we need to know our enemy. But violent revolution cannot be tolerated, and that's why we have to protect the community from the radicals.

Things are complicated by the presence of yakuza in the area. Kanamachi Ikka is the most powerful group. It's part of a national organization, and the boss of Kanamachi is currently its chairman. They fought a lot of turf wars with other yakuza and came out on top. They've also fought with Sōgidan. Our job is to see that a balance is maintained between the yakuza and the unions, and to adjust our response to their movements as needed.

There have been some disturbances in Kamagasaki lately, as you probably know, and so we prepared ourselves for anything that might happen here. Nothing did happen, but we were prepared. As long as we have sufficient time, we can dispatch forces in such a way as to seal off the entire area and contain the disturbances to this locale alone. Our police box would work the western flank, and we'd be supported by Minami Senjū Station to the north and by Asakusa Station to the south. The Sumida River provides a natural barrier to the east. We can box everybody in from all sides and make sure that no disturbance spills over into the neighboring communities.

If things get really hot, we can call in the riot police. They came here every morning in their buses when Sōgidan was parading about the streets on a daily basis awhile back. But let me remind you that we're not here to make enemies. We like to help out when we can, by giving directions to laborers who are new to the area, for example, or by dispensing blankets and clothes. We look on the laborers as humans, even if they do wear work gloves.

The one thing we don't do, by the way, is make arrests. If we did, the laborers might start screaming that we were torturing him or something like that, and soon we'd have a mob on our hands. If the man is drunk, we take him to the detox center on the other side of Nihonzutsumi. There are no police there, just doctors in white coats. If we suspect someone of criminal activity, we haul him straight to Asakusa Station and let the police there deal with him.

We have learned to treat the laborers with great care. One tiny spark can flare up into a conflagration. If one of our officers oversteps his authority, then we've really got a problem on our hands. That happens once in a while. It's my biggest headache.

For the most part, the laborers here are a docile group. Sōgidan does its darnedest to stir the embers, but when you come right down to it, the union is a bunch of hypocrites. Everybody knows they're dyed-in-the-wool communists, but they insist on hiding their true colors. They may be right about capitalist exploitation, but they ignore the very first page of the Communist Manifesto, which states plainly that communists should demonstrate their commitment to direct word and direct action without pretense and without trying to conceal themselves. That's what really irks me. But you know, the laborers are getting wise to Sōgidan's ways, too. They see that they're being taken for a ride. They also know that union support can backfire on them. For example, a laborer might get injured on the job. Of course, he's not covered by any insurance. At that point, Sōgidan moves in and jawbones the subcontractor into giving the laborer, say, a month's worth of compensation for an injury that will heal in a week. The subcontractor complies in order to avoid any hassle. Sounds good for the laborer, right? Wrong. The next time the subcontractor recruits help, it avoids San'ya altogether and starts hiring out of Takabashi or Takadanobaba. That means everybody in San'ya ends up losing.

The facility you see here went up in 1960. It served its purpose, but it's gotten old and tired and it's time for a new one. We're getting just that across the street, in the lot catty-corner to us. It will be about five times as large as the present structure, and it will accommodate riot police right on the premises, instead of having them sit out in their armored buses at curbside like they do now. There's talk about a protest movement against the new police box. But it'll go up. Don't you worry about that.

Missionaries

SENDAI. LATE FORTIES. CHRISTIAN PASTOR AND RESTAURANT MANAGER. AT THE RESTAURANT. APRIL 1990.

I started this restaurant two years ago. It's open every day except Sundays and holidays for breakfast and dinner. The food is good, if you ask me.

Darned good, in fact, for the price. We're open just mornings and evenings, like most places in San'ya, but even that schedule keeps us plenty busy. I've hired two people full time to cook. The rest are volunteers—maybe thirty or forty in all. I'd be obliged if you signed up for a shift. You wouldn't be the only foreigner. I've got several working for us and they're from all over the world. Most of them are here in Japan doing missionary work and I get them to come here a few hours each week in their spare time.

The restaurant's still relatively new, but I myself have been living in San'ya for about a decade. This place is the fruit of my long association with the area and a symbol of what I think is most needed here. That, in a word, is nourishment. Of course, I see my ultimate mission as helping others to feel the presence of God and to join the faith. But let's face it: it's hard to nurture your faith on an empty stomach. And there are a lot of empty stomachs here in San'ya. So for me right now, offering sustenance *is* my mission. I realized this after taking part in a winter soup kitchen operated by the United Church of Christ in Japan a few years back. People get hungry all the time, you know, not just in the evening during the cold months.

What brought me to San'ya? God brought me here, of course. That's my only answer. I moved to Tokyo from Sendai in the early 1960s and started out in an ordinary office job. I first came to San'ya as a volunteer working with children. You see, there used to be many more families living in this area than there are now—even among the day laborers. Ever since they moved out of the doya, though, San'ya has become a much grimmer place.

Anyway, my sense of commitment grew over time and I eventually quit my job to enter divinity school. After graduating I worked in Kotobuki-chō in Yokohama for a while. I've been in San'ya for about ten years now and work as a day laborer. That's really the only way to understand how the men here live and think.

Three principles have guided my life here. The first is what you might call networking. I may have come to San'ya by chance, but once I got here, I wanted to make the most of it by meeting and getting to know as many people as possible. The second principle is hands-on experience. The only way to get to know the men here is to participate in their lives, and so experience for me has meant working myself as a day laborer. The third principle is securing a livelihood. As I said, I'm associated with the United Church of Christ in Japan, but I'm not funded by the church. Those of us who work here do so in its name, but we have to make ends meet on our own. It's tougher that way, but it results in closer bonds with the people we live with. We can't get bailed out by some charitable windfall. We have to deal with boom and bust just like everyone else here.

Without a doubt the most depressing thing about this place is the abuse of alcohol. Alcoholism is a terrible disease. You get mad at the men for how they act under the influence, but it wrenches you to see what liquor does to them. The Japanese government's policy—if you can call it that—is terribly backward. It's a travesty, in fact. If my work at the restaurant ever settles down to a dull roar, I'd like to visit the United States and Europe and study social policy in those countries, especially their policy on excessive drinking. No doubt I could learn a lot.

Sure, I admit to having a drink myself now and then. After all, it's the grease that keeps the social machinery moving in this country. And it does calm you down. Sometimes you need that. You said you're overnighting in a doya this evening. If you think you'll have a hard time getting to sleep, just have a cup of saké before bedding down. That'll settle your nerves.

After having lived here for a decade, I can tell you this. The people here are treated like old rags. You're used until you can't sop up any more grime and then you're just tossed away. Recent changes in government policy have made it all the harder for the weaker to survive. If you get sick or hurt, you're done for.

Oh sure, you can always ask piously just what made these men come here in the first place. After all, nobody forced them to, right? So maybe you'd want to argue that the yoseba is actually a convenience for people who seek it out as a refuge of last resort. But I would answer that you're only looking at the half of it. Free will works all right in the abstract, but you can never call all your own shots, especially in this country. San'ya's not just a repository for men who for a variety of reasons don't fit into the rest of society. And it isn't just a labor pool ripe for capitalist exploitation. I think it's both. In fact, it couldn't be one without the other. And that's what makes this place indispensable to society at large. Quite the system, isn't it?

QUEBEC. MID-FORTIES. CATHOLIC MISSIONARY AND PHYSICIAN'S ASSISTANT. SAN'YŪKAI EXAMINATION ROOM. JULY 1990.

Quebec, who works at the Maryknoll Order's San'yūkai free medical clinic in Kiyokawa, has become a San'ya institution. Lacking the oversized (by Japanese standards) physique of many Westerners and truly fluent in the language of his patients, he blends in well with his surroundings. Every greeting, every gesture, suggests a deep knowledge about and engagement with his clientele. He casually alerts a patient leaving the clinic, for example, who is getting on the wrong bicycle. Quebec does not speak much English. I do not speak French. Our lingua franca is Japanese.

When I prepared to do missionary work for the Quebec Foreign Missions Society, its custom was to offer three choices for a residence abroad. I picked Chile, Peru, and Japan, and I ended up in Japan. I worked all over the country

Man slumbering on Old Streetcar Boulevard. Early morning, and the shops are still shuttered.

and didn't make it to San'ya until six years ago, which was about the time that San'yūkai was founded. I began working on a volunteer basis, but one thing led to another and now this is my only job. I work here full time.

We used to be located at a tiny place near the Jōhoku Welfare Center, but last year we finally collected enough donations to purchase land here and build this clinic. The senior citizens' center [Iwashita Center] that used to be based in Minowa is located upstairs. The clinic's waiting room and examination room are both downstairs. Dr. Katori is the director. You may have heard of him, since he's well known for his work with alcoholics and a rather amazing person. He's getting up in years now, but he still sees patients on Saturdays. He also works at the Center one day a week.

San'ya can be a rough place, but things have been pretty peaceful around here of late. There was of course that bitter feud in the mid-eighties between Sōgidan and Kanamachi Ikka. After the Sōgidan leader was killed, the union changed its face. What used to be a laborers' union has turned into a group headed by idealistic students singing a revolutionary tune but lacking practical experience. I think the workers realize this.

Kanamachi Ikka, though, is doing just fine. In fact, they're making money hand over fist. They've got a lock on the jobs that men get off the streets in the morning, and they do a good business in off-track betting, too. Anyway, it behooves us to keep on friendly terms with them. After all, we've set up shop on their turf. We try to be cordial, and they respond in kind. We receive gifts from them now and then.

I live within pretty easy walking distance in a little apartment just east of the Sumida River. My salary comes from two sources: the San'yūkai itself and my Quebec mission. It's not much, but it's enough to live on.

I've lived in Japan for twenty years, and I've put down a lot of roots. I enjoy myself here. I regard the men I see at San'yūkai not just as patients but as buddies, too. And I think that most of them see themselves not so much as patients at a clinic but as members of a special club. That's why they take it upon themselves to pitch in and help out when the occasion calls for it, without anybody asking. When we moved here, for example, several of them just showed up and offered their services. They hauled everything from furniture to filing boxes.

That's why it hurts when you lose one of them. It happens all the time. I'd guess that 20 percent of the total San'ya day-laborer population use the clinic. And of this group maybe twenty-five pass on each year—many right on the street. So figure out for yourself how many die altogether in any given year. It's frightening. You want to do everything you can for these men. On the other hand, you know it's not going to do any good to give anyone a free lunch. But just where do you draw the line? It's a tough question, and I don't really have the answer. I just try to encourage them.

Give them a nudge. Try to help them get back on their feet. Sometimes it works. Sometimes it doesn't. Usually it doesn't. But you keep trying. You have to.

Other Voices

SHIMIZU. EARLY SEVENTIES. FREELANCE WRITER AND FORMER DAY LABORER. AT HIS DOYA. MAY 1990.

Shimizu is a sprightly man who radiates enthusiasm and intelligence. His three-mat room, crammed with books, papers, and bags of clothes, barely has space for a futon in the middle. When he is not resting, he is likely to be poring over a manuscript at a tiny table below the corner window.

I've lived the last forty years here in Tokyo, and most of them have been in San'ya. It hasn't been the best of lives, but it hasn't been the worst, either. I wouldn't have chosen this life when starting out, but I can't say that I have any regrets.

Not that I haven't done anything I don't regret—far from it. It's just that the line dividing a life without incident and a life gone astray is a tenuous one at best. Frankly, I think that people who manage to steer the so-called straight course in life really don't do much steering at all. They're just lucky never to have been hit by a stray bolt of lightening which strikes without warning.

When I was young, the brightest of futures awaited me. My father was a graduate of Tokyo University Medical School who embarked on a distinguished career as a surgeon. He was the deputy director of one of the best-known hospitals in Shizuoka Prefecture before illness ended his life when I was still very young. Not only my father but nearly all my relatives on my mother's side were in the medical profession. I was encouraged to become a doctor myself, but I didn't pass the entrance examination into the medical faculty at Tokyo University. I ended up going to Waseda University and majoring in economics.

I was already out of school when the war broke out and I had my stint in the military like everyone else. But I spent most of my years with a special technical unit in Urawa [just north of Tokyo] and never even went to the front. I certainly led a charmed life in those days! After the war I was able to return to the job I held at the Shimizu branch of Mitsui Bank and Trust. And a very good job it was. I got married to a school teacher I met when I was with the army in Urawa and was all set for a career among the elite.

Then the roof caved in. You see, I learned the real story about my mother. People in my family had always told me that she had left home to teach music after Father died. But in fact she ran off with one of the doctors working in my grandfather's clinic. The news hit me like a ton of bricks. It turned out that everyone in the family knew about the scandal except me. I not only felt betrayed by my mother but deceived in the bargain by everybody else.

Everything fell apart after that. I started living a life of debauchery. I took up with all sorts of women and drowned myself in drink. I went through a lot of money as well—far more than I could come up with on my own. Eventually I got caught with my hands in the Mitsui coffer, and that was the end of my job. My family disowned me, and my wife divorced me. I was finished.

I couldn't stay home any longer and so I drifted to Tokyo. I found myself in Asakusa, which I'd frequented during my university days. I learned about San'ya from a vagrant who was sleeping out near the temple and dealing in stolen goods. "You need work?" he asked. "You'll find it in San'ya. They'll hire anyone. And you can sleep in a doya there with the money you've made—no references required."

And that's what I did. This was back in 1951. I worked on and off as a day laborer as long as I had my health. I also had a go at other jobs. I even worked as a clerk at one of the doya here. I kind of enjoyed that job. But good things never last, do they! The owner got mad because I was about to put up a vagrant who'd drifted over from Ueno Park one rainy evening. He had the money, but he was dirty. The owner didn't like that. He had his standards. This was in the late 1960s. The city had been rebuilt, the Tokyo Olympics had been held to showcase Japan to the world, and vagrants were under constant pressure to move out of areas like Ueno Park where they might sully the view for a growing number of foreign tourists.

Anyway, I was shocked by the owner's attitude. Here I had thought I'd hit bottom, only to learn that San'ya was actually a rung or two above the muddy floor. But after I got over the shock, I became furious at the owner. Who was he to judge a person by his looks? And so I quit my job then and there, packed up everything I owned—which wasn't much, of course—and moved to Ueno Park myself. I had to see with my own eyes what life among the lowest of the low was really like. I ended up staying there for seven years.

I was one of about thirty vagrants who made Ueno Park their home— double that during the cherry-blossom viewing season in the spring or festival time in the summer. I was astonished by how easy it was to eke out a living on zero income. Food was plentiful once you knew when and where to get it—and once you learned to rid yourself of shame. That's the real trick. Scavenging was a nighttime job, so we'd sleep a good part of the day. It wasn't at all like San'ya, where you have to get up at the crack of dawn.

Some people would sleep on the park benches that line the walkways. Others would sleep right on the ground with cardboard or newspapers for bedding. They'd get their food from the garbage thrown out by the hundreds of restaurants doing business near the park.

You'd be amazed at how much perfectly good food and drink the restaurants dump every night. We'd get to know the staff at each place when we made our nightly rounds. Some were pretty decent. They'd have a can of leftovers waiting for us. Others—well, you'll find a rotten apple in every barrel. Once in a while we'd get a bottle of beer with cigarette ashes dumped in it. You couldn't tell by looking, because the glass is tinted dark brown. But you found out in a hurry when you took a swig. It tasted odd and made you sick!

We never lacked for drink, what with all the near-empty beer bottles standing in crates outside each restaurant and bar. You don't believe me? Well, think about it. Every time a waiter or hostess brings a new order of beer to a table of guests and clears away the other bottles, there are usually a few drops in the old bottles at the very least, and sometimes a lot more. The patrons don't mind. They're not watching that closely, and besides, they're more interested in having fresh cold beer and having a good time with their friends. So their waste is our profit. We'd pool the dregs of each crate, and soon we'd have a dozen big bottles-worth to divide among us.

I met all sorts of interesting people while I lived in Ueno. And in the process I was "discovered" by a newspaper reporter from the *Yomiuri* who was covering the area at the time. That meeting led eventually to my own column in another paper and acquaintances with numerous celebrities. I even hob-nobbed with a few literary types, including the likes of Endō Shūsaku. Would you believe I appeared in one of his collections of dialogues with "men of culture"! Soon I had enough material to fill a book. It caused quite a stir in its day, and so I came out with a sequel. I was interviewed several times on radio and TV.

But that, too, is past. All that good food and drink in Ueno finally caught up with me. I contracted diabetes and gout, spent a good long time in the hospital, and have never been the same since. I'm living on a small welfare dole now because of my physical disability, and am just making ends meet with the extra income I get from a monthly column on San'ya I'm writing for a magazine. Needless to say, I don't drink anymore, but I can't simply switch to soda pop or juice, because of the diabetes. My solid diet's restricted as well. You can see that I've hardly a tooth left in my mouth!

To get on welfare I registered with the ward office and have established residency in San'ya. But I'm in the minority. I'd guess that only about one out of every five men living in this doya is registered. That's more than before, though. I used to be the only one.

There's a big divide between the day laborers who've registered and get their work through the public hiring agencies and those who haven't and get their work off the street. The first group doesn't make as much money, it's true, but they're covered by unemployment insurance when they're out of work. The other group has to go it on its own. There's plenty of work right now, but when business goes slack, they'll be out of luck. The only place left to work then will be the *hanba,* and they're only one step up from forced-labor camps.

The situation is actually more complicated, but you may be aware of that already. At any rate, San'ya has changed over the years on the surface, but it's still the same place I've always known underneath. This is where men trade their lost hopes on a little freedom. They're thinking all the while they can beat the system but eventually getting ground to the bone.

Changed but same underneath

TAMAHIME. MID-LATE SIXTIES. VAGRANT. TAMAHIME PARK. AUGUST 1991.

I am eating a lunch of rice balls and barley tea on a Tamahime Park bench. The heat is oppressive. Several men walk by me and eye me surreptitiously. Tamahime is the only one who acknowledges my presence. We do not engage in conversation, however: the exchange is in fact a one-sided monologue, delivered on the stroll. Tamahime walks excitedly in front of me and talks in fits and starts, his speech interspersed with snatches of English, German, Chinese, and Korean. It is the speech of a madman. Reflection reveals a suggestive pattern in the madness, however: Taiheiki *is the fourteenth-century chronicle of a revolt by a branch of the imperial family against the throne and of the throne's defense by a famous supporter, Kusunoki Masashige (also known as Nankō). The camphor tree in Japanese is called* kusunoki. *The* sakura *(cherry tree) is of course a widely invoked symbol of Japan. Other images suggest wartime experience on the Asian continent. Tamahime carries with him a Styrofoam bowl filled with dried noodles, to which he eventually adds tap water from a nearby faucet. His unbuttoned shirt reveals a lean, wrinkled, and deeply sun-tanned torso. The index finger is missing from his right hand.*

Hey, you! What are you doing here? Who said you could come? Not me, not me! Go home, will you, go home! Where are you from? Germany? Italy? I know all about those places. I was in the army. I went through the war. Do you know your history? Well? Well? *Taiheiki.* Ever heard of it? Nankō. Kusunoki Masashige. Who is the most important character in *Taiheiki*? Do you know? Do you know? Hey, what's this tree here? [He points at a tree next to us in the park.] A *sakura.* No, wait—it couldn't be a *sakura.* No bugs. A *kusunoki,* that's it. Bugs don't come near it. *Sakura* are no good. All they do is attract bugs. No good, no good. You know your history? Who's the biggest shot of them all? Hitler? How about Hirohito? Is he great? Is he strong? Ha! Who gives a damn about the emperor! Look what I've got. Know what these are? That's right, noodles. No, of course you don't eat them dry. You gotta cook 'em. And that's what I'm gonna do. Here, can you read this? "Sanuki Konpira *udon.*" This is lunch. I'm having something else for dinner. What are you eating? [He glances at the remnants of my meal.] What, *onigiri!* That's too heavy on the gut. It's not dinner time yet! Don't eat, don't eat! Listen, here. Take down some notes. [I have had my pen out, thinking to write down some thoughts during lunch.] *Taiheiki.* Who's the biggest big shot? You don't know? You don't know? Don't come here. We don't want you here. I ate mutton and dog and rat [he uses the English words]. You weren't even born yet. What were the big shots doing? Godfather. [The English word used: "God," pronounced "goad."] Goat. [The English word used.] Sheep. I ate sheep. Don't eat. Don't write. Don't come here. We don't want you here. Look, this is all I have. All copper. Yi, er, san . . . [He counts his ten-yen coins in Chinese.] Whew, it's hot. Where's the shade? Where's the shade? I'm going to rot! Rot to bits!

AIRIN. LATE THIRTIES. CARTOONIST AND DAY-LABORER COUNSELOR. IN THE KAMAGASAKI YOSEBA AND NEARBY TENNŌJI, OSAKA. AUGUST 1991.

I know of Airin, who works full time at the Airin Welfare Center in Kamagasaki, through his well-known comic strip that depicts life in Japan's largest yoseba. Our conversation begins at the Welfare Center and continues at a restaurant nearby. Airin's account reveals a wide knowledge of the yoseba in general as well as of the specific differences between Kamagasaki and San'ya.

When I was young I had no ambitions of being a cartoonist or anything else. I didn't study in school and I had no goal in life. All that changed after I started working here at the Welfare Center. I began meeting people who told me memorable stories I thought worth preserving. I took to drawing sketches so that I could remember the men I talked with during the day. I didn't have any special training. I wasn't an art major in school and I never took drawing lessons. But one thing led to another and I was soon publishing a strip in the Welfare Center paper. The cartoons have always been an avocation. But without a doubt they're what's kept me going.

Let me show you some drawings. [He pulls out a large sketchbook filled with portraits.] This one here's typical of the older generation in Kamagasaki. He lost everything in the war. His home was flattened in an air raid, and his entire family was wiped out. Yet for some reason he was convinced that his sister had survived the bombing, and he devoted his life after the war to locating her. He was even featured once on TV. But nothing came of it. He's a great baseball fan, and he keeps his life together by rooting for the Hanshin Tigers every chance he gets.

This second man is a *hibakusha*. He suffered constant headaches, so he quit school at an early age and began doing the only thing he was capable of doing, which was physical labor. He's no longer with us, though. He was only in his fifties when he died.

The next here is the son of a priest who became a yakuza. He wasn't exactly a model of his profession, though. When he was asked to knock somebody off, he got cold feet. He was a half-baked gangster any way you look at it. Even his body tattoo is unfinished.

Here's a drawing of a guy who was continually caught in the ebbtide of the Japanese economy and was eventually washed up on the shores of Kamagasaki. Talk about bad luck! He graduated from Kyushu University in 1955 and was about to join a prestigious bank in Fukuoka when he decided at the last minute to go into his father's coal-mining business. It seemed like a good idea at the time. Business was booming, and he would be helping out his dad. What he didn't know was that Japan was about to abandon coal for oil as its primary energy resource. The family business went belly up three years later. So he took a job in steel. Another seemingly good idea. But then the steel industry bottomed out in the late sixties. Next he started working for Ishikawajima Harima Heavy Industries, one of the biggest shipbuilders around. Guess what happened. The shipbuilding industry crashed in the mid-seventies, after the first Oil Shock. He struggled until the 1980s before finally coming to Kamagasaki. He's done pretty well for himself here, all things considered. He works as an electrician and makes good money at it. But you've got to wonder how things would have turned out if he'd gone ahead and taken that job with the bank. I bet he'd have done well—at least until it was the banks' turn to meet with hard times.

This next group of sketches shows a new breed of day laborers. Unlike the previous generation, they didn't go through the war and they don't come from the provinces. They have very specific interests in life and they work to support them. Take this man here. He's in his fifties, but he leads the life of the younger generation I'm talking about. He's crazy about traveling. He comes into Kamagasaki and arranges to get work at a *hanba* for maybe a three- or four-month stretch, which earns him enough to finance a trip abroad. When he runs out of money he comes back to Osaka, gets a job at another *hanba*, and starts saving up all over again. This man here is a university graduate in his forties who rejected the corporate ladder. He's a dyed-in-the-wool mountaineer, and works only as much as he has to in order to finance his treks. This next man here's also in his forties. He makes his home in Thailand, would you believe, and he returns to Japan just long enough to earn what he needs to support himself in his adopted country. This last sketch is of a forty-year-old surfing bum. He quit his office job a few years back to surf every chance he could. He started following the waves when he was thirty, and he's been going strong ever since.

So you see, you really do get all kinds here. How did I come to Kamagasaki? Actually, I've answered that question in one of my comic books. I trace the lives of several men who wind up in Kama and I don't forget to include myself. I graduated from a university in Kyoto in 1974. The first Oil Shock had just closed the book on the "high-growth period." It wasn't easy to find a job then, especially for someone like me who never cracked a book in school. Anyway, I looked around a bit and frittered the time away and it finally came down to two choices. One was a teaching job at a women's college in Yamashina. The other was a job here. Positions at the Welfare Center were going begging because—well, let's face it—this place just doesn't appeal to most prospective employees. I thought it over. The teaching job seemed to have more appeal on the surface, but I could see problems lying down the road. I fantasized about a scandal with one of my students which would make me lose my job and wind up in—where else?— Kamagasaki! Might as well come here voluntarily, I reasoned.

The interesting thing about the yoseba is that no matter how isolated it appears to be from mainstream society, it reflects that society with brutal accuracy. The tremors from any general social or economic shakeup are felt here immediately. Kama's own development is emblematic of this linkage. Back in 1903 a major exposition was held in Tennōji, which the Meiji Emperor was scheduled to grace with his presence. Well, his parade was routed just north of here, right through what is now Nippombashi. It's a place people know today as Electric Town, where you can get electronic appliances at a deep discount—something like Akihabara in Tokyo—but it use to be a slum where lots of homeless people and day laborers lived. The local authorities took it upon themselves to rid the area of undesirable elements. So all the vagrants and ramshackle lodging houses were moved out. Of course, cleaning up one part of town of the so-called dregs meant finding another place to accommodate them, because they just don't disappear into thin air. In the case of Osaka, that place was Kamagasaki.

Kama is big because it's the central yoseba for the entire Kansai region. Amagasaki has a small yoseba, but it's not a rival the way Kotobuki-chō rivals San'ya. There are something like twenty-five thousand day laborers living here. I'll tell you how we come up with that estimate. There are about fifteen thousand white cards in circulation, which means a minimum of fifteen thousand laborers. That figure is fairly reliable because the men have to reregister once a year. But not all men have a card, of course. In fact, fewer and fewer of them do. The reason is that the gap between the wage you can make on the street and the daily unemployment compensation has widened in recent years. In Kamagasaki you now make ¥12,500 a day minimum for work as a *dokata*. That's rock-bottom. Unemployment compensation is still pegged at ¥6200, which is now way below the daily wage, and you have to put up with all the bureaucratic hassle to get it. Our best guess is that 40 percent of the day-laborer population doesn't bother to get a white card. Some put the figure higher than that. But let's stick with the 40 percent. That brings the total to twenty-five thousand.

We also estimate that Kama is fed by about three thousand newcomers a year. Of this group only about half get a white card. You hear a lot about how the yoseba population is aging. What you don't hear is that the average age of the man who first sets foot in Kama now is forty-six. That's right—forty-six. That means he's already had a career—or maybe several careers—under his belt, and he's seen a lot of life even before arriving. He probably has a family somewhere, too. In the past most men came here when they were young and still single.

The composition of the yoseba population is also changing. You see a lot of foreign workers here now. Filipinos especially are here in big numbers. They stay in the more expensive business hotels, like the Sun Plaza, which is located just to the east of Shin-Imamiya Station, or the Penthouse 1-2-3, just to the west. The foreigners don't mind paying more because they sleep several to a room. They're young and strong and do a lot of loading work, and they get it through recruiters on the west side.

Another group you'll find nowadays in Kama are the so-called free arbeiters, or "freeters." These are the young kids with the punk-rock look who'll come to Kama in the morning and pick up work near the station but have nothing to do with the Kama way of life. I think you'll be seeing more of this type in the future, now that seniority and lifetime employment are becoming things of the past, even in the big corporations, and more and more young people turn down their noses at full-time jobs in favor of short-term stints. I guess this means that the dividing line between Kama and mainstream society will become blurred as more of this group comes into the day-labor force. I guess it also means there's room here for other groups that haven't been a part of yoseba life before. Women, for example. More and more are entering the labor force, and sooner or later they'll be meeting with hard times, just as the men do. And what will happen to them? The idea of a female day laborer might seem odd to most people, but it's certainly not unthinkable. After all, women are already working in many jobs that were thought to be the province of men only a few short years ago.

I've seen a lot of changes in my sixteen years here, both in Kamagasaki and in society as a whole. I know that changes will continue to take place, and I'm anxious to monitor them. That's what keeps my interest. And that's what keeps me going with both jobs, at the Welfare Center and at the drawing board. What started out as a kind of fluke—a haphazardly chosen job in a lean hiring year—well, it's turned into a life work. That of seeing Japanese society from the bottom up. To view all of Japan through the lens of Kamagasaki. I don't think I'll ever lose interest.

CHAPTER 3

❋

ACTIVISM

Labor-Union Workshop

December 16, 1989. Thirteen people are gathered in a room far too large for us on the eighth floor of the Tokyo Metropolitan Government Annex in Iidabashi. The occasion is a workshop on San'ya sponsored by Santōrō. The venue: the Central Labor Administration Hall (Chūō Rōsei Kaikan). Located in a clump of high-rises in the center of Tokyo, very near the "bull's eye" of the Imperial Palace which dots the circle of the Yamanote Loop Line, the Annex—a large office building you will not see the likes of in San'ya—and the area itself, a bustling, brightly lit section of town, reminds me of what the rest of Tokyo is and what San'ya definitely is not.

The workshop has fewer guests than hosts. Among the thirteen present are Santōrō's three union officers, five union cadres, three university students who had chanced to pick up fliers on the workshop, a writer who has published on San'ya, and myself.

The workshop begins with a film viewing, the seating for which defines the relationship between hosts and guests. The shabbily clothed rank-and-file sit on one side of the viewing area, their handsomely dressed audience on the other, and the modestly but neatly dressed union officers in the middle—the physical and psychological buffer between the two groups. The film, a forty-minute, eight-millimeter documentary titled *Nagasarete*

(Cast Adrift), features the 1984 Spring Festival, held as usual in Tamahime Park. It opens with shots of the Ginza, followed by shots of a Hibiya Line subway train moving away from the glitter of Tokyo's most glamorous shopping district to Minami Senjū Station and the grime of San'ya—all this to the accompaniment of John Coltrane's breathtaking "My Favorite Things," the soprano sax veritably soaring over the frenetic metropolis.

The film then presents a series of interviews with men in the park who are celebrating the arrival of spring. They speak with pride and with shame. A day laborer in his mid-fifties from Hokkaido is the primary focus. He came to San'ya after having worked with a construction firm that paid him so poorly that the switch to yoseba life seemed like a move up. At first, he thought of San'ya as a temporary abode and regularly visited his home in Hokkaido. As time went by, however, it became more difficult for him to return, lacking anything to show for his work, and he has not been back for seven years. He maintains occasional contact with his family, calling his wife now and then and asking about the children, who are now grown.

The man interrupts his reminiscences and enters the karaoke competition atop a makeshift stage. He can hardly carry a tune, he admits, but he will sing his heart out, and that's what counts, he assures his interviewer. On finishing his song, belted out in a miserable but passionate voice, he pants, "Boy, do I feel great!" The film closes with a shot of the gray, dingy Shokuan, where a long line of Yama men are picking up the day's unemployment compensation, their faces without expression.

Following this cinematic tour of San'ya, the three union officers make their presentations on behalf of the rank-and-file. Tottori commences with an incisive if somewhat hackneyed analysis of what makes business tick in Japan. "Employees in the larger corporations are the envy of Japanese society," he begins. "They receive big salary bonuses and ample retirement benefits. The problem is that the medium- and small-sized corporations have to support this arrangement. When business is good for the big corporations, the smaller ones get paid off in the form of increased contracts. But when business is bad, the contracts dry up. The subcontractors are at the bigger corporations' mercy and have to rely on their good will. But business can't be conducted on the basis of good will alone. And if that's true for the subcontractors, it's all the more true for us Yama men. What we need is a safety net."

"You can say that again!"

"You tell 'em, Tottori! That's the least we should expect."

After a flurry of remarks from the chorus line of day-laborer cadres, Tottori, at first taken aback by the zeal of his followers, takes stock of his audience and forges ahead with his presentation. "Morning starts early in San'ya. The men must find a job and be at the work site by eight o'clock no matter where it is. They get their work from places like the Shokuan and the Welfare Center or off the streets from labor brokers. Jobs from the public agencies come with written agreements. The problem is that there aren't very many of those jobs available, and what few there are don't pay well. You can get a better-paying job off the street, but verbal agreements about wages are broken all the time. There are laws in the books about this sort of transaction, but they're flagrantly disregarded. . . . "

"Hey, we already know that!"

"Yeah, that's old hat."

Tottori sits down and mops his brow, but not before the cadres have expressed their view on the subject.

"Now tell them what we're doing about it!"

"That's what I was just going to do." Osaka comes to the rescue. It is his turn to speak.

"We at Santōrō have been able to improve matters considerably, especially in the area of wage rates and wage collecting. But San'ya is changing rapidly and we're doing our best to cope with the new realities.

"Now you're cooking, Osaka."

"Let's hear it for our fearless leader!"

"All right, men, just let me get my message out. . . . The first problem is deteriorating living space. In San'ya there are still a lot of wooden apartments built right after the war, as well as the old-style bunkhouses that sleep eight to a room, and even some rickety lodging houses on the Arakawa-Ward side where the men are all cooped up in a single room. They're cold in winter and damp in summer, and naturally they're breeding grounds for diseases like TB."

"Tell us about it, Osaka. They're regular germ boxes!"

"Okay, okay, now just let me continue. I'm sure our guests will be interested in what I have to say. . . . The second problem is an aging day-laborer population. The average Yama man is over fifty years old now. Working for a company, you'd expect your salary to increase with age and time on the job, right? Well, it doesn't work that way in the yoseba. In the world of manual labor, an older man is worth less, not more. Some firms don't even hire men over fifty-five, and the ones that do pay them a much lower wage. There's got to be a better way."

"No retirement age in this business, you know. That's the goddamn' problem."

It is Osaka's turn to mop his brow, but he is not finished. "The third problem, and it stems from the other two, is an increasing street population. San'ya's in the middle of a construction boom, and business hotels are now replacing the old-style lodging houses. That may sound like an answer to the housing problem I was telling you about before, but the big issue is their cost. A room in a business hotel goes for three times what you'd pay for space in a bunkhouse. Well, for that kind of money you could rent an apartment with twice the space that a business hotel offers."

"Maybe *you* could rent one, Osaka, but we couldn't."

"That's what I mean. You can't become a tenant unless you show the landlord you've registered with the ward office or come up with the name of a guarantor. But there aren't too many Yama men who've established residency here, and, well, if they *were* able to come up with a guarantor . . . "

" . . . we wouldn't be here!"

"Thanks for you attention, men. . . . But it's not only that. If you live in an apartment, you have to pay several months' worth of rent in fees up front. Well, it's all a lot of men can do to pay for a single night's lodging. More and more can't afford even that and have to sleep out. We have a name for these men . . . "

"*Aokansha!*" The chorus line is definitely paying attention.

At this point Osaka passes the baton on to Kobe and takes his seat. The hour is late; the guests are getting a bit restless, and the chorus line is becoming more vociferous by the minute. Kobe's solution to the problem is to talk faster.

"Right now Japan's in the middle of the biggest construction boom since the Tokyo Olympics, but Yama men haven't been able to cash in on the good times. A lot of the men are getting up in years, and they don't have family to fall back on. That's why Santōrō is pushing for the right of single men of all ages to live in public housing. Right now there are all sorts of restrictions meant to exclude them. You have to be over sixty years old. Or you have to be handicapped. Or you have to prove that you've lived in San'ya for at least a year, which means registering with the ward office, and that's something a lot of men don't want to mess with. Anyway, since housing continues to be a problem, we've always felt that the only way to get at it is to run one of our own candidates in the ward-assembly election and make our case directly to the city government. Unfortunately, we've lost both times we tried."

"Have no fear—third time's the charm!"

"There are other problems, too. Like the lack of medical care in the area. A recent newspaper article reported that 746 men have died on the streets of San'ya in the last five years alone. . . . "

"And nobody gives a damn."

"Blah, blah, blah . . . "

"Can't we call it a day?"

Kobe does not want to call it a day quite yet, but the Yama men are losing patience. They have heard all this before, even if the guests have not. More important, they have experienced in the flesh what Tottori, Osaka, and

Kobe have been trying to put into words. Are the union officers simply preaching to the converted and boring them thoroughly in the process? Or are they making a vain attempt to reach a few outsiders who, because of nonresidency, would be ineligible in any event to vote in the next Taitō Ward Assemby election? Either way, their efforts seem futile.

The officers' presentations have been interrupted not only by assorted comments from the peanut gallery but also by an altercation within the gallery itself. Aizu and Sakata, two of the rank-and-file, are having a running dispute, the focus of which appears to be the large intake of alcohol on the part of Sakata, who has been providing much of the background noise this evening. This is unfortunate in the eyes of Aizu, who seems painfully conscious of his guests. Halfway through Osaka's presentation, he stalks angrily out of the room. Later he returns, but sits apart from the rest of the group, his face sullen, and sips on a bottle of booze. The drunker Aizu gets, the quieter he becomes. He is a slow burner.

In the midst of Aizu's subdued tantrum, which occurs during Osaka's presentation, a latecomer appears. This is Naga-san, as he is known to his colleagues—a day laborer in his forties with a kindly face, a winning smile, and a joint missing from his left pinkie. He defers to the union leaders during their presentations but squirms in his seat all the while. Now that Kobe has finished his remarks, he wants to have his say.

"People avoid us like the plague. They say we're dirty and smelly and dangerous. Okay, we may be smelly and we may be dirty. There's a reason for that, you know. We can't afford to take baths as often as you. But we work hard, and we take the jobs that nobody else wants. We think this kind of life ought to produce some tangible benefits. That's what it boils down to. It's no fun sleeping out in the cold. But it's hard for a lot of us to find enough work to afford a roof over our heads, especially when we get older. Now don't get me wrong. If you're young and work hard, you'll have no problem making it. You're a member of what I'll call the 'A' generation and you make good money. You live well and sleep in a business hotel. But if you're in the 'B' generation, your body has already taken a beating. You're in your middle years now and you can't wield your pick like you used to. You force yourself to work a few days a week and hope that you can fill your white card with enough stamps to qualify for unemployment compensation the rest of the time. In other words, you just break even. And then there's the older generation—the 'C' generation. You're a has-been. You're sick or disabled or just don't have any place else to go. You can't work. You can't afford to stay in a decent place where you can rest your bones and steel yourself for the next job. If you're in this generation, you've been in San'ya too long. I say that by this time you've paid your dues to society and you deserve something in return."

Construction in Tokyo: workers at rest (Ueno).

Naga-san sits down. The gallery has been quiet throughout. This is a hard act to follow, and no one tries. Hosts and guests mingle for the first time, and we share a few soft drinks. The exchange is rewarding, but all too brief. The room must be closed and it is time to leave the building. We descend the elevator to the street below, near Iidabashi Station. I take the train home to my rented house in south Tokyo. The writer boards a train headed for the western suburbs. The students take the subway north to their apartments near the university. The Yama men and the union officers climb into two taxicabs and tell the drivers to head east for Kiyokawa. A discussion ensues between drivers and passengers. The drivers, learning the destination, want to beg off. The passengers eventually win out. I wave good-by to Kobe, my closest acquaintance among the officers, and salute Naga-san, who has stolen the show.

Union Planning Session

December 22, 1989. It is early afternoon. I am killing time at the Santōrō union headquarters waiting for Kobe, who has invited me to attend a meeting at which members will discuss the upcoming Winter Survival Struggle.

The headquarters are located on the ground floor of a small, two-story building east of Tamahime Park. A shoemaker lives upstairs. The downstairs apartment is a rude dwelling with a dirt-floored entranceway the size of a six-mat room, a four-and-a-half mat tatami-covered anteroom in back, a small storage area (it can hardly be called a kitchen), and a toilet. There are no partitions, and the rooms are in a sad state of disrepair. The union headquarters double as lodging space for some of the members. Shimokita, from Aomori Prefecture, is under the quilts in the anteroom this very moment. A temporary visitor, having his own apartment, he has only recently returned to San'ya after a lengthy stay in the hospital for liver disease. No longer able to work, he is on welfare and receives ninety thousand yen a month for rent, food, and incidentals, all of which he can afford now that he is on the wagon and can save what he used to spend on liquor. He is a wide-eyed, soft-spoken man of few words. A thick accent unmistakably reveals his place of origin.

I am making conversation with the other three men. We share the small table in the entranceway, trying to keep ourselves warm around a kerosene stove and eyeing each other uncomfortably. This is not the first meeting between any of us, but previous encounters have always been mediated by one of the union officers, usually Kobe. Now we are on our own. The conversation becomes animated over time, however, as Kobe is very late. I listen and I look. Or should I say ponder and stare. I ponder what these men are saying and doing and I stare unreservedly at their faces.

Aizu (short for Aizu-Wakamatsu), a slender, sickly-looking man from the picturesque castle town in Fukushima Prefecture, a hundred miles or so north of Tokyo, is pulling rank within the organization and playing host. Just as at last week's workshop, he is extremely self-conscious. As long as he dons a hat or cap and hides his bald pate, as he does even now indoors, he does not look too much older than his forty-five years.

Sakata, from the seaport in Yamagata Prefecture, is a lean, sinewy man whose terry-cloth *hachimaki* is twisted about a thick head of faintly graying hair. He, too, was at the workshop, the principal object of Aizu's wrath. He appears at first glance five years younger than Aizu, despite the deep creases in his forehead. Perhaps he is actually fifty and, given his baby face, simply looks forty. I have a hard time deciding which.

Hamamatsu, a burly, bear-faced man from Shizuoka Prefecture, is the group's senior member, at fifty-eight. He looks seventy. His stubbled, deeply creased face is covered with scabs, mostly on the cheek and forehead—the result of a recent fall, he explains. Hamamatsu does have difficulty keeping his balance, the result of constant drinking. I know for a fact, however, that some of the scabs are the product of cigarette burns—the malicious act of those who would take advantage of a jovial but weak-willed man seemingly always begging for punishment. He briefly puts down his cigarette—he has one constantly lit—and proudly shows me his white card, which is plastered with small-sized unemployment-insurance stamps of the sort obviously purchased on the black market. Having thus duly entertained the guest, he leans over on the table and promptly falls asleep. This is no cat nap. He eventually keels over right onto the floor, to a chorus of guffaws. Aizu, heaving a sigh of disgust, grabs Hamamatsu's cigarette butt, which is still lit and is burning a hole in the sleeping man's coat, and presses the lit end against his nostril, making one of the scabs bleed anew. Hamamatsu seems barely conscious of his fresh wound.

Sakata, who is also nearly always in his cups, speaks to me in stuttering monosyllables and in a gravelly voice. He tries to impress anyone who will listen that he is in far better shape than he looks, and utters a stream of unsolicited comments in an attempt to become part of the conversation. That failing, he changes his tune, coming out simply with a "Yeah, yeah, that's right. That's right!" or a "Sure, that's okay," often accompanied with a wink. But everything is clearly not okay. He cannot walk straight. In fact, he can barely stand up. Several ticks animate his already expressive face. His uncontrolled speech and behavior inevitably get him into trouble, especially when he is in the company of an abrasive soul like Aizu.

Of the three men at the table with me, Aizu, although hardly what you would call eloquent, is certainly the most coherent. I try to draw him out, and he obliges with a paean to his home in Aizu-Wakamatsu, in Fukushima Prefecture. It is a most beautiful part of Japan, he beams. He remembers little, however, because he moved when he was still a child to the neighboring prefecture, where he went to school until he was seventeen. From there he left the area entirely for Yokohama, lived in Kotobuki-chō, and worked on the docks for two decades as a stevedore. It was a tough life, and he was never able to get ahead. The debts began to pile up, and he ended up escaping to Tokyo in the middle of night. He did eventually pay back the money he owed on his rent, though, he tells me proudly. He has been in San'ya for six years and a member of Santōrō for five.

Aizu's recitation is frequently interrupted by Sakata, who seemingly cannot resist comment on any remark Aizu makes. Sakata clearly means no harm, but Aizu is just as clearly miffed by the unwanted attention. The latter tries to go on talking, and I am eager to learn more about his life, but his momentum has been broken by one too many "Yeah-yeah-that's-right's" and "Sure-that's-okay's," uttered with an altogether atrocious sense of conversational rhythm, by the former. Aizu warns Sakata to restrain himself or else, and prepares to venture onto more technical ground—the details involved in coordinating the upcoming Winter Survival Struggle—but he is tripped up by yet another volley from his tormentor.

"All right, Sakata, I've had about all I can take. I'm telling you one last time to shut up or get the hell out of here." He slaps Sakata across the face, decides that the gesture is insufficient, and proceeds to bang the man's head with a large, empty tin can that happens to be lying nearby.

Sakata stares blankly at Aizu and quiets down for a time. Then he apologizes profusely. "Sorry, sorry. It won't happen again. So sorry."

But it does happen again. Scarcely a minute after his scolding, Sakata unleashes a stream of chatter as if nothing were amiss. Shimokita, who has been awakened by the ruckus, joins the argument on the side of Aizu, but in vain. Shimokita then avails himself of the opportunity to berate Hamamatsu, for the latter has regained consciousness and enough strength to teeter precariously as before at the edge of the table. Sakata thinks this is hilarious and begins to mimic Hamamatsu with a skill that is nothing short of professional. I am not surprised to learn later that Sakata performed as a circus clown before coming to San'ya.

Aizu thinks none of this funny at all. More scolding and more slaps. "I'm not going to put up with this anymore," he snarls. "Why do I have to do everything around here? You've lived in San'ya a lot longer than I have and you ought to know the ropes. But all you do is kid around. You're absolutely useless to this organization! What have you done for the Winter Survival Struggle? Not even a single phone call! But how could you when you're so damned drunk? You can't even string two words together! You drink and you sleep. That's your whole show, and for that you expect a free ride. Well, the free ride's gonna stop. You get on the phone right now and call the Taitō Ward office and see about the equipment they promised for the Festival. Right now, you hear? I'm sick and tired of having to do everything. Look, here this man has come all the way from America to hear our story and offer his support, and I can't even talk to him without your interrupting every other second. Now get on that phone and start dialing!"

This tantrum may very well be grandstanding on the part of Aizu, trying to create a scene in front of the guest in an attempt to get more mileage out of his request for help. But there is no question that his anger is real. The explosion has been building up for at least a week, ever since the workshop at Iidabashi, where he walked out halfway through in disgust at Sakata's unsolicited stream of comments. The display of anger seems to overwhelm Sakata, who is easily the stronger of the two and who could parry Aizu's tin-can blows with little difficulty were he of a mind. But he is not. He merely cowers before the physically weaker Aizu and whimpers, "Sure, that's okay!"

Sakata stumbles over to a narrow ledge to one side of the entranceway, where the telephone sits atop a bookshelf, and proceeds to dial the number, listed with several others, on a bulletin board hanging above the ledge. He is unsuccessful. Drink has robbed him of his coordination. He knocks a notebook off the ledge. An enraged Aizu kicks Sakata and in the process knocks over the bookshelf and spills its contents. He orders Sakata to clean up the mess. Sakata clenches his fists for an instant, then lowers his head in submission. "Clean it up, I said!" Aizu shouts. Sakata mumbles an apology and puts the fallen books and other items back on the shelf. Then he begins sweeping the area below. It is a dismal job. Aizu then walks up to our table, kicks it in disgust, and sends a saké cup flying.

By the time Kobe arrives, things have calmed down, more because of exhaustion than anything else. Aizu explains the situation to Kobe, who has noted with audible surprise the headquarters' more-than-usually tattered state. Once again, Sakata seemingly cannot resist comment: "Yeah, yeah, that's right. That's right!"

The actual planning session for the Winter Survival Struggle was conducted without incident after this, but I remember almost nothing of what went on.

Maria Restaurant

April 20, 1990. I have volunteered to work the evening shift at Maria (Mariya Shokudō, in Japanese), a tiny restaurant located southwest of

Namidabashi just off Old Streetcar Boulevard and run by a Japanese Protestant missionary who had opened it for business two years earlier. The cozy, wood-paneled room is barely large enough to accommodate the nine tables that seat up to thirty-six customers, all of them Yama men, who come for a square meal reasonably priced.

Maria is just one of the half dozen or so Christian-sponsored facilities in San'ya. The Missionaries of Charity (Kami no Ai no Senkyōsha Kai), for example, located near the Jōhoku Welfare Center, is affiliated with the organization headed by Mother Teresa and staffed principally by volunteers from India. It provides, during the limited hours it is open, space for fellowship and distributes blankets and clothes to Yama men. The San'ya Gospel Mission (Seisen Kirisuto Fukuin Kyōkai), located just off Iroha Arcade, is run by Morimoto Haruko, a minister who has provided worship services and food for her San'ya parishioners since the 1970s. She claims numerous converts among the day laborers and has been featured on national television. The Catholic Maryknoll order runs the San'yūkai, Japan's only accredited free clinic. The San'ya branch of the United Church of Christ in Japan (Nihon Kirisutokyōdan) and the medical consultation room affiliated with it provides a variety of services to the area. This last is the organization with which the manager of Maria is affiliated, although it provides no financial backing.

Looking more like a coffee shop than a restaurant, Maria is unique among San'ya eateries: it serves no alcohol. Many men will not come here for that reason. The ones who do, however, can expect a lot of food for their money: ¥220 buys a basic dinner of rice, soup, dried laver, a raw egg, and one extra dish; ¥350 buys the menu of the day, which includes a more substantial meat dish or an item like curried rice. The price is half of what a customer would be charged anywhere else, and the food is good. The restaurant does a smart business both during breakfast hours (seven to ten) and dinner hours (five-thirty to seven-thirty), Monday through Saturday year-round.

Two cooks, the restaurant's only fulltime employees, work the kitchen, while anywhere from two to four volunteers work the tables serving customers and the sinks washing dishes. The volunteer staff, along with outside donations raised specifically on the restaurant's behalf, combine to keep the price of a meal well below market level. In addition to the Japanese volunteers, there is a global cross-section of missionaries: today I am working with a young man from Mexico and a young woman from New Zealand; I have met others from Europe and the United States. Most of the foreign volunteers are in their early twenties, although I have waited tables with a nun in her sixties. All speak Japanese to some extent; the nun speaks it very well. Some of the volunteers work on a set schedule; others, like myself, work when they can or when the mood strikes—the more the merrier would seem to be the manager's creed. Although the foreign volunteers tend to be students, Japanese volunteers come from all walks of life: I have shared duties with an employee of Mitsubishi Electric, and I have been served, when off duty, by Shintani Noriko, a socially conscious professional singer whose career has spanned two decades. All but the two young cooks, who rent an apartment in Minami Senjū, live outside San'ya, some of them very far away.

You will find an assortment of comic books tucked under the tables or in the corner magazine racks, as you would in any coffee shop and many neighborhood restaurants in Tokyo. You must look closer for signs of the restaurant's Christian connection: a small portrait of the Virgin Mary on one of the walls; a crucifix near the restroom in back; a bookshelf in the corner with a selection of Christian literature, from *The Story of the Bible* to *The Silence*, a novel by the well-known Catholic writer Endō Shūsaku.

Most of the customers appear to be regulars who are here for at least one meal every day. These men know one another and they know the volunteers. A few customers approach the restaurant tentatively as they might a soup line they had not frequented before, trying not to attract notice. The restaurant in fact evolved from a soup line that the manager helped run on weekends and holidays until he came to the realization that the appetites of those he served were not abated by occasional meals prepared at the convenience of the volunteers.

A few men come not to buy dinner but to beg. The manager obliges them, passing out sealed dry biscuits from a cubbyhole near the restaurant's entrance, which also contains underwear, shirts, and other essentials for life in the yoseba. One man, venturing no further than the door, asks me if the restaurant sold just bread and water—even ¥220 for the basic dinner was too steep a price for him. I tell him no. Once again the cubbyhole is opened. The recipient has to step over a man in his late twenties who lies sprawled out on the street, his head shaven and his face scabbed and puffy. The manager tells me that the man lying there unconscious is an alcoholic and mentally retarded—easy pickings for *mogaki* and others who would do mischief. I have seen him walking about Namidabashi and Iroha Arcade, sometimes alone in a drunken daze, sometimes with others.

Last time I was here I washed dishes. Tonight I wait tables. The work comes naturally. I have done it on three continents: as a summer job in New England in the 1960s when still in college; trying to make ends meet when living in London in the 1970s; and now here in Tokyo. The temptation to chat with customers is great, but brisk business and a rapid turnover make me concentrate on the task of taking orders, serving food, and clearing tables.

The temptation for some of the customers to chat with me would appear to be equally great. Several men brag about their gambling exploits. Others talk of life in general. "I was riding home on the train today and sitting on the 'Silver Seat' [specially marked seats for the elderly and disabled]," one man laments. "And what do you think happened? Someone had the gall to ask me to move. I'm sixty-four years old and don't tell me I don't look my age!"

There are some, however, who clearly do not want to be bothered. They order their meals in monosyllables, eat silently, and leave. One leaves without paying. He has not even finished his dinner. The manager keeps the order slip and posts it above the cash register, warning the staff to be on the alert and make the culprit pay up the next time he comes in. That there will be a next time is not in doubt, since he is a regular.

Half an hour later the culprit appears, dragged in by the man who was sitting at the same table with him. He is not here to pay his bill, however, but to explain: he has no money to spare right now but will square up as soon as he gets some. The manager accepts the explanation and dismisses him.

As business winds down and the closing hour draws near, I turn my attention to the other volunteers. I have a long talk with the woman from New Zealand, who had studied Japanese before coming to Tokyo and who has lived here for eight months. It must be difficult being married to a Japanese, she says, when she learns of my marital status. Having spent time with a family during her first months in Japan has made her realize just how much adjustment to the culture is necessary. Not at all, I reply. The real difficulty is in being married, period. It is not easy living with someone else. It is not easy seeing things another person's way. It is not easy bending to another's will on a regular basis and not just when one is feeling generous. Nationality is of secondary importance. It's the same thing, whether you are trying to adjust to a personality or to a culture. What counts is simply being able to adjust.

I can feel myself warming to the subject. I recall leading a seminar on cross-cultural marriages years ago for a Tokyo-based social organization where Japanese and foreigners could mix. At the time I was between degrees, out of school, and working freelance in Japan. Several couples, each with a Japanese and non-Japanese partner, had gathered to discuss the rewards and the trials of "international marriages." By that time I had been a married man myself long enough to have transcended the honeymoon stage and to have made more than my share of mistakes. I thought I knew all the answers then. Knowing the answers did not necessarily make me any smarter about marriage, however. I might have been aware of the right thing to do or say, yet still not do or say it. That seems to be the problem now just as much as then. Here I am quite arbitrarily volunteering my time in a neighborhood in which my wife has never set foot and about which I talk to her with some difficulty. San'ya is as foreign to her as New Guinea. But the difficulty in communicating my impressions of San'ya stems less from her own prejudices about it than from her inability to understand why it should interest me in the first place. The fact that this is a part of Japan she does not know, would perhaps never know, is appealing. It is a territory all my own.

The possession of such a domain is an extravagance, I have to admit, that taxes the resources and patience of one's partner. Was not the precious time I volunteered here in San'ya not better spent with my family, after all? I wonder aloud if it is solely because of my spouse's silent sacrifice that I have adapted quite well to life in Japan generally—taking off by myself to visit friends around the country, not to mention coming and going at will here in the city. Am I the sole possessor of the right to go off on my own and blow off steam? Is this what I mean by "adjusting"? I am afraid to answer the questions I have put forth, but fortunately the volunteer from New Zealand is preparing to leave and I simply bid her farewell.

It is time to close the restaurant. Business has been good. I linger after hours, talking with the manager and the remaining volunteers. One by one the latter leave the restaurant. I am the last one out. Unlike so many of the diners, I cannot say I have no place to go. I dare say I am lucky to have a place with a family that I can return to any time. That makes me linger all the more.

Citizens' Patrol

June 16, 1990. It is a few minutes before eight o'clock on a Saturday evening. The night is fair—a brief respite in this, the monsoon season, which in Tokyo lasts a month or so from mid-June. This afternoon's torrential downpour has cleansed the air, but not cooled it.

I am part of a "citizens' patrol" (*jinmin patorōru*, commonly abbreviated as *jin-pato*), which tonight comprises eighteen volunteers: members of Sōgidan (the labor union), San'yūkai (the private medical clinic), a missionary group, and some university students recruited through an outreach program. We are gathered at the Iroha Arcade's east entrance in front of the San'ya Workers' Hall, still under construction, and we are here to monitor the area's homeless population. Tonight's patrol, the first since winter, inaugurates a series of weekly missions scheduled throughout the monsoon, which, along with the winter season, is the most life-threatening time of year for Yama men braving the elements.

Our task is to determine the number of *aokansha*—men sleeping out—and to distribute tea and clothing to those who want them. We are also here to field the men's complaints. Our route covers three parks, two public buildings, and two shopping areas—all common haunts of the homeless. The stout, bearded F-san, a regular supporter of Sōgidan activities, pulls a large, canvas-topped cart laden with boxes of clothing and a huge cauldron of cold barley tea. He is relieved occasionally by I-san, a sixty-four-year-old San'ya institution who spends his free time sweeping the streets around Namidabashi. U-san, a Sōgidan member and tonight's leader, decides that we should split up in order to approach the men without creating a commotion. A couple of the university students are here in San'ya for the first time. Several appear ambivalent about their role as volunteers and scarcely interact with the men they encounter. As the evening wears on, more and more spend their time chatting among themselves.

Our first goal is Tamahime Park, where we count ten *aokansha*. Two of them are lying on the ground, two or three more on the cement near the public toilet on the park's north side, and the rest on the few short benches that line the caged playing field. The benches are so short, however, that they can barely hold a human frame. The men are in various states of undress, from the fully clothed, with only shoes or sandals removed (and usually arranged neatly next to the pieces of cardboard on which they lie), to the nearly naked. One trouserless man sleeps on a bench *sans* briefs, his bare legs dangling over the edge.

The faces of these reclining figures are barely visible in the dim light; yet there is one I recognize: a man whom I had met earlier in the day at this very same spot. He is fifty years of age and sports a week-old stubble. I had been talking with another man from Yamanashi, who kept repeating that he wanted to die, when this man appeared and started raving about American movies and about actors I reminded him of, much to my amazement. He then offered me a swig from his *shōchū* bottle, which I accepted.

Now he is lying on the damp ground under a slender row of shrubbery, his shoes for a pillow and his only possession a small plastic bag filled with his belongings. It would appear that he has been nursing the *shōchū* bottle ever since we parted company this afternoon, and it takes a few seconds for my presence to register. When it does, he becomes chatty, and all I have to do is listen.

"So, what brings you here this time? Barley tea? Ah, come on. I've got my *shōchū*. Now, if you had some nibbles to go with the *shōchū*, I'd be happy to accept. . . . You don't have a thing? Look, I can put up with a patch of bare ground for a bed, but a man's gotta have something to eat! I can't work until my ankle gets better. Sprained it two months ago and it's still tender here. . . . Of course I had it looked at. Over at the clinic—you know, the

Caged playing field at Tamahime Park. Two jobless men gaze at middle-school children playing inside.

San'yūkai. Didn't go near the Welfare Center. It won't take people like me. I like my *shōchū* and they won't let you through the door if you've been drinking. Here, want a swig? No? Okay, suit yourself. Anyway, I've been sleeping here in the park ever since hurting my ankle. Stayed at the Palace before that. . . . Nah, it's no big deal sleeping out. The mosquitoes don't bother me much. I think the alcohol in my blood keeps them away. . . . The rain? Yeah, the rain is a problem. We sure get a lot of it this time of year, don't we? But tonight is pleasant enough. It cleared up real nice after that downpour this afternoon. . . . No, I don't think there's anything on that cart I need. . . . What do you mean, go check it out myself? Come on, I'm dizzy enough as it is just lying here. Listen, why don't you bring me something—you say they've got underwear? . . . Thanks. Let's see here—what, only one pair? . . . Yeah, sure, these are fine, just fine. Oh, by the way, give me a cigarette while you're at it. . . . Look, I don't care if you don't have any. Go bum a couple off one of your friends. And make it snappy, you hear?"

Our next stop is the Shokuan, where more than twenty men, many of them in their fifties and sixties, are spending the night. Some look to be asleep and doubtlessly do not wish to be disturbed. Silently we place cups of barley tea next to them. I offer some tea to one man whose "bunk" is sandwiched between several others in a space of cement lined with cardboard and sheltered by the building's concrete eaves. The man, perhaps forty years old, wears a long-sleeved, brightly patterned sport shirt and dons a short-billed racing beret. Both his sandaled feet are tightly bound at the toes.

"This is one hell of a place to spend the night, isn't it?" he says to me. "I don't have any choice, though. I burned the toes on both my feet a week or two ago and I can't work. So I'm stuck here until I get better. It's gonna take time. I go to the San'yūkai for treatment. Got my toes rebandaged there just yesterday. Now, if I can just get this sock over everything . . . "

I ask if it wouldn't be better to undo the bindings and air the wound out as long as he is off his feet.

"What? You've gotta be kidding. This is no little scrape, mister! This is a *serious* injury, understand? *I'm* the one who's hurting, so I ought to know. Damn it, you just think I'm playing hooky because I stubbed my little toe or something, don't you? Look, you bastard, I'm not sleeping out because I want to. You got that? I'd be doing just fine if I could work. But I can't. If you don't believe me, then go ahead and unwrap this bandage and take a look for yourself. And after you've taken a good look, you can put your money where your mouth is and get me a regular doctor to fix this burn!"

I apologize. I had no intention of insulting him, I say, and then ask if he received unemployment compensation in the meantime to tide him over.

"Who the hell are you, anyway, asking questions like some cop! You go snooping around like that and you'll get yourself into a heap of trouble. Look, I got my reasons for being here. But I . . . I can't say what they are. And I can't—I can't tell anybody I'm here, either. . . . I just can't. So don't ask, okay? [He wipes his eyes.] You don't have to bother about me. I can take care of myself. And I've got friends here who'll spare me a bite to eat. So things could be worse. Anyway, you just go on your merry way and don't give me another thought!"

I excuse myself, but not before repeating that I am sorry for what I said and that I really want him to get better and to take care.

I leave in pursuit of the patrol wagon, which has long since continued its procession down the dimly lit streets. As I turn the corner of the Shokuan, I run into an acquaintance: Aizu, a member of Santōrō, the other local labor union, who has been out of circulation because of a long hospital stint. He has been relieving himself against the Shokuan wall and is just turning around when he sees me and says hello. We are about to part company after a brief chat when the man who has just given me a tongue-lashing appears at my side and takes my hand in his. "Thanks for coming by," he says, his eyes still red. "I really mean it. Thanks."

We continue our rounds. A "Keep Out" sign is posted in Ishihama Park. Another sign: "It is illegal to sleep in this park or engage in any activity that creates a nuisance to other users. In the event of trouble please dial the emergency police line: 110." We count three men here, of whom only one is actually sleeping. The other two are merely resting, and pondering where to go next. One of them has come all the way from Kizarazu across the bay in Chiba Prefecture. A dozen or so children are playing noisily on the jungle gym and the merry-go-round nearby.

Next stop: Nihonzutsumi Park. We have come via Asahi Street, where an unusually small number—only half a dozen—are spending the night beneath the protective awnings. Several of the shop fronts have been watered down. In the park a man sleeping on the ground jumps up at the sound of our approach. Three others are perched precariously on tiny park benches. Four more have camped out beneath a large plastic tarpaulin in the corner closest to an elementary-school playground, which is surrounded by a fifteen-foot fence. The two men lying down in back are not interested in talking. The two sitting in front and drinking are more than willing to chat.

"We have it pretty good here, thanks," one of them says. He is wearing the colorful garb of a *tobi shoku*: bright-blue knickers flared at the hips, light-gray sweater, and terry-cloth *hachimaki* twisted around his head. Even in the dim light I can tell that he is dressed with an eye for fashion. "We still have all our stuff, too. The police didn't get it when they made their round a few days ago. They come every month to clear the place out. We knew they were coming and we were here to protect our things."

The man goes on to tell us that he was severely injured the previous year while working on the underground extension of the Shinkansen tracks from Ueno to Tokyo Station. He was perched on some scaffolding and pulling on a guy wire when he lost his balance and fell to the floor below, breaking his hip and wrenching his neck. He was hospitalized for two months and received compensation to cover hospital bills. "I guess I'm lucky to be alive," he concludes. "Got this liver problem now, though. That may be a lot harder to clear up."

The injured man and his cohorts run a tight berth. The tent has an assortment of bedding, along with a wardrobe that includes a neat row of shoes and sandals. The concrete slab on which they rest is carpeted with cardboard and newspapers. The "cupboard" is filled with saké, soy sauce, and tinned food, and the trash is stowed away neatly in bags. The bivouac-like accommodation is immaculate in its way.

Our final stop is Iroha Arcade, our starting point, which we now enter from the west end. We count about fifteen men sleeping the length of the arcade. Here, too, some of the shop fronts have been watered down. One drunk near the east end is sleeping practically underneath an automobile parked in the arcade. I try to wake him up, but he will not be revived. His breathing and pulse are normal. I succeed only in making him roll over and vomit out of the corner of his mouth. He still does not gain consciousness. I put his sandals, kicked away and lying askew on the street, next to him, and hope that he does not get run over when the car's owner drives away.

During our three-hour patrol we have counted some seventy-five *aokansha*. This is a small portion of the total number in Tokyo, and even of the total in this district. Union members tell us that a section of the river-bank to the east of us beneath an overhead expressway is home to about fifty men each night.

June 30, 1990. I am in San'ya again to participate in another Citizens' Patrol two weeks after the first. It is much cooler this evening and there is a breeze: the monsoon weather has returned in earnest after an unseasonably hot spell.

Less than ten volunteers have shown up this evening. The initial good-samaritan enthusiasm seems to have worn off. There are no university students among us. Once again the leader divides us up into groups: three this time. The first group will cover the Sports Center near Sumida Park and "Cardboard Box Village," a haunt of many homeless on the other side of the Sumida River east of San'ya. The second group will cover the west side— Iroha Arcade and Yoshiwara Park, located just outside San'ya in Senzoku. The third group will concentrate on the south side: Tamahime Park, the Shokuan, Asahi Street, and the Welfare Center in Nihonzutsumi thrown in for good measure. I am with the third group. All of us distribute fliers announcing who we are and showing the tally of *aokansha* taken during the previous week's patrol. Tonight is a simple affair: there is no cart, no clothes, no tea. The first group has not returned when the other two groups reassemble in front of the Workers' Hall, and so I do not learn the number of *aokansha* in their precinct. The second and third groups alone have counted over seventy. We field a variety of complaints. One man sleeping out in Tamahime Park has an injured left hand and cannot work because he is left-handed. Another man, new to San'ya, left his *genba* early because the job he was forced to do was not the job advertised (a common occurrence, I am told), and came away with no money at all.

I am teamed up with a young man who was born and raised in Kiyokawa just south of the doyagai and the area we are patrolling. I know him from before; it is he who arranged for me to see a videotape of the Sōgidan film that cost the lives of two of its producers. He describes a documentary he saw recently on NHK about *karōshi* (death from overwork), which has been afflicting white-collar workers and which has been making headlines of late. The program reported that *karōshi* had claimed the lives of fifty "salarymen" during the past year in the Marunouchi business district (near Tokyo station) alone. A sensational figure, the program would have its viewers believe—until I recall that three times that number drop dead every year on the streets of San'ya, whose population is a fraction of the white-collar population in Marunouchi. "So you see who counts in this society," he tells me with no little sarcasm. "But even fifty is a significant number, don't you think? Let's face it, no matter where you live in Japan and no matter what you do, people are treated like animals."

❋

RITES

All is not grim in San'ya. The men's work is hard, the fatigue palpable; but there is a time for joyous celebration here as anywhere in the city. Four ~Festivals~ major festivals are held in April, August, November, and New Year's. The spring, fall, and particularly summer festivals (*haru matsuri, aki matsuri, natsu matsuri*) are lively affairs, while the New Year's festival is a more somber undertaking, as its very name, Winter Survival Struggle (*Ettō tōsō*), suggests. All are sponsored by the two San'ya-based labor unions: Santōrō and Sōgidan, whose members can be seen at festival time soliciting donations to help defray costs. Prior to the actual event they are also busy collecting the essentials for a successful festival, in the form of gifts or loans: clothing, foodstuffs, utensils, bedding, medical supplies, generators and lamps, wood for bonfires and saws to cut it up, musical instruments, loudspeakers, amplifiers, and other stage items.

The perennial setting for these observances is Tamahime Park. The caged playing field's off-limits rule is lifted only during the Summer Festival (see next chapter), when students at the middle school across the street are on vacation. For as many as six days in mid-August the gates are thrown open and the Yama men take over. The unwritten agreement with the city is for the labor unions to "liberate" the caged area during this, the Obon holiday (the Buddhist Festival of the Dead) and the semiannual trek by Tokyo residents out of the city to visit relatives in the provinces. The playing field is thus in low demand among local users.

Against the tide of this exodus, Yama men are returning to San'ya. Construction work comes to a standstill during the holiday, and *hanba* in the provinces empty out. The Summer Festival boasts the largest crowds of the year—upward of a thousand each night. In addition to the music, dancing, and food typically enjoyed anywhere in Japan on festive occasions are the games (wheelbarrow races with heavy loads, for example, mimicking the work at a construction site) and sheer liveliness that mark this particular celebration as unique.

Fall and Winter Festivals

The festivals held in spring and autumn incorporate the same sorts of activities but on a smaller scale. The Fall Festival, which I attended in 1989, is held on November 23, the national holiday Labor Appreciation Day (Kinrō kansha no hi). The festival competes with an annual shoe bazaar, a lively event held on the same day at Tamahime Inari Shrine, which borders the park on its south side. To say it "competes" is perhaps to give a false impression, because the clienteles differ entirely. The bazaar attracts middle-class bargain hunters from all over Tokyo and beyond. Many come by car, and many more by chartered buses that shuttle passengers to and from Asakusa and Minami Senjū stations. Either mode of transport to an event such as this is unusual in urban Japan, given the crowded thoroughfares and abundance of public transportation; it is evidence that San'ya is considered otherwise inaccessible and a place that the average Tokyo resident would hesitate to walk through. Yet while it is true that San'ya has the ingredients for violent crime—given the presence of the gangs, militant unions, and general poverty compared with the rest of the city, as well as a history of worker flare-ups in response to a variety of provocations, it is simply not the danger-ridden area it is often made out to be.

There is certainly little danger of any criminal activity today, what with both uniformed policemen and plainclothes detectives (easily spotted, with spiral notebooks in hand and wearing distinctive vests and caps) present in such great numbers. The Yama men are gathered at the park's eastern end. Most of the attention is directed at a makeshift stage, erected in the shadow of the playing-field cage and on which a variety of groups will perform: a five-member band that includes two women (which by my count amounts to a quarter of the entire female turnout at this gathering); a two-man theater troupe, both in drag (after the *onnagata* of the Kabuki stage); a male

Summer Festival: dancing caps a night of activity.

dancer in the traditional style, dressed in an ornate kimono; and finally, the union members themselves, dressed in eye-catching red livery with the union logo prominently displayed in white on black lapels. The park is adorned at one end with numerous slogan- and information-bearing plac- ards and overhead with two crisscrossing guy wires studded with red-and- white paper lanterns.

The stage has been set up by Santōrō. Although they both champion the day laborer, Santōrō and Sōgidan have little to do with each other. During the spring and fall festivals the two unions hold forth in separate sections of the park and take turns making speeches and offering entertainment. About the only display of mutual cooperation is their scheduling of activities in advance so as not to overlap. But schedules have a way of going awry, and sometimes speeches can be heard from both parties over the loudspeakers simultaneously, which is in effect to hear nothing. During the larger-scale Summer Festival, Sōgidan and Santōrō split duties down the middle, each managing the festival for three days rather than pooling their resources. For today's Fall Festival, Santōrō has provided a soup line that serves free cur- ried rice (a popular item on such occasions) to everyone on the premises. Funds for the soup line and other expenses come out of the union treasury, which is fed by dues and by contributions made at this and similar events.

It is five o'clock and already near dusk. The air is chilly but not bone cold. The men have queued up a good hundred feet for the soup line. Several cauldrons are filled to the brim with curried rice—more than enough to feed today's crowd. While the men are still being served dinner, Santōrō union members ascend the stage and make speeches. Many of the men are still in line when two dozen of the rank-and-file, accompanied by as many supporters, leave the park and begin parading through the neighborhood, chanting slogans and waving an assortment of flags and banners. I do not join the parade, but I can imagine now what it was like, having joined another during the Winter Survival Struggle the following New Year.

That parade followed a prescribed route: a thirty-minute, quarter-mile circuit through the narrow streets of Kiyokawa. The marchers, about fifty of us, chanted rhythmically every inch of the way. We were hemmed in on all sides by several platoons of kidōtai troops in full riot dress. The latter were there, I was later told, to prevent marchers from venturing too close to the headquarters of Kanamachi Ikka, San'ya's dominant yakuza gang, lo- cated a short walk north of the park. A few rowdies, encouraged by liquor and the presence of supporters, attempted to bust their way through police lines, but the results of this sort of pushing contest were never in doubt: they were easily beaten back by the kidōtai troops with a few flicks of their shields. Santōrō officers took turns hollering out slogans through a megaphone, and workers punctuated each phrase with affirmative yells and raised fists:

"We're gonna make it through the winter!"

"The doya rates are way too high!"

"Don't take away our unemployment pay—say 'no' to registration!"

"Come on, everyone, let's eat together in Tamahime Park!"

"We're gonna make it through another year!"

"We can do it!"

"We can do it!"

The intended audience would seem to have been the doya proprietors, but as far as I could tell, none was inspired to sup with day laborers in the park. Indeed, the streets, blocked at every end by riot police, were deathly still.

The autumn air has turned nippy. Most men have finished their dinners and are eyeing the stage expectantly. The ground in front is covered with pieces of cardboard and rows of thin straw mats. Many have removed their shoes and are sitting on the mats, much as Japanese anywhere might do when picnicking or viewing spring blossoms or autumn leaves with friends in parks elsewhere in the city. At the foot of the stage, several men dance, gesticulate, and otherwise make merry. Some men in back watch approvingly while warming their hands at one of the bonfires. Their smiling faces glow in the flickering light. Many sing boisterously along with the five-member Bridge Band; they shout encouragement to the man dancing in the traditional style in a lavishly decorated kimono; they go into stitches while watching the two-man troupe in drag; and they listen politely to the speeches of union officials. Except for a couple of very minor alcohol-induced flare-ups, the atmosphere is relaxed and peaceful—more peaceful, in fact, than at the white-collar drinking parties under the cherry blossoms, say, in Ueno Park, where men in suits attack the branches in their struggle for souvenirs or yell at the top of their lungs without concern for the neighboring parties.

The group assembled here in Tamahime Park might be considered the day-laborer "middle class." Those better off are no doubt relaxing in their centrally heated business-hotel rooms and watching TV. Those worse off have probably camped out on the street already, about to spend another night on an empty stomach and a bloated liver. It is clear that a good many men here know one another. They have done all this before and look forward to doing it again. They are under no illusions about why they are here. But they are eager nonetheless to enjoy the conviviality and fellowship of the moment. After the entertainers leave and the union members clean up, the men go their separate ways: most to their rude accommodations in the

mengo separate ways after celebration

doyagai, a few to their apartments outside San'ya, and some to a corner of this very park, where they will spend the night—perhaps several nights.

Like the Summer Festival, the Winter Survival Struggle (December 28– January 4) is held when school is not in session, but the caged playing field remains closed. The city's policy is to encourage men to leave San'ya altogether during that same eight-day period and lodge in specially built quarters near Ōi Wharf in Tokyo Harbor. Union leaders and many Yama men question this policy, however: could not the same sum of money now being spent on temporary barracks and the transporting of some fifteen hundred men out of the area be used instead right here in San'ya, on accommodations in the nearby gymnasium or other local facility—or even better, on a permanent facility?

Although a happy season for ordinary citizenry—a time for feasts and gifts and visits with relatives and friends—New Year's is a stark reminder to Yama men that they have no place to call home. The reminder comes at a very inhospitable time of year, when a biting wind blows in from Siberia and temperatures at night dip below freezing. The number of *aokansha* swells during the holiday season, when there is no work. Bonfires are scrupulously tended by both volunteers and Yame men the whole night through for the many who sleep in Tamahime Park. The entertainment, which generates its own welcome warmth, is even more appreciated than at other times of the year.

On January 3, 1990, I take a break from my own holiday schedule and make a visit to Tamahime Park, at the cost of reneging on a promised outing with my family. This being the only possible time during the holiday to make the visit, I tell myself that its rewards will outweigh the wrath of my wife and the disappointment of my son. After writing out a mental rain check for a future outing with them, I tell my family that I will return this evening at an early hour.

I participate in the neighborhood march, described above, which takes place daily at five o'clock, and then I partake of the stew being served at the soup line from five-thirty. At six-thirty the evening's entertainment begins. Boisterous applause follows each act, whether deserved or not—not that some acts lack a certain professional quality. Shintani Noriko, who gained fame in 1969 as the singer of "The Case of Francine" ("Furanshiinu no baai"), an immensely popular ballad, is here tonight for her annual appearance. She became active in a number of left-leaning movements, from day labor to antiwar, to the detriment of her career. She is singing for free in San'ya, and she begins her concert with "Article Nine," a song that sets to music the stirring words in the Japanese Constitution renouncing war and the maintenance of military forces. She continues with a selection of

Korean songs and concludes with a medley of songs made famous by Japan's most popular *enka* singer, the late Misora Hibari. She does not forget "Francine" along the way. Nor does she flinch when one man, then another, jumps on stage and runs up to embrace her. She manages to untangle herself from the two rivals, back away from the ensuing scuffle, descend the stage to the ground while union members restrain the combatants, and mingle with the crowd—all without skipping a note. The band, of course, plays on.

The hour-long stage entertainment is followed by the "sermon": Tottori's lecture on union activities and on the yoseba's potential as a permanent home. His words are seconded by the rank-and-file members, who stand behind him, fists raised and shouting their approval. Aizu, Hamamatsu, Sakata, Naga-san, and Akita—the last a particularly vociferous participant at these activities—are among the faces I recognize on stage.

The festivities are over at eight o'clock sharp. About half the men file out of the park to their doya, leaving those who will bed down here in Tamahime. A small crowd is taking in a documentary presented by Sōgidan on San'ya, which includes scenes from this very park. Some of the men point to themselves on the portable screen.

It has gotten very late. High in the winter sky, a nearly full moon casts its pale light over the park. A piercing chill inhabits the night air. The middle-school gymnasium, completely dark, is dimly visible beyond the park through the cage's wire mesh. I find myself becoming obsessed with the cage as I converse with a group of men who are preparing to spend the night here. I am tempted to spend it with them. But I have told my family I would be returning home. I am angry at myself for having to leave. I am angry at the vacant cage. I am especially angry at the unused gymnasium. Following the example of other men, who have been using the shrubbery at the base of the cage's eastern edge as the urinal of preference all evening, I observe a call of nature and relieve myself after what has seemed an eternity. The steaming stream drenches the wire mesh.

No sooner have I made my way to the park entrance, resolved at last to return home, than I am confronted by K-san, a short, powerfully built man in his late forties from the island of Kyushu and a long-time resident of San'ya. His thick, coarse hands tell anyone who shakes them of much toil. He enjoys shaking hands. I heard him talk at length earlier in the evening about life in San'ya and about life in general. He has not had an easy time of it, but his mood was upbeat; after all, it is festival time. Now, however, he has become teary in his cups. His face is black with soot from the bonfires. "Happy New Year," he shouts as he approaches me. He shakes my hand again. "The best to you in 1990." Then he gives me a bear hug. He does not let go. "The sky is beautiful tonight," he whispers in a voice choked with emotion. "I want to go up there and join the stars. I want to know peace."

"It is not time yet, K-san," I caution him. "You'll get there soon enough. There's a time to go and a time to stick it out. This is the Winter Survival Struggle—surely now's a time to stick it out."

"Yeah, I guess you're right," he sighs, finally letting go of me. "Okay, I'll stick it out for now."

Year-Forgetting Party

December 26, 1989. I have been invited by Santōrō to its *bōnenkai*, a party to "forget" the old year. It is the sort of occasion celebrated by Japanese throughout the country, at offices, schools, and clubs. Our venue is an eight-mat room (twelve-foot-square) rented for the evening in a tiny building that faces the JR Shioiri switchyard.

The room is cold. After applying in vain his considerable ingenuity to the computerized thermostat, Kobe, the officer who invited me, pays a visit to the manager next door. I tag along. The manager listens to Kobe's complaint through the closed door, but refuses to offer help or even talk to us face to face. "Well, it must be broken, then," is his only comment. "There's nothing I can do about it."

"Shit, the bastard won't lift a finger for a Yama man," my host mumbles beneath his breath as we return to our room. Nor even look at a Yama man, apparently.

The expected turnout was twenty men, but only ten actually show up. No matter: the dues of a thousand yen per person have been collected in advance, providing an unexpected largess that makes for more food and drink, already bought and delivered, for the rest of us. We are determined that no leftovers remain. There is one other nonunion member in attendance besides myself who, at age thirty, is the youngest of the group by nearly a decade. A frequent visitor to San'ya, he offers an acupuncture service to Yama men free of charge.

Other than the acupuncturist, I know everyone here: the three union officers—Osaka, Tottori, and Kobe—and five rank-and-file members: Aizu, Hamamatsu, Sakata, Naga-san, and Akita. Akita, who was charged with making purchases earlier in the day, has brought with him a mountain of fresh salmon roe along with canned herring roe and steamed scallops, all purchased at Ameyoko, the buy-in-bulk bazaar below the tracks between Ueno and Okachimachi stations on the Yamanote Loop Line. He has also bought a dozen large bottles of beer, four large bottles of saké—no One Cups will do tonight—and a case (thirty bottles) of *umeshu*. The consensus is that we have gotten a lot for the money. "Yeah," groans Akita, "but let's face it. The roe's second rate. Way too salty." He is right. It *is* second rate, but we wash it all down with what is of course the central attraction anyway: the first-rate saké—or, for those with a sweet tooth, the *umeshu*. Aizu, who has a particularly sweet tooth and who worried at first about the low turnout, seems quite content now. About an hour into the party, he dozes off. The room could never have held twenty people anyway.

Despite the incident next door which nearly ruins the party before it starts, we have a nearly perfect evening. Liquor, body heat and conviviality provide the warmth. Naga-san and Hamamatsu provide the entertainment, belting out various numbers in the traditional (*min'yō*) and popular (*enka*) repertoire. A boom box, its volume kept low, serves up the accompaniment, and the rest of us keep rhythm with chopsticks on our beer bottles and saké cups. We also chat, reminisce, sing along, and finally dance. When asked to sing a number myself, I dig into my memory and come up with a song by Woody Guthrie, "This Land Is Your Land." A paean to wide-open spaces and equal access, the song strikes me as the perfect antidote to our restricted quarters. I try as best I can, as a near-native of California and sometime native of Tokyo, to explain the lyrics. We end with several impromptu, randy verses sung to a melody everyone knows: "Donpan-bushi."

During the singing and throughout the evening, Aizu and Sakata prudently seat themselves at opposite ends of the table. Hamamatsu, a huge scab on his cheek, manages to keep conscious for the duration of the party. He is clearly having a good time, occasional ribbings by his cohorts notwithstanding. Naga-san smiles broadly and accompanies his own singing with smart claps of the hand. Akita is complaining vociferously as always about this and that, but no one takes him seriously. At the conclusion of each song, we applaud ourselves liberally and reward ourselves with more drink. There are no teetotalers here tonight. After eating our fill, we sing and dance and clap and chat still more. But we do not engage in rabble-rousing. The manager has nothing to worry about. Not that he really could have been expecting trouble. After all, he did let the room. And he knew from the beginning to whom he let it. The building is in San'ya. The clientele cannot possibly have been a mystery to him.

The party over, we all pitch in to clean the room: our goal is to leave it in exactly the same condition we found it in. It is not because of what the manager thinks. To hell with what he thinks. It is because that is what the members always do, whatever the occasion and whatever the venue—be it Tamahime Park at festival time, or at a workshop, or at a private facility such as this. We fold up the center table and put it away. We store the cushions, wash the dishes, clean out the sink, sweep the floor. The room is immaculate. My host accompanies me and the acupuncturist to Minami Senjū Station. We salute the officers at a police box on wobbly feet along the way.

Transferring at Akihabara Station to a train bound for south Tokyo, I nearly bump into two men in business suits pissing the beer they probably drank at *their* Year-Forgetting Party that evening—not on the tracks below but right onto the platform. They race to get on the train. My train. I am in no hurry, I decide, and wait for the next one, choosing a bench far removed from the widening puddle.

Requiem for a Yama Man

June 7, 1990. Hamamatsu is dead. Mourners are assembled in the Taitō Ward Office Annex multipurpose room in Kiyokawa, just south of the doyagai near the Asahi Street shopping district. I am a late arrival this afternoon, having been sidetracked by a self-proclaimed former yakuza who insisted on sharing a drink at a vending machine not a stone's throw from the annex.

A makeshift altar stands against the rear wall. Its centerpiece is a monochrome photograph of Hamamatsu, an extremely good likeness draped in black crepe and prominently displayed alongside a bronze incense burner, a couple of saké bottles, and several bouquets. A U-shaped table (actually several low tables placed together end to end), with the bottom of the U nearest the entranceway, nearly fills the tatami-covered room. I remove my shoes and sandwich myself between the other mourners at the bottom of the U. Some twenty Santōrō members sit to my left as I face the altar. Perhaps fifteen others—union supporters and friends—sit to my right. We are packed shoulder to shoulder and the skin on our shirt-sleeved arms is sticky to the touch with the humidity of the season.

Tottori is master of ceremonies. His voice cuts through the steamy air with the aid of a portable amplifying unit. After showing us photographs that feature Hamamatsu participating in a union-sponsored activity, he leads the offering of incense. We all pay our respects, at a deliberate pace, to the man each of us had known in his own way. The offering is followed by short speeches by several union members. Kobe suggests, in a voice audible to all present, that I say a few words as well. I am not prepared. Kobe had informed me only the day before that the service would be held, and I had my doubts about attending at all. Today is Thursday. I have been asked to address an organization of foreign residents on San'ya this coming Monday—my first formal presentation. Prior commitments rule out any preparation time over the weekend. I had been planning on spending this, my only free day, to think about the talk.

I stand up and walk to the altar. After bowing, as the others had done, to the photographic likeness of the man I had known for over a year, I turn to the audience. "I guess I should tell you what I had planned on doing today in order to explain how I feel about Hamamatsu . . . and . . . about San'ya in general."

I am having difficulty stringing my words together. I look again at the closely cropped portrait draped in black. I recall my various encounters with Hamamatsu last year and in particular the planning session at the Santōrō union headquarters. My memories are disturbing ones. In my mind lurks the vision of a man whose body had been wracked by both alcohol and the frequent abuse of his peers. Perhaps now, at last, he is resting in peace.

I confess to the mourners that it had been my intention to spend the day at home preparing a lecture for the members of a society composed of scholars, businessmen, diplomats, and professionals who I was told were interested in becoming more familiar with an area of the city they knew very little about. But I abandoned my plans when I got the call from Kobe. Several times in my life I'd lost out on the chance to pay my last respects to someone I knew. I had regretted it each time. I did not want to regret it again if I could help it. I had decided that it was more important to come and be part of what was going on here than to stew in my room over a talk for an audience I didn't even know. . . .

Here I stop. This is not a particularly good place to end a memorial, but I can think of nothing more to say and I sit down. Tottori takes the cue and quickly ushers in the next part of the program: a concert by some musicians who frequently perform at festival time in Tamahime Park. One plays harmonica, and he is followed by a singer accompanied on a guitar. The applause, offered merely out of politeness after the memorials, is unrestrained after the entertainment. The funeral mood that shrouded the ceremonies at the beginning has been transformed into a celebration.

It is time to eat. Fat bottles of beer and slender bottles of juice adorn each of the low tables at which we sit. The saké bottles on the altar are respectfully removed and redistributed about the U. The man squeezed in next to me, a latecomer like myself, is a day laborer in his late fifties I have not seen before. He seems anxious to talk, and his warm smile and kind eyes overcome my embarrassment at having just delivered such a lackluster speech. While we eat I find out why we have not crossed paths. He has just returned from a long stint in the hospital, where he underwent a battery of tests for stomach cancer. There will probably have to be an operation. But in the meantime, he is free to do as he wishes. He likes his saké. He is drinking right now. It is I who am doing most of the eating. His arm is febrile against my skin.

Several people exchange seats during the course of the meal, offering their saké cups and pieces of the puzzle that was Hamamatsu. I move about myself, trying to put the pieces together. Hamamatsu collapsed on the street in March and died in a hospital on May 31, succumbing at last to the symptoms of exposure and advanced alcohol poisoning. Being a notorious snorer and very self-conscious about it, he was a regular *aokansha*, sleeping out on the street by preference. Better to brave the night air than bother his buddies in a doya, he had always said. Such a practice took its toll over time. So did his drinking, as we all knew.

Hamamatsu's cremation, which took place on June 3, was attended by two of his sisters from his home town. It was their first "meeting" with their brother since he had left home, nearly thirty years earlier, for Tokyo. While watching the smoke trail out of the crematorium chimney in south Tokyo, they reminisced with the union members also in attendance. They had known their brother only as a lazy good-for-nothing who could not hold down a job and who sponged off family, fellow workers, and short-lived friends. They were therefore surprised to learn that he was a union member in San'ya and an active supporter of day-laborer causes. Could he really have changed that much? Hamamatsu's colleagues replied that they couldn't say for sure whether he had changed or not, because they did not know the "old" Hamamatsu. They did know that he worked hard when he could still work, but that the money he made went mostly to support his drinking habit. Nobody liked him when he was drunk—not because he was a mean drunk but because he was so self-destructive. When he wasn't hurting himself, he seemed to encourage abuse by others, as I had seen during my visit last December to union headquarters. It was a frightening sight.

When we have all eaten our fill, Tottori turns the microphone over to Kobe, who says he has an announcement to make. By this time the audience has grown weary of speeches, but Kobe takes the lack of interest as a challenge. Unlike the rest of us, he has thought a great deal about his subject and he will have his say no matter what.

"I've lived in San'ya for eighteen years, and I've been with the union since it began in 1977. I turn forty this year. I'd like to say I've made a contribution to the quality of life here, but unfortunately I've seen many things go from bad to worse. . . ."

"Sure, tell us about it, Kobe!" The hecklers are feeling their oats.

Kobe is not to be upstaged. "Okay, you guys, just hear me out. If the city of Tokyo had taken the trouble to build more public housing in this area; if it let single workingmen live in it and do things like invite their friends for a visit without worrying about a curfew; in short, if it were more interested in getting men off the streets and under a roof than in simply trying to cover up this embarrassment that is San'ya, then Hamamatsu might still be alive today. And even if he did die, at least he wouldn't have had to die alone! That's what's so hard about living here, you know. . . ."

everyone on their own

"You don't have to remind us, Kobe! Got any better ideas?"

"I sure do. Everybody's on his own in this neighborhood. But that's the system, isn't it? You come drifting into San'ya on your own and you live on your own. The work wears you out and the elements wear you down. And before you know it, you're on your deathbed, facing the great unknown by yourself."

"Don't rub it in, Kobe!"

"You forget it at your peril, Ibaraki." Kobe directs his words at his principal heckler, a man who hails from a prefecture northeast of Tokyo. "I'm telling you, that's no way for a man to die! Sure, we all have to go sometime. And when we do go, we yearn for peace of mind. We yearn to be surrounded by family and friends. But can any of *us* go home?"

"We know the answer to *that* question, don't we, boys!"

"Always gotta put in your two bits, don't you, Ibaraki. . . . Well, the answer is, no, we can't. If we *could* go, we'd sure as hell get out of this god-forsaken place. But we're stuck here, aren't we? So we've got to make the best of it. That's why I'm telling you we need city-funded housing, and we need it now. The doya are getting too damned expensive. Half of them are business hotels. But all that twenty-five hundred yen a night buys you—which is to say all that seventy-five thousand yen a month buys you in this neighborhood—is a three-mat room!"

"Ha! D-don't worry about me." Sakata, who has been waiting to get a word in edgewise, finally succeeds after a fashion. "Hey, I've got a p-plan! I'll just . . . take off! Wheee!"

"Sure you will, Sakata! So you're going to fly back home? Don't make me laugh! And stop trying to outdo Ibaraki. You haven't got a prayer. Just pack up your bags and leave right now, if you can."

"But I've got a better plan!"

"Okay, spell it out."

"I'm . . . just . . . not . . . going . . . to . . ." Sakata can hardly sit up at the table.

"Die!" Another voice finishes the sentence for Sakata.

"He's *not* going to die. Ugh—that's the problem!" This from yet another heckler.

". . . d-die!" Sakata belatedly finishes his own sentence.

"Oh, what the hell, you're all crazy! The whole place is crazy! But it's not going to do any good to sit and moan. If we want something to happen, we've got to make it happen. We can't wait for someone to take our complaints to city hall. *We're* the ones who've got to take the initiative, so long as there's a single breath left in our lungs. If we don't, you can bet your life no one else will, and the city would be very happy to close the book on us. The city can afford to wait until we all die. Can we afford *not* to act now?"

Doya resident in three-mat room.

"Hey, the big talk sounds good, Kobe, but what can we really do? The city holds all the cards, and we don't have a single ace."

"I never said it would be easy, Ibaraki. But look at the alternative. Go ahead and sleep on the street when the dough runs out. Sleep there until you pick up pneumonia. Then get tossed into a pauper's ward and be given up for dead even before you've breathed your last. Don't you see what I'm saying? Death is staring us in the face every day. Now doesn't *that* motivate you?"

"It motivates me to take another swig from my bottle! Shooting for the stars just makes it hurt all the more when you come crashing to the ground."

"Okay, Ibaraki, go ahead and drink. Rush to your death, if that's what you want. I admit that I'm tempted myself—more times than I can say. But I also want to live out my allotted life span, thank you, and I know I'm not going to make it the way things are now. There's something else I know— that we're not going to make it by depending on other people's favors. Nobody out there gives a damn if we live or die. If we want something done, we've got to do it ourselves. That's why I'm running for a seat in the Taitō Ward Assembly."

"Hooray!" Whistles and applause from around the table.

"I officially declare myself a candidate for office. The workers here need a voice in government. I'll be running hard and running scared, because I'll be running for life itself. You see, I want a place I can call my own in this town. San'ya is no Ginza . . ."

"You can say *that* again!"

". . . but it's home. It's the only home I've got. It's the only home you've got. So what do you say we give it a try?"

Kobe takes his seat and the party continues, but the mood is once again more subdued. It has long since grown dark outside. We have all enjoyed the get-together. Some express their envy of Hamamatsu. "Do you think this many will gather at my funeral?" one man remarks wistfully to no one in particular. We have also enjoyed the food and the drink, not to mention the hoots and hollers. But we have absorbed the grim message as well, doled out like a dose of bitter medicine, by Kobe. It is time to break up, but no one is in a hurry to leave.

On my way to Minami Senjū Station, I bump into Ibaraki, the heckler who had earlier so outrageously interrupted, and deliciously spiced, Kobe's speech. He is headed for Ōtone, a tavern opposite the station, and invites me to have a drink with him. I hesitate. I have a talk to prepare, after all. The obvious excuse seems to hold the least currency, however, and I end up following him through the door. We chat for the longest time. To hell with the talk, I tell myself.

Ridge-Raising Ceremony

July 15, 1990. A crowd has gathered at the Iroha Arcade's east end to celebrate the near-completion of the San'ya Workers' Hall (San'ya Rōdōsha Fukushi Kaikan). The rainy season is not yet over, but the clouds have parted today and warm, hazy sunshine filters through a white sky. I am standing next to a waist-high mortar placed on the pavement and watching its doughy contents being pounded with a large wooden mallet by an officer of Sōgidan, one of the San'ya Workers' Hall sponsors. He is followed by several day laborers, not a few of whom I have seen around before and who are always present at festive occasions such as this, having a nose, as I do, for food and drink and good conversation. Sendai, manager of Maria Restaurant, is next. Today is Sunday and the restaurant is closed. The crowd numbers perhaps forty or fifty people—large enough to attract attention and yet still small enough to remain intimate. I recognize several volunteers I have worked with on the Citizens' Patrol, as well as several men I have seen on the job at this very construction site.

Mochi (rice-cake) pounding is all in a day's work for the Yama man, who is typically a jack-of-all-trades and attacks any chore with gusto. No doubt many men have memories of pounding rice cakes at home in the provinces during the winter holidays, when they were home and could partake in a delicious seasonal dish called *ozōni*, for which the glutinous rice cakes, prepared in the cold weather right before New Year's, are a principal ingredient.

The Workers' Hall is being built with labor recruited by Sōgidan and funds raised by the United Church of Christ in Japan. I have visited the construction site several times before to inspect progress and am familiar with the layout. The ground floor will house a small restaurant named, simply, Yama, to be run by day laborers and their supporters. Upstairs, one floor will house a medical-consultation room and office space for the United Church of Christ; the other, supplementary office space for Sōgidan and a multipurpose room, where we will gather shortly to celebrate the building's progress with food and drink.

During a visit last April, I ventured through a door marked "No admittance," and after ingratiating myself with the group of workers on duty that day, who fortunately took kindly to this sudden intruder, I received a guided tour of the building. I accepted the cup of tea offered me during their break but declined a portion of the stew they had just prepared, thinking it impolitic to accept food without having done any work. "Okay, then just be sure you drop by sometime for a meal when the restaurant's open before you leave Japan," my guide told me. He then pointed to one of his fellow workers: "This man here cooks a mean dish of *horumon-yaki!*"

Labor on the building has been performed entirely by volunteers. Many men make it a habit of stopping by the Workers' Hall after trying to get work off the street that day. Some have even forfeited jobs to help out. The volunteer labor has saved a great deal of money, which is needed for materials. (The land itself is owned by the United Church of Christ in Japan, bought with nationwide contributions from parishioners.) In theory, all Sōgidan members are supposed to chip in with elbow grease. But in fact the burden has fallen on a relatively small number of men who have pitched in far more than their fair share. Not everyone likes to work for free, as one worker explained to me that April day during break—not that there is no reward. "Let's just say that the hours spent here are an investment. I'm sure we'll get paid back somewhere down the line—right, U-san?" He directed a knowing glance at the Sōgidan member in attendance.

The building was to be finished by the end of the month, but it is behind schedule. That fact has not dampened the spirits of anyone present, however. The rice-pounding ceremony drawn to a close, we partake of the fruits of the men's labor: a mouth-watering, stick-to-your-ribs assortment of *mochi* and *dango*—skewered *mochi* covered with red sweet beans or sweetened soybean flour.

It is time for a tour of the premises. We make our way past the usual crowd of drunks who line both sides of the arcade's east end (some of whom are oblivious; others are only too happy to join in the festivities once they have been roused to their senses), climb the narrow stairs single file, and view the unfinished rooms on each floor. We even have a look at the rooftop, which, like many buildings in Japan, is a functional part of the architecture: flat, spacious (albeit cluttered with utility closets, pipes, and tools), and affording a view of the surrounding area, including the arcade roof running toward Senzoku and the gray expanse of buildings extending to Namidabashi.

Someone on the tour asks a Sōgidan member, "Why build the Workers' Hall when the Welfare Center is located just up the street?" "It's very simple," he is told. "We may have what look like similar facilities, like job- and medical-consultation rooms, but our approaches to what goes on on this neighborhood are very different. They are a bureaucracy. We are a cause. We want to be able to do our own thing. And the best place to do it is right here in the arcade, in the heart of San'ya."

The tour ends in the multipurpose room, where an ample spread of food and drink awaits today's guests. The room is not large enough to accommodate everyone comfortably, and after the obligatory speeches and toast, the overflow makes its way back to the rooftop, liberal portions of beer, saké, and hors d'oeuvres in hand. It is much pleasanter up here. The stench of raw concrete is far less noticeable, and the urine-stained streets are mercifully distant.

I have brought my camera along with me today and begin taking pictures when I notice a man bent over in a corner vomiting. At first I suspect that the food has not agreed with him, but then I realize it is because of drink. The man is retching painfully; yet no one seems to notice. I put my camera down and kneel at his side. "Let me get you a glass of water." "No, thanks," he says. "I've still got some of this left." He points to his One Cup jar of saké, which is still half full. I do not argue. The man tells me that he is a plasterer by trade and that he has not been working recently because of a rib injury. He shows me his hands. They are very rough, and his finger tips are broad and flat.

The festivities wind down toward evening. The building is closed up, but many of us continue chatting on the street corner at the arcade entrance. A frail, wizened man perhaps in his late forties but who walks with the ginger movements of an eighty-year-old, cuts in on a conversation I am having with someone else and asks me to do him a favor, to drop by the watch shop run by his sister in Kameari and give her his regards. He is serious: he insists that I take down the address. I do. It seems he has not seen her in several years. Kameari is a half hour by train from San'ya.

Our chat takes place over an extended period, but the actual number of words exchanged is small. His request and subsequent comments are interspersed with a running commentary on my character and breadth of understanding: "You're really beyond help, you know?" and "You just don't get it, do you?" He claims to know all the *tehaishi* working the area and insists that they cannot look him in the eye. He further insists that he has connections with all the yakuza syndicates in the area. He does have that look about him, despite his present physical state. His left leg has been severely burned. He pulls up his pant leg and shows me the skin grafts taken from other parts of his body. "I thought the leg'd have to be amputated," he tells me, "but the doctor said 'Leave it to me, leave it to me!'"

He then asks me if I want to go drinking and if I know of a good place. I assure him that he must have a superior knowledge of San'ya's watering holes. We head north, in the direction of the Welfare Center, but get only a short distance before he pulls up in the middle of the street and begins talking about nothing in particular. When I realize he has no goal, I decide that it is time to part company. He asks me if I want to go gambling. I tell him I am not interested. "You're really beyond help, you know. You just don't get it, do you?"

He is right, of course. There is a lot I do not understand, and I hesitate to rebut him. Yet there is no need to take his remarks personally, I finally decide. Something about the way he says them suggests a great deal of practice on many compatriots who are similarly beyond help and who just don't get it.

I head back to the Iroha and chat with some of the stragglers. During a conversation I am having with a man from Numazu, a man takes ill a few feet away. He is vomiting and having convulsions, and someone calls an ambulance. It arrives shortly and takes him to a nearby hospital. The excitement over, Numazu and I continue our conversation. In seemingly no time, the man who took ill is among us again, returned by the same ambulance that had whisked him away. "Well what do you expect from Shirahige [the name of the hospital], anyway?" he explains with a sheepish grin that quickly transforms into a dour look. "They didn't even check me over. They could've examined my stomach at least. But no, they said I was having a fit of alcohol poisoning and told me to stop drinking and to be on my way. And then I had to shell out two thousand yen! Shit, what a waste!"

Some of those listening to him laugh aloud; others shake their heads. The man makes his way unsteadily to the edge of the street and starts vomiting again. Numazu and I resume our conversation and then opt for more congenial surroundings: a tavern on the Street of Bones. Despite the scene I have just witnessed, the saké tastes very good this evening.

Farewells

July 27, 1990. I am in San'ya for the last time this trip. After today I must begin in earnest packing up two years of life in Tokyo with my family for the journey back to the States on August 1.

My friends in Santōrō have invited me to a late lunch near Minowabashi. We gather at a restaurant overlooking the trolley station and feast on *okonomi-yaki,* a pancake-shaped concoction with vegetables and meat or fish that we cook to taste on the grill at our table. It is a dish native to western Japan and thus popular with my friends. It is popular in Tokyo, too, especially in winter, because of the warmth generated by the grill. In today's searing heat, however, business is slow and most tables are empty. We temper the heat with frequent rounds of ice-cold beer served in giant mugs.

I enjoy myself thoroughly and am touched by my friends' gesture. The conversation is wide-ranging. Kobe outlines his campaign strategy for a place in the Taitō Ward Assembly. I tell them of my plans to return to San'ya next summer to work if possible as a day laborer. We part company a little after four o'clock. From Minowabashi I head south, cross Meiji Boule-vard, and make my way east through the Nihonzutsumi doyagai. Unlike previous visits, this time I regard the area not with a mind to discover something new but rather to implant firmly in memory the many scenes I will not be witnessing again for at least a year.

I have several errands in the neighborhood. I have promised to deliver a snapshot to a man I met two weeks earlier at the San'ya Workers' Hall ridge-raising ceremony, doubting all the while that he would ever receive it, because he gave me no address and merely instructed me to attach it to a lamppost at the Iroha Arcade's east entrance, where I met him. I have also promised to deliver another snapshot I took at the ceremony to a second man, who wisely instructed me to leave it in care of San'yūkai. I have promised as well to pay a final visit to Shimizu, a man of letters living in Kiyokawa. As I make my way through the doyagai, I marvel at how my forays into San'ya, tentative and almost whimsical at the beginning, have engendered bonds—some lasting, some not, but bonds just the same.

I keep my visits with Shimizu in his doya and at San'yūkai short. I have to be home by evening. I am needed, of course, to help with the packing. There is no daylight savings time in Tokyo, and the sun is already low on the horizon. I cross Old Streetcar Boulevard from Kiyokawa back into Ni-honzutsumi for my last errand in the arcade. A breeze has cleared the air and the ordinarily hazy summer sky has been transformed into a cobalt blue. The late-afternoon sun gives the streets, the few trees, the buildings, the residents, a warm luster I have rarely seen here before. The haunting strains of the five-o'clock chime, which can be heard anywhere in Taitō Ward, reverberate from the middle-school loudspeaker.

With the evening, the arcade's east end has come alive. Nodaya, the stand-up bar just outside the entranceway, is already packed. I eye the lamppost, then the snapshot in my hand.

"Long time, no see!"

Startled, I look up at a bearded face. The man in front of me wears the flared knickers of a *tobi,* a long-sleeved, dark-green sweater, and a small, yellow terry-cloth towel around his neck. It is not the man whose picture I was to put on the lamppost.

"Remember me?"

For a moment I fail to recognize him. Then I notice the crew cut and the glassy eyes. Then the voice—that piercing, throaty voice. And it all comes back. Nine months after my first encounter, Shiga has appeared before me again, not fifty steps from the spot outside Sen'nari, where I had first met him.

"Of course I do. And I remember how much I'm in your debt."

"Don't mention it. You still taking pictures?"

"Yes, I am," I answer with a grin. "But I'm also talking to people. In fact, I'm doing a lot more talking than picture taking these days. Looking back on it, I think of that little incident last year as the start of something important. I'm truly grateful."

The "little incident" flashes into memory, as does the aftermath. Four days after the events described in the Prologue, I had returned to the photo shop in the Iroha Arcade to pick up my slides. Shiga had not removed the incriminating picture—the deal he'd insisted on. With developed slides in hand (I left the last shot at the photo shop), I had made my way down the arcade toward Sen'nari. Once again, the scene I found there was of warm camaraderie. No one greeted me with the fierce stares I had anticipated for four sleepless nights. Shiga was not there, but I learned from the proprietor where he was lodging: a tiny business hotel not far from the arcade. I immediately paid the hotel a visit but, as Shiga was not in, ended up leaving a note in care of the manager expressing the hope that we get together sometime under more favorable circumstances.

We had maintained indirect contact in the interim. I received a reply to my note in the form of a message from the Sen'nari chef, who hailed me one day about a month later as I was passing through the arcade. "This is from Shiga," he told me, and handed me the slide I had taken that October evening. "He picked it up from the photo shop." I was dumbfounded. "He says that the picture looked harmless enough," the chef continued, "and he wanted you to have it back."

I reversed my steps and paid the business hotel another visit, only to leave a note once again in Shiga's absence. Sometime later I spoke with him on the telephone. But our paths had never actually crossed until today.

"By the way, are you still staying at that hotel?"

"Not right now. Can't afford it. I'm working only a couple of days a week. It's too damned hot in the summer to do more. I'm staying in a bunkhouse on the other side of Namidabashi. It's only eight hundred yen a night. The hotel cost three times that. When it cools down again I'll start working more often and move back into a single room. But it's just too hot now. Say, how about a beer?"

"Thanks, but first I've got to take care of this snapshot. You see, someone asked me to take his picture a couple of weeks ago and now I'm trying to deliver it. He told me to stick it right over there on that lamppost."

"You shouldn't take that kind of request seriously. The guy was probably drunk at the time and won't give it a second thought."

"He may have been drunk, but he was very persistent, and I'm sure he won't forget. Anyway, that's why I'm here. I'm set on leaving it."

Just then the man whose snapshot I had just delivered to San'yūkai happens by in his usual summer garb of sleeveless white undershirt and knapsack. I tell him that I have made the delivery and he seems very pleased.

Shiga, who has been observing this exchange, understands that I am serious about my deliveries and hastens to put a plan into effect. Just as he did last October, he wants to take charge.

"Listen," he tells me. "It's no use hanging the other picture on the lamppost. Somebody's just going to tear it down. And it won't do any good to leave it with someone here on the street. They're all just a bunch of drunks." I think I detect the sheepish grin of a man not unaware of the irony of his statement. But then I recall my own sheepish grin just moments ago. "Come with me," he continues. "I have a better idea."

The "better idea" apparently is to have a beer at Nodaya. We make our way to the counter and he orders the large bottle, which I gladly pay for. Then he gets down to business, asking the proprietor to hold onto the snapshot and hand it to the man in question the next time he shows up.

The proprietor, who is working the counter, protests. He does not want to be bothered with random requests. But as the conversation progresses, he begins to take interest. Finally he agrees. He actually knows the man, he now claims, and he'd be happy to get the picture to him. By the time we leave, he radiates confidence: "You can depend on me!" More than at the proprietor's display of authority, I marvel once again at Shiga's way of handling people.

We chat for a while outside Nodaya. Shiga grew up in a village near Lake Biwa and moved to Kyoto after finishing middle school. He became so enamored with the famous city that he took to introducing himself as "N, from Kyoto." He worked for a while in a small company, got into some "trouble," and eventually wound up in San'ya, where he has spent the last sixteen years. He has not returned to his home in Shiga Prefecture for twenty-five years. He is the youngest among his male siblings, all of whom hold down respectable jobs. One of his brothers is a ranking bureaucrat in the prefectural office. He never knew his father, who was drafted late in the war and went down with his ship immediately after departing for the Pacific Theater, when Shiga was still in his mother's womb.

We shake hands at length when we part. I notice for the first time that he is missing a finger joint. I suspect that this part of his anatomy is connected with the "trouble" he mentioned earlier.

He offers to show me Kyoto the next time I am in Japan. I believe that the offer is a serious one. He tells me that he reads a lot on his own about the city's history during his free time.

As I walk away from the arcade toward Namidabashi and Minami Senjū Station, I resolve one day to take him up on his offer. We have, of course, set up no definite time. That would be impossible now anyway. I will be leaving the country in a few days. But I will be back. And there will be other chances. I have no doubt that I will see Shiga again. He has not left me an address, and even if he did, it would change. I believe nonetheless that I could reestablish contact, because I know some of his haunts and I know people—including the proprietors of Nodaya and Sen'nari—who know him.

In a way, it is not important that I see Shiga again. What is important is that I did get to know him. I believe that as long as his spirit inhabits me I shall always be close to San'ya, and that whenever I come to Tokyo, before going to Shinjuku, or Shibuya, or Roppongi, or the Ginza, I will head this way first—as I would do the following summer to work as a day laborer at several *genba* in the Tokyo and, later, Osaka metropolitan areas.

CHAPTER 5

※

WORK

4:40 a.m.   Rise, dress in street clothes, and carefully pack my shoulder bag with the duds I plan to wear at the job: a long-sleeved shirt to prevent sunburn, light-weight work pants, *jikatabi, gunte* (coarse cotton gloves), and a small terry-cloth towel. I have made arrangements the previous evening with Tottori to try our luck together getting work he knows about at an expressway construction site near Shinden Station in the city of Sōka, a bedroom town north of San'ya in Saitama Prefecture. Tottori has worked at the site before. The doya at which I lodge already bustles with activity. Tenants make their way sleepily out of their rooms to the toilets and sinks down the hall.

5:30 a.m.   Rendezvous with Tottori outside the doya. We proceed up the street to Meiji Boulevard and meet Minami-san, a lean, wiry man in his mid-fifties who has been elevated to the position of "quasi-foreman" (*jōbi*) and who uses this corner just east of Namidabashi to recruit workers for the expressway construction site. After Tottori introduces me, Minami-san slowly sizes me up and finally agrees to take us both on for the day. We grab breakfast at a shop across the street that sells *onigiri* and miso soup served in Styrofoam cups.

6:10 a.m.   Walk to Minami Senjū Station with Tottori, Minami-san, and several other day laborers, take the Hibiya Line to Kita Senjū, and transfer to the Tōbu Isezaki Line bound for Shinden.

6:45 a.m.   Arrive at Shinden Station. We walk twenty minutes along a very busy street to the construction site, which is a ramp leading up to the half-finished expressway, an elevated highway about fifty feet above ground supported by huge, reinforced-concrete posts that are connected by steel girders with their protective undercoat of red-zinc paint still showing. A guard eyes us as we pass through the gate, and a fence surrounds part of the site, but security is lax compared with office-building construction sites in Tokyo, which are typically surrounded by corrugated-aluminum sheets and invisible to passersby. I survey the premises. To my left stands a prefabricated barrack that serves as an office; to the right, another barrack filled with tools and rubber boots and which some of the men are using as a changing room; and in between, a scaffold tower with stairs leading up to the highway pavement. Inside the office is a table, a few folding chairs, and a wall lined with hard hats, some marked with the company emblem, which regular employees use, and others, unmarked, which we day laborers will wear. A sign in the office, meticulously lettered, reads: "Jōban Expressway, Sōka Interchange, Ramp No. 2."

7:10 a.m.   Change into the work clothes I brought in my bag, go to the toilet (I have my choice of two portable outhouses, both filthy, near the gate), chat with Tottori, and wait for work to begin. Among the day laborers I see two Chinese students who I later find out attend a Japanese-language school but work full time during this, the summer holiday.

7:50 a.m.   Employees belonging to the sub-subcontractor, mostly electricians and other *shokunin* (skilled workers), arrive at the site in a light truck. They are in their twenties and thirties and therefore younger than most of the day laborers, and dressed in colorful uniforms. The foreman, the most colorfully dressed of all, is a stout, robust man in his late thirties who can do any kind of work. He is deferential to the electricians and other *shokunin*, condescending to the day laborers. There is no intermingling between the two groups. They will do their work and we will do ours.

8:00 a.m.   The site manager, a short, heavy-set man in his late fifties, leads the group (about twenty-five men, of whom fifteen are day laborers) in "radio calisthenics," a recorded exercise regimen that nearly every Japanese knows. Exercise is followed by a brief pep talk/job description, plus a lengthy explanation, complete with chalk-board diagrams, of safety rules. This avuncular, kindly looking man works for T-Industries, the main subcontractor of SK Enterprises, which is the firm hired to build this portion of the expressway. Below T-Industries is I-gumi, headed by Mr. I himself, the robust foreman who supervises the *shokunin* and pays our wages. Below

Shinden construction site: elevated highway and ramp.

I-gumi and at the bottom of this hierarchy are we day laborers. Minami-san serves as mediator between us and the rest of the workers.

8:15 a.m.   Donning an unmarked hard hat that hangs on the office wall, I follow everyone up the fifty-foot tower, which is decked out with banners advising "Safety First" and proclaiming "National Safety Week," to the highway surface. I learn from a fellow worker that someone fell to his death just a few weeks ago at a site farther down the expressway. Day laborers have been assigned various jobs. Some help pour concrete. Others dismantle the wooden molds of sections that have already been poured. My work for the day is scraping away cement that has splattered onto the girders beneath the expressway. Along with the others on the same assignment, I collect a fistful of tools in storage atop the expressway, then lower myself through an opening onto the narrow plank catwalks below that run as far as the eye can see in either direction. Beneath the catwalks are nylon nets that look strong enough to snag tools and other objects and to slow down, but not break, the fall of anything larger.

I am with a team of six day laborers. We split up initially into three pairs, but rearrange ourselves from time to time. In addition to Tottori, I work mostly with Koshigaya, a talkative man in his mid-fifties who keeps up a constant banter about his sexual exploits, and with Mitaka, a thirty-year veteran of yoseba life who commutes from a suburb in west Tokyo. The latter is all business and takes it upon himself to act as my mentor. I learn from him the names of the tools we are using and how best to scrape the cement. I begin at a slower pace than the rest but finally get the hang of things and gradually get up to speed. We cover perhaps a hundred yards before the ten-o'clock break. The two hours seem an eternity. Although the day is not swelteringly hot—we are just barely out of the monsoon—it is steamy beneath the expressway girders and we are quickly bathed in sweat.

10:00 a.m.   Break. Someone brings up a bag of canned soft drinks. A couple of workers take a quick snooze; the rest of us chat.

10:30 a.m.   Resume work. Now that I know what is expected of me, the work goes faster, as does the time.

12:00 noon.   Lunch hour. We retrace our steps to the opening in the highway surface and descend the scaffold tower. Box lunches arrive and are distributed to all workers on the site. We day laborers, keeping to ourselves, seek refuge in the shade directly below the expressway and eat our food, which is abysmally poor. Then we stretch out. Some use plywood boards stacked nearby for mattresses and take an extended nap. Silence reigns. The shokunin eat their meals quickly and then relax on straw mats, some reading girlie magazines, others pairing off for hanafuda, a traditional card game that is often played for high stakes.

1:00 p.m.   Resume work. A long two hours again. The job is slowed by several hard-to-remove splatters of cement.

3:00 p.m.   Short break. Another round of soft drinks.

4:30 p.m.   Time to quit. Put away tools.

4:45 p.m.   Descend scaffold tower and clean up below, using two faucets next to a ditch behind the office shed. Stripped to the waist, we form two lines by the faucets. For the first time today I am self-conscious, not in the presence of the other workers but in the presence of passersby on the street. There is no fence on this side, and we are in full view of the ordinary citizen. It is not so much that I am a foreigner and easily recognizable as such but that I am here working illegally. Eyes peeled, I keep my back turned toward the street, wash up quickly, and retreat to the rear barrack out of view, where I change into my street clothes.

5:00 p.m.   Collect cash wage: ¥14,750 (¥15,000, plus ¥250 allowance for bus fare, minus ¥500 for lunch). Also collect unemployment-insurance stamp. Several of the men immediately affix the stamp on their white cards. Not owning such a card, I put the stamp in my wallet to save for a rainy day. Its face value is ¥146, but I'm told it is worth up to a thousand yen on the black market.

5:30 p.m.   Some men, including the two Chinese students, have already left the site for Shinden Station on foot. The foreman drives a van for those of us who have waited. No one uses the city bus for which we have collected the ¥250 allowance. I join Tottori, Minami-san, and a few others at a vending machine outside a liquor store near the station for a round of ice-cold beer to celebrate the end of a hard day.

6:30 p.m.   Back in San'ya. Dine with Tottori at Mitoya, an eatery in Nihonzutsumi, on tomato salad, pork cutlets, and chilled tofu seasoned with ginger and bonito flakes, and wash it all down with two tall highballs called *chūhai—shōchū* cut with plain seltzer or with mineral water in a variety of flavors. We congratulate ourselves on a day's job well done, curse the nature of the work, and hope for better assignments in the future.

8:00 p.m.   Return to the doya, well before the eleven-o'clock curfew. I survey my room: a six-by-nine-foot cubicle, like all the rest, complete with futon, electric fan, and a small color TV. It sets me back eighteen hundred yen per night, which is standard for these accommodations, or about 12 percent of my daily wage. Rent is by no means an onerous burden—I spend a far greater portion of my income on housing in the States. In fact, my income greatly exceeds expenditures at this juncture: ¥15,250 versus a total of ¥5,550 for lodging, meals (¥3,280) and transportation (¥470). Not a bad ratio, and it leaves plenty left over for extras—assuming, of course, that I stay employed. What I have heard from others seems to be true: you need to get work every third day to break even—less if you are staying in a bunk-house, more if you are staying in a business hotel or if you indulge in other distractions—playing *pachinko* or playing the horses, bar hopping or brothel hopping, karaoke singing or serious drinking. Come to think of it, the distractions are prodigious.

10:00 p.m.   After counting my money, bathing, rearranging my room, and taking down a few notes, I retire. My sleep is very sound.

SUNDAY, JULY 21. SUNNY AND HOT. HIGH TEMPERATURE IN THE MID-90S.

5:00 a.m.   Rise and prepare for work.

5:30 a.m.   Rendezvous as before with Tottori, proceed to the street corner on Meiji Boulevard, and find Minami-san, who agrees to take us on again. Tottori and I continue walking about the yoseba to observe the exchanges between day laborers and *tehaishi*. We breakfast at Yamagataya, a small eatery a short way in from Old Streetcar Boulevard on the Nihonzu-tsumi side which is known for being a hangout of members of Nihon Gijintō, a yakuza syndicate. Tottori attacks a bowl of *tonjiru* (¥130), while I sample the *suiton* (also ¥130). The food is competitively priced, but it will win no awards.

After breakfast we talk to a curly-haired *tehaishi* who is probably associated with Gijintō and who holds forth next to Yamagataya. Work is available, he says, although at a lower wage (¥14,000) than what we make. I file the information away for future reference. Back on the boulevard, we encounter Matsui-san, a *tobi shoku* and Santōrō member, who treats us both to an ice-cold vitamin drink. It tastes very good, because it is already quite warm out. The sun has been up for an hour. Matsui-san, in his late forties, is a whirlwind of activity, chatting with this person, ribbing the next. Tottori tells me that he is an excellent worker and that he lives outside the doyagai in his own one-room apartment, from which he commutes daily to the yoseba.

7:45 a.m.   At the *genba*. I have something of a scare before work begins. A yakuza-type, replete with pompadour and loud shirt, is chauffeured to the work site in a big American car and begins casing the joint. No doubt he has his hand in the business. He takes one look at me and demands to know what I am doing here. Working, of course, I tell him. Where are you from and where's your work permit? he asks. From the United States, I answer, and I don't have a permit. You'd better bring your passport tomorrow, then, he says, so he can take care of things. Letting him and his ilk "take care of things" is the last thing I want done. I may never see my passport again. Worse, it would blow my cover. I am here on a research visa, which makes my stay in Japan quite legal but renders me vulnerable to charges of spying

Breakfast at an open-air restaurant. Menu items with prices in background.

on their activities. I acquiesce to his demand, however, since I do not have to cough up anything right now. He finally drives off. I inform Tottori of what has happened. He says not to worry. It is true, he tells me, that the major construction firms won't allow foreign workers on their work sites. What does that say about SK Enterprises? I ask. Very simple, is the answer: it's a third-rate operation!

I have to smile at this worry about my sticking out like a sore thumb, accustomed as I am to the market value of Americans in Japan making a living here *because* they are American (especially white American) and can speak English. This privileged position never set well with me. I recall my few halfhearted attempts at teaching English conversation to uncomprehending groups of businessmen during an earlier stay in Tokyo and realize with certainty how much better suited I am to my current job, in which language is the conduit it is meant to be rather than a barrier to communication, and through which physical effort, exhausting though it is, clears the mind as well as the pores. I mop my brow and prepare for calisthenics.

8:15 a.m.   Work begins after the obligatory "radio calisthenics" and review of safety hazards. I recognize half-a-dozen day laborers from yesterday. Today's job, dismantling the wooden molds on the expressway ramp soundproofing wall, is far more dangerous than yesterday's, and much hotter. I am teamed up with Tottori on a catwalk that skirts the outer side. We begin by removing the scaffolding pipes from the molds covering the wall, which runs the entire length of the ramp and the expressway itself. The pipes are heavy and the hands easily pinched. There is nothing between the catwalk and the ground below. A stray bee, braving the heights, makes a nuisance of itself for several minutes. I repeatedly alert myself to the very real danger of falling, and reflect on the words of the job manager this morning: Sundays are accident prone, because people's minds tend to be on other things. There is no protection from the sun. With each trip back to the ramp I do not fail to make a stop at a makeshift table holding a large, five-liter thermos jug filled with ice water. Fortunately, the day passes without incident, and the work, although far more strenuous than yesterday's, goes faster. After work, several of us repeat the "cocktail hour" at the liquor-store vending machine near Shinden Station.

6:00 p.m.   Returning to San'ya, I dine again with Tottori, this time at a cafeteria-style eatery on Old Streetcar Boulevard called Makotoya. The fare at this inexpensive tavern is simple: boiled vegetables, salads, garnished tofu, grilled fish, miso soup, and rice. From there it is a few steps to Takara, a karaoke bar with drab walls, hard seats, and the latest in laserdisc equipment: a five-foot pillar of amplifiers, equalizers, and other controls topped by a twenty-four-inch monitor showing the visuals that dramatize the lyrics. After listening to the guests (all appear to be regulars, and some sing well enough to cut a record or two), I decide that I am out of my league and foist the microphone handed to me on Tottori. The food is so good and the atmosphere so congenial, however, that I promise myself to return when I feel less self-conscious.

MONDAY, JULY 22. CLEAR AND HOT.

Another scorching day, which I decide to take off. I arrived in Japan in good physical shape but am exhausted by the previous two days' work. I learn later that Tottori has also taken the day off. It is more than exhaustion that ails me, however. I am worried that I will be interrogated further by the yakuza-type who pestered me yesterday. If I do not show up today, then maybe he will forget about me, and perhaps *he* won't show up the next day, when I plan to work again.

In the morning I get only as far as Hifumi, an eatery located just down the street from the corner where Minami-san holds forth, and sit down to a breakfast of steamed rice, miso soup, stir-fried eggs, and a salted plum—the last to replace body salts lost in the sweat that pours off my back in this heat. The helpings of rice are generous. Mine comes in an oversized bowl: the "regular" helping. For those who order the large helping, the bowl is capped with an extra mound of rice. The waiter, who works a small, U-shaped counter, bids each customer a hearty *"Itte'rasshai,"* the standard sendoff to men in the morning, whether they actually work or not.

After breakfast I spend some time tidying up my tight quarters in hopes of making room for something besides the futon. I had an idea of what extreme confinement is like, having once shared a densely furnished four-and-a-half-mat room for a month with a Japanese college friend, but living alone here with nothing more than the bedding, a fan, and a small TV to clutter the room is proving to be the more confining experience by far. There is nothing quite so unnerving as being cooped up in a space where you can literally reach out and touch both walls. Not a few jail cells are larger than this. The window at one end provides welcome ventilation, but it opens out immediately to the next doya, less than an arm's length away.

TUESDAY, JULY 23. SUNNY AND HOT. TEMPERATURES IN THE MID-90S.

4:30 a.m.   Rise and prepare for work. I proceed to the street corner on Meiji Boulevard near Namidabashi on my own. I exchange glances with Minami-san. He does a double take and then nods. That is my pass.

6:00 a.m.   After breakfasting at Tatsumi, an eatery like Hifumi located right on Meiji Boulevard, and being "sent off" to work (*"Itte'rasshai!"*), I take a stroll through the flea market next to Tamahime Park.

8:15 a.m.   At the *genba*. I am back again beneath the girders scraping dried cement. Tottori is here, too, but working with another team. This is the first time we are separated. After finishing the scraping, we plug up the exposed bolt holes with mortar. I work with Mitaka, who pushes me to the limit. Before lunch we both work at filling the bolt holes. After lunch he suggests that I do the rough work, leading the way, while he finishes up behind me. The idea is to bring the mortar to a fine gloss, he says. We make good progress. It is even steamier beneath the girders than it was three days ago, but still better than being under the direct sunlight. This is the last day that I receive an unemployment-insurance stamp. The site manager announces a new company policy when handing out wages after work: no white card, no stamp. We are told that tomorrow the trucks will be here to pour concrete. The yakuza who accosted me Sunday does not show up. I am safe, at least for the time being.

WEDNESDAY, JULY 24. VERY HOT AND HUMID. TEMPERATURES IN THE MID-90S.

5:30 a.m.   Set out from my doya in search of a job. I assume that work at the Shinden site is available for the asking, but have misgivings about baking atop the expressway as well as about another encounter with the yakuza. I make the rounds along Old Streetcar Boulevard looking for other work and strike up a conversation with a day laborer who immediately relays my wishes to a *tehaishi* standing nearby. He doesn't bite. A man who looks like a former yakuza standing next to me, his lip bleeding from a fight—or is it some disease?—offers me a drag from his cigarette. I take a toke on it and hand it back. Anything for a lead on a job, I tell myself. But no dice; he can't help out. I continue walking and run into Mukōjima, with whom I had a conversation a year earlier and who is wearing the same *tobi* garb I remember him in before. I am not surprised to see someone I know; the yoseba is a compact place ideal for fortuitous encounters. A few yards farther up the street I spy Minami-san, who has strayed from his regular post to look farther afield for workers. He is having difficulty recruiting because of the heat. I am not the only one with misgivings, apparently. "Any work today?" I ask, relenting. "Yes, go on ahead," he answers. That is the extent of our conversation.

6:00 a.m.   Breakfast at Tatsumi. I fancy the esprit of the manager and head waiter, a strong, sinewy man in his late fifties who looks as though he could hold his own at any construction site. He wears the traditional garb of the Shitamachi *shokunin*, complete with indigo apron, and keeps up a constant banter with his customers, teasing and cajoling them by turn in a brash yet inoffensive manner. When a man who sits down beside me complains about the weather, the manager immediately takes him on. "You say it's hot? Why, of course it's hot! It's summer, isn't it? What do you expect? If people grumble about the heat, it's because they don't eat right. You're not going to make it through summer just by gulping down water. You've got to have nourishment. That's right, calories! Remember that. Here, I'll warm up your tea for you. Don't worry, I won't make it too hot. [Turning to me] Here, I'll give you some tea, too. You can cut it with water if it's too hot. [To the first man] Finished? Okay, that'll be ¥470. Yeah, you heard right. See the sign? We raised our prices as of today. Ten yen per dish. No, we're not trying to boost our profits. We're just trying to stay even. The price of food keeps going up. You understand, don't you? Good. See you now. "*Itte'rasshai!*"

6:30 a.m.   After purchasing a long-sleeved shirt and undershirt at the flea market, I proceed to the *genba,* making a pit stop at the Shinden Station toilet on the way. I make it a point now to use this well-kept facility, which is infinitely preferable to the portable outhouses on the site.

8:15 a.m.   I am one of seven day laborers chosen to assist with the day's concrete-pouring activity, which is a section of the sound-proofing wall along the ramp. We remove our *jikatabi* and change into rubber boots. The work is very strenuous. First we tote the wooden molds to their proper location. The molds are extremely heavy and dig into the shoulder. Then we tote the compressor. It takes four of us to lift it. We then wait for the cement mixers to arrive. They dictate our schedule. When they start pouring, we hurriedly compact the concrete into the molds with broom handles, shovels, and compressor-powered vibrators—long steel poles attached to heavy rubber hoses—making sure to leave no air pockets. Agility is a must in this job. I am slow in the beginning to get out of the way when the concrete firm's foreman squirts cement in my direction. The foreman is assisted by two Iranians, who wear the firm's blue uniform. I learn during break that they have been working, without documentation, for nine months, at ten thousand yen per day plus room.

11:30 a.m.   Break. Spreading the concrete takes everything out of me— and everyone. Only now have we been allowed to rest. The concrete must be poured as soon as the mixers arrive, and they have been arriving thick and fast. The break goes right into lunch. Nearly everyone, including me, takes a nap. Minami-san promises that work will end early today. As soon as the last truck empties its load, we can go home, he says.

1:00 p.m.   I man one of the vibrators all afternoon, working beneath the catwalk. I am rewarded with a couple of cement baths for my trouble, getting splattered from above. A four-man team from SK Enterprises is doing an on-the-job inspection of the pouring and taking numerous photographs. One of the team, a quintessential company man and looking very smart in his buff-colored uniform, hard hat, glossy boots, and fashionable glasses, yells at me to hurry up with the vibrator. I try to stay out of camera range.

3:00 p.m.   Break. It is very hot, and the ration of soft drinks much appreciated, but they are quaffed in the twinkling of an eye. After moving the thermos, which holds a treasure of ice water, to a shady spot beneath its makeshift table, I chat with some of the other workers. There is Niigata, a seventy-three-year-old man who grew up in Manchuria and has worked as a *dokata* for six decades. He is a veteran of such major construction projects as the Jōetsu Shinkansen (the bullet train) and the Jōetsu Expressway to Niigata. He claims that he is still up to any job, vibrator included, even at his advanced age, and that he is doing "easy work" today (smoothing the edges of the freshly poured slabs) only because he has been so ordered. Then there is Kagoshima, who keeps shouting at me gleefully, "Japan is number one! Japan is number one!" Japan and Germany are the only two countries in the world worth their salt, he tells me. Korea comes in third. The United States is a distant fourth at best, way down the line and slipping farther back. He seems absolutely ecstatic about this pecking order. Finally there is Chōsen, a North Korean about sixty years old who mentions by the bye having killed an American during the Korean War. He is very friendly. We speak in Japanese, of course. "My proficiency in Korean is 100 percent," he explains. "My proficiency in Japanese 90 percent, in Chinese 30 percent, in English 0 percent." And his proficiency as a laborer? "Second to none!"

3:30 p.m.   Back on the job. I hoard the ice water and husband my strength. The time does go faster, though, now that I have a few days here under my belt. I am frequently asked, both during breaks and while on the job, why I am doing this kind of work at all. How come I'm not teaching English in some air-conditioned office? It's simple, I answer. I hate teaching English. Construction work is a paradise by comparison. My cohorts cannot believe their ears. But I know it is true, having tried my hand at teaching when living in Tokyo in the mid-1970s. I worked mainly as a freelance translator but succumbed on occasion to the temptation of high wages for what looked like an easy job. Most corporations and many language schools would hire seemingly any warm-blooded Caucasian body they could lay their hands on. Call it the law of supply and demand; and the "all-American" type, particularly one with even a modicum of Japanese at his disposal, was in great demand. As it so happened, I fitted readily into his version of "all-American" type, not because of what I was (short, skinny, plain), but because of what I was not: black, brown, red, or yellow—which is to say, anything but Anglo-European. I did not like the students who attended such schools and I hated the stress of having to be nice when I wasn't in a good mood, which turned out to be most of the time when I was teaching English. I was also uncomfortable with the idea of being qualified automatically, just because of my nationality and the color of my skin, for a job that in fact required considerable skill.

I am very candid with the men here about my teaching experience and my opinions concerning it, but somewhat less than candid about chronology. I do not let on the fact that my English-teaching days are almost two decades old and that it is only my feelings about the work that are still fresh. I also do not let on to the fact that I am here on research and teach at an American university. Only a handful of people know this—Tottori and a few others associated with Santōrō who are not around. Tottori is aware that such information could very well get in the way of what I am trying to do here. This is my little secret, but that is okay. Everyone here has his secret, and this happens to be mine. I must admit that my home institution seems very, very far away right now, as does home itself, and family. I find that I don't want to talk any more about teaching English and keep trying to change the subject.

"You're just feeding us a line," one of the workers announces with a calculated grin on his face. "You're probably so used to speaking Japanese these days that you've forgotten your own language. Maybe you have a Japanese girl friend and are spending too much time with her to be worrying about English. You couldn't even hold your own in a classroom, I'll bet!" There are laughs all around. I take this ribbing as a cue from a very kindly soul. I have been let off the hook. "Yeah, I guess you're right," I agree, deadpan.

4:00 p.m.   Work proceeds slowly. Minami-san's words this morning are an empty promise. We do not finish spreading the concrete until five o'clock, which is to say half an hour *after* the usual stopping point. We are pooped.

THURSDAY, JULY 25. BLISTERING HEAT. TEMPERATURES IN THE UPPER 90S.

4:30 a.m.   Rise. I have set my wrist-watch alarm for five o'clock, knowing that I could use the extra half-hour of sleep, but wake up at the usual time anyway. Getting up is an effort, however. My whole body aches.

5:20 a.m.   Minami-san is not at the street corner where he usually holds forth. I wander down Old Streetcar Boulevard and bump into Matsui-san near the Mammoth box. He tells me that if I cannot locate Minami-san he'll try to get me work elsewhere. I retrace my steps to Meiji Boulevard and this time see Minami-san. "Go ahead by yourself." I breakfast on my own at Hifumi, making sure to order an *umeboshi* to replace the body salts I will lose during the day. *"Itte'rasshai!"*

8:00 a.m.   Work begins without the usual pronouncements on safety or "radio calisthenics." The cement mixers have already arrived and the pouring begins at once on a section of expressway pavement. We are to lay a slab of concrete ten yards wide, more than one hundred yards long, and one foot thick. The two Iranian workers are here again, manning the sluice. I help man one of the compressor-powered vibrators. Two day laborers are on each vibrator, one holding the head and working the concrete into the grid of reinforcing steel, and the other holding the long hose so that it will not get twisted or in the way of things. As soon as the truck empties its load, we rush to smooth out the concrete. The work is grueling, the heat infernal. The vibrators are unwieldy, the concrete heavy, the sluice treacherous—as I was to find out when it rips my pants and lands on my toe after jerking loose from the foreman's hands.

10:00 a.m.   There is no break, but we wait a few minutes for the next mixer to arrive. Our ration of soft drinks is delivered just as the mixer drives up. We pour down our drinks and race back to work.

10:15 a.m.   My toe is throbbing. The heat is intense, and with the sun now high up, the battle against dehydration commences in earnest. I am gulping down water every ten minutes. The cement mixers continue to arrive well past noon.

12:30 p.m.   Break at last for lunch. We descend the scaffold tower and look forward to a long summer's nap.

1:00 p.m.   The mixers are back. There is no respite. We rush back up the tower to man the vibrators. Our movements are furious. The last mixer empties its load at two-thirty or so. Then the long, drawn-out process of cleaning up begins. We put away the compressors, cover the fresh concrete with long felt mats, water the mats down, and finally secure them with boards.

4:00 p.m.   We finish work "early." But we have had only a thirty-minute lunch break and no afternoon break at all. Everyone is exhausted and walks about in a daze. One older man lets out a torrent of complaints. "I'm taking off tomorrow. This work is a joke. No breaks. No lunch hour. I've never been to a *genba* like this."

4:30 p.m.   At the station. I have a beer at the usual watering hole with Minami-san and a couple of others. He encourages me to come tomorrow and promises an easier day, although he admits he has no control over work content or scheduling. The others have a chuckle over my concrete-bespattered *gunte,* which are now useless. I'll have to buy another pair, along with some tape for my battered toe.

FRIDAY, JULY 26. HOT.

5:00 a.m.   I feel punch-drunk. This is the first morning that I am awakened by my wrist-watch alarm. I proceed to Meiji Boulevard, "pick up" my

Morning market.

job, and try out the cuisine at Iseya, a tavern on the west side of Old Streetcar Boulevard, where some of the men are breakfasting on beer. Later, I scour the morning market for a pair of decent work pants to replace the ones I ripped yesterday on the job. I am unsuccessful. The cheaper ones are unsatisfactory. The satisfactory ones are prohibitively expensive. The *gunte* are cheap, however, and I buy a second pair for insurance. There is no tape in sight.

7:45 a.m.   I reach the work site very late. There are only about ten day laborers here today, nearly all of them new faces. Most of those here yesterday are nowhere to be seen. "Does that mean more work for us?" someone grumbles. Minami-san acknowledges the problem but then tells us he actually turned down at least four or five other men who asked for a job. "It was all they could do to walk," he says. "They'd be useless here." Minami-san would rather be short of help than strapped with dead wood. I am surprised to see Mitaka among today's crew. He has not shown up the last two days. I spied him earlier today near Iseya looking for other work and had jokingly accused him of ditching us at Shinden during the two toughest days on the job. That was the whole point, he had replied with a grin. I told him rumor had it that there would be no concrete pouring today. My information seems to have influenced his decision to come. He says he declined an offer to work at another *genba* for the same fifteen thousand yen, because it was farther out and the conditions, he confessed, were even less attractive than those at Shinden.

Today the work is easy. Concrete pouring is being handled by another crew. I team up with Mitaka and dismantle the catwalks under the completed sections of the expressway ramp. The catwalk boards are very heavy, but we work in partial shade and can rest at will, without being harassed like the sorcerer's apprentice by the concrete mixers.

10:00 a.m.   The conversation during break two days ago centered on my credentials as an English teacher; today it is on my eligibility as a family man. One worker begins by asking my age. You mean you can't guess? I reply. No, he says: it's so difficult to tell a foreigner's age. A quick poll produces estimates ranging from thirty to fifty. Why not split the difference, I tell them. They'd be pretty close to the truth, then, especially if they added a couple of years for good measure. Old enough to have a family, one of the men volunteers. Yeah, I reply, old enough for that. The men usually do not probe one another's backgrounds, because that is what many have come here to escape. The same men who will give you an earful about everything from lunch at today's *genba* to the current political scandal are generally tight-lipped about their pasts. But curiosity about my situation has given some men the courage to make a few casual inquiries. I oblige with a few casual replies. Quid pro quo. Yes, I am married, if you really must know, and I have a son who is seven and of whom I'm very fond. I am working hard to earn money and am going to buy him a present. Plausible story. Which also happens to be the truth, at least as far as it goes. But there is no need to press the truth any further than necessary.

I do not volunteer the fact, for example, that my wife is Japanese, born and raised in Japan. After all, no one asked, at least not in so many words. A couple of the Santōrō officers know, but they keep it to themselves, bless them. I might have taken her with me to San'ya any number of times during our most recent stay together in Tokyo, when I was visiting the neighborhood on a regular basis. Surely no one would have minded. She herself had expressed interest—or should I say a bewildered curiosity—on occasion. But something had always held me back, and I did my subtle best to discourage her. The only one who minded, then, was me.

And so I have yet to bring my wife to San'ya. Unlike earlier times, these days San'ya is no place to bring a wife or to be with a wife, period. It has become a place to escape from wife, family, any previous life. But it is more than that. Seen with a foreigner, she might be loathed and despised and taken for what she is not. Not by the people who know my circumstances, necessarily, but by everyone else. That should not matter, I suppose, but it does. It matters a great deal that the person standing beside me is seen as my wife and not as a mistress. This is silly, of course, for me to think and them to imagine. But think it I do and imagine it they must.

Why? Because both sides still live with the memory of the war and its aftermath, whether we have experienced it directly or not. I reflect on all the conversations I have had over the years with Japanese, not just in San'ya but all over the country. Sooner or later they bring up the same subject: the U.S. presence in Japan during the Occupation years. As an American I become part of that presence. With people actually calling me or likening me to General MacArthur, I have no choice but to confront my inherited identity of conquering warrior. I do not want to be associated with it and I might argue that I have nothing to do with that history, but I am sucked into it all the same. I could harangue every passerby, knock on every door, and plead my case at the top of my lungs and still not reach everyone, I am sure, still not get my message across. And what is my message? That she and I are not some GI/bar-girl vestige of the Occupation? That we are lawfully wedded husband and wife? That we have every right to be together, even if she *were* a bar girl? Even if she *were* an affront to her country? Which of course she most certainly is not—even though she has had a career of her own, and has resided outside Japan for many years, and is living with a foreigner. Our neighbors, unaccustomed as they were to mixed marriages, may have been thinking all this when we were both still in Tokyo. But I did my level best to correct any wrong impressions. As for San'ya—I simply decided to take no chances. And that meant not bringing her here at all.

10:30 a.m.   After break, which is at the usual time today, Minami-san assigns us an easy job: plugging bolt holes on the ramp sound-proofing wall with mortar.

12:00 noon.   Lunch break. No amount of heat or exhaustion makes these insipid box lunches taste any better. I brave the sun overhead and walk to a convenience store on the main drag, where I shop for snacks to supplement lunch.

3:00 p.m.   I venture once again to the main drag to telephone a news-paper reporter who has requested an interview. By the time I return I have missed my soft-drink ration. There is nothing to do but steel myself for a liquid-less final shift. There is almost no water left in the thermos.

5:00 p.m.   Quittin' time. The day's work has been far easier than yester-day's concrete pouring, but I am just as tired. The fatigue of four straight days on the job has taken its toll. At one point it looks as though we will have to work overtime because of the delays in the other crew's concrete pouring, which hold everyone up. We are getting cranky and the thought of earning a little extra money holds no attraction to any of us. All we care about is returning to the doyagai and resting up. Late in the afternoon, Mr. SK Enterprises, the smart-looking company man who yelled at me the other day, barks at me again for being slow to report to his work area when beckoned. I have visions of being interrogated about my visa status, but he just wants me to hold a makeshift spout so that he can take a picture of Mr. I of I-gumi pouring a bit of mortar. His arrogance enrages me, but I control my temper and keep my face out of camera range. Fortunately, the concrete pouring ends on schedule after all. We stagger down the tower and clean ourselves up. On the train home I hint to Minami-san that I will be taking the next day off. I refrain from telling him my decision to take Sunday off as well.

As I alight the train at Minami Senjū, I run into several fellow workers who were riding in the next car. After chatting outside the station for a while, we decide to go out drinking at a tavern just up the street near the JR Minami Senjū Station. The group consists of Arakawa and Kagawa, both in their forties; Shiga Kōgen, in his early sixties; and Kumamoto, a witty if somewhat loud-mouthed man from Kyushu in his fifties, who exhorted me yesterday to work with any team but his (he wanted nothing to do with foreigners) and who today, once he got to talking with me and found that I spoke Japanese, would not let me go.

We observe a ritual before entering the tavern, each of us anteing up two thousand yen, then charging one of our group to play host and "treat" us. It is still early, but the tavern is jammed. Most customers are dressed in apparel like ours, but there are a few business suits in the crowd as well. The waitresses rush about taking orders, stepping to the sound of clapping hands hailing them from all directions at once. We can hardly hear our own voices above the general din. Our "host" barks out the first order: a round of "dynamites"—huge, one-liter mugs of ice-cold beer on draft. Plates of *horumon-yaki* arrive soon thereafter, at which point we order another round of "dynamites." The four men, who call themselves the "fearsome foursome," tell me that they are fast friends and often work the same job together. Arakawa and Kagawa in particular are close buddies. They are good talkers, and know how and when to inject a humorous note into the discussion. Thanks to our libation, it is not the least bit difficult to detect the humor in nearly everything. Now Arakawa, now Kagawa light the fuse, and the rest of us explode with laughter.

7:00 p.m.   I am very late for my appointment with the newspaper reporter, whom I find pacing the subway station entrance in front of the wicket at Minami Senjū. He has learned about me through a mutual acquaintance living in San'ya and he has pressed hard for an interview with this foreigner working out of the yoseba. I am not enthusiastic. We chat—or should I say spar?—at Mitoya, he over beer, I over *shōchū*. He says that a photograph traditionally accompanies such an interview. No dice, I tell him. And everything I am saying now is off the record, I tell him further. I am fearful of spoiling my cover, not to mention jeopardizing the anonymity of the men I have talked to or worked with. He expresses surprise that I would turn down a chance for this kind of publicity. I reply that it is not the first time; I have declined a similar interview with another major newspaper. The reporter resigns himself and orders another beer. Tonight's meal is Dutch treat.

MONDAY, JULY 29. SLIGHTLY LESS WARM.

5:45 a.m.   After my two-day rest, I pick up my job at the usual spot and then think about breakfast—will it be Hifumi, Tatsumi, or Iseya?—when I am intercepted by Kagawa, who spots me on the street and drags me and a couple of others already in tow to Minami Senjū Station.

6:00 a.m.   Kagawa clearly wants to talk and he breaks the news on the train to Shinden. T-Industries, SK Enterprises' principal subcontractor and the firm directly in charge of construction at the expressway site, gets a bigger-than-usual cut for each job it farms out to day laborers. Because its share per worker is ¥21,000, it is in effect skimming ¥6000 off the daily wage of each day laborer, who ends up with ¥15,000, with the exception of Kagawa and Minami-san, who get ¥17,000. Kagawa learned of this last night when he went out drinking with a *tehaishi* he knows. The *tehaishi* bawled him out for working for such a stingy outfit, he jokes, and then tells us that Minami-san should be pushing on our behalf for a higher wage. So who pockets the extra dough? I ask. You know, Kagawa replies, the site manager—yes, that avuncular old fart who explains the safety regulations and leads the group in "radio calisthenics."

6:30 a.m.   Buy breakfast (two rice balls and a boiled egg) in Shinden at a convenience store on the way to the construction site. I overtake another day laborer on the way who hails from Akita and who is a veteran of many large-scale construction projects, including the underground portion of Ueno Station a few years back. He has been working at the Shinden *genba* without a break for twelve straight days, he tells me. He is no grand physical specimen and he must be pushing fifty, but he never lets up. I silently take my hat off to him. He will work through Thursday, he tells me further, and at that point take a day off, reason unspecified. He is something of a loner, and I am surprised he has told me this much. He goes on. He is pushing himself now because of the long holiday (Obon) coming up, when there will be no work to speak of for a week. Obon comes in the middle of the week this year, and chances are that construction firms will also shut down on the weekends both before and after the holiday.

7:00 a.m.   I breakfast at the *genba*. Day laborers trickle through the gate in groups of twos and threes. It is less hot today, and about twenty show up. That means ¥120,000 for Mr. T-Industries and his underlings. A cool thousand bucks.

8:00 a.m.   About ten day laborers are bused to another site where concrete is being poured. I remain at Ramp No. 2 with the other ten to do cleanup the entire day. I work mostly with Mitaka. Boards, bolts, plywood molds, supports, beams, and other recyclable items all get moved down the ramp and stacked. Wire, concrete shards, and wood scraps all get dumped overboard. I enjoy the dumping no end. It is a great tension reliever to hear the scraps, some quite large, crashing to the ground fifty feet below.

10:00 a.m.   Morning break. The heat wave has abated. I am taking in less water now, and only once every twenty minutes.

3:15 p.m.   While not as hot as last Friday, it is still plenty warm, and I jump at the chance after break to help Mitaka do clean-up down below in the shade. He teaches me the names of various tools used in scaffolding. "How can you become a *tobi*'s assistant if you don't know your way around?" he lectures me. Now thoroughly groomed, I am ready to test my mettle. When will I get the chance? I wonder.

5:00 p.m.   Work ends without incident and on schedule. Instead of riding in the van I walk back to the station with one of the Chinese workers, who has been here every day during summer vacation. He is in the country legally as a Japanese-language student, but earning money illegally on the side, taking advantage of the high demand in Japan for unskilled labor.

6:00 p.m.   At Nodaya, a tavern situated just east of the Iroha Arcade entrance with its own liquor store right next door, I am drinking with an American colleague, also in Japanese studies, whom I have known for years and whom I have promised a tour of San'ya. It is his first visit. We met a few minutes earlier at Minami Senjū Station. I recognized him long before he recognized me. As I descended the pedestrian bridge I could see him furtively eyeing his surroundings from his perch atop the station steps and squinting in my direction, not believing that the figure he saw was in fact me. I do look different. He would not be the only one to have difficulty recognizing the wiry, tanned figure, clad in tattered shirt, work pants, and *geta,* that stood before him.

A tour will follow the obligatory round of libations. We are equally uncomfortable at first. Here at the bar it seems strange to have this foreigner in "our" midst. I order the usual—a *chūhai*—size large, please—drain it, and quickly order another. I explain that this concoction of *shōchu* and seltzer water was born in San'ya. He orders one as well. I introduce him in a low voice to the proprietor, who has been eyeing us curiously and is duly impressed with my connections. The proprietor has deep roots in San'ya. His family began the shop sixty years ago. After the war the shop was designated as a ration outlet, and people would form long lines awaiting their dole of provisions.

7:00 p.m.   My colleague and I crisscross the doyagai in Kiyokawa and then close out the tour at Mitoya across the way in Nihonzutsumi for supper. We continue drinking. He is fascinated by what he has seen, but he does not seem anxious to visit again.

How different my own situation, I think to myself. It is not a matter of visiting. I am stuck here for the time being—of my own accord, to be sure. I have promised myself to earn my keep while doing research here, to live as if I were indeed entirely on my own. Which I am, in a sense. I am a long way from home and out of touch with my family. I can get hold of my wife if need be easily enough—she is just a telephone call away—but she would have difficulty getting hold of me. The doya where I am staying has a telephone in the corridor and the manager can take messages in an emergency, but he clearly does not relish the role of receptionist. I make all my calls from outside. Inconvenience is built into the task of communication. I find that I am quite comfortable with this arrangement.

9:30 p.m.   It has been a long day, what with work and the guided tour. I have escorted my acquaintance back to Minami Senjū Station and am alone now once again. I will sleep soundly tonight.

Yes, sleep is my great reward—but not before taking a bath. The doya bath is already closed by the time I return, so I make the walk to one of the local public baths in the neighborhood. There are at least half a dozen, and I have sampled most of them. None is particularly attractive—the bath at the Palace puts them all to shame—but each has the advantage of being open until midnight. I buy myself a cold drink at a vending machine on my way home. It is a race to get the liquid down me before it turns tepid. The heat, even at night, is infernal. It simply will not cool down. The electric fan in my room merely succeeds in pushing the hot air around.

TUESDAY, JULY 30.

4:45 a.m.   Rise and prepare for work.

5:50 a.m.   Go to pick up my job a bit late and am turned down by Minami-san. "Take the day off," he tells me. "I'm taking off, too. If you still want to work, then try your luck down the street." I certainly will, I decide, after recovering from the initial shock. Trying not to look too desperate as I stroll down Old Streetcar Boulevard, I reach the place I saw Mitaka holding forth the other day. There I stand, cursing my complacency. No job offers, and no Mitaka. Then I look for Matsui-san across the street. He is not there. It is well after six now, and I assume he has gone off to work. But then I spy him on a back street behind the boulevard. I tell him my predicament and he immediately checks with a labor broker he knows. Too late: the broker has all the workers he needs for the day. Matsui-san knows about another job, but he advises against taking it. "The pay's way too cheap," he warns, "and the foreman will drive you into the ground." I want to believe him. He excuses himself and dashes off to his own job.

6:30 a.m.   I am resigned to my unemployment. Is Minami-san miffed because I took off Sunday as well as Saturday? It is hard to say. And I will probably never find out. So this is the meaning of *abure*, I tell myself. I am out of work. I breakfast at Iseya. The *"Itte'rasshai"* yelled at my back rings hollow today.

7:00 a.m.   The day free, I drop in on Kobe, who is preparing to leave for a bus stop near Asakusa, where he greets potential constituents once a week, although the next election for the Ward Assembly is still nearly four years away.

7:45 a.m.   At the Matsuya Department Store bus stop. For the next hour and a half I watch Kobe, dressed in coat and tie and with banner mounted on bicycle, greet all bus and taxi passengers who alight here and descend the stairs into the subway station below. During the first few months after the election, which he lost by a surprisingly small margin, he was here every morning greeting commuters. "I don't like all this bowing and scraping," he tells me, "but that's what it takes to get elected." His head bobs down and up with each passing commuter. "I don't want them to forget me," he adds. "After coming that close, there's no way I won't run again."

10:00 a.m.   Kill the rest of the morning and part of the afternoon with Kobe at a coffee shop in Nihonzutsumi. Chat with the proprietor.

4:00 p.m.   Visit the Fulbright office in Akasaka, which has kindly offered to hold mail for me even though I am no longer affiliated with the organization. There is a letter from my wife. I have been thinking, for the purpose of this trip, that no news is good news. Now there is news, and it is not good. The house we are trying to sell in advance of our move from North Carolina to California still has no takers. I am getting nervous, since I have committed myself to a position with the University of California starting this fall. As everyone tells me, this is a golden opportunity, no doubt, but I find my enthusiasm waning. To begin with, the thought of pulling up stakes and moving across country is daunting, and I am saddened by having to part with some very dear friends in the bargain. My wife, on the other hand, is quite keen on leaving, even though it means parting, if anything, with more friends than I. The lure of California, where we spent five years before moving east and where she worked full time, is very strong. Either way, the strain of the impending relocation is telling on our relationship. "So off you wander again while I'm stuck here with the house," she said to me more than once, in a tone I came to dread, before I left.

She is right, of course, at least about the house, which has been on the market for months. I am sick of keeping the place immaculate for prospective buyers who might show up at any time, and waiting by the phone for offers our agent hints at but never come. How do I react to these events? By ducking out at the critical moment. The timing of my trip to Japan might be ideal for my research, but it is disastrous for my domestic life. We parted company at the airport in stony silence, having exhausted ourselves in a bitter argument before my flight to Tokyo. Better for me to be out of your hair while you fret about a matter we can't control, I said in the casual manner I have been cultivating in recent years in an effort to distance myself from familial duty. Better for you to be out of our lives altogether, she retorted, if irresponsibility is all you have to offer this household. As usual, she pressed for confrontation—and ultimately, resolution—while I maneuvered for disengagement. I do not know why I felt trapped, like some cornered animal; I just knew I had to escape. To hell with the move, I thought. To hell with the family. Why force myself to do something that did not feel right, to be something I did not want? Better indeed for me to be out of their lives altogether, if self-deceit was the only casualty. Clearly, the time had come to be alone.

And so here I am, in Tokyo, living on my own in a section of town where the single life is the norm. It feels liberating, yet also a bit frightening.

Leaving the Fulbright office, I walk about Akasaka in a daze. I have known this section of Tokyo for nearly a quarter century. I once commuted to this very same building, which then housed the exchange program I was on in the late sixties. This was of course long before I met my wife, and familial duty, whether of the Japanese or American sort, was something I still had the luxury of being able simply to observe rather than be beholden to. My home stay was in Akita, the rural northern prefecture famous for its saké and its scenery, where so many of the San'ya day laborers I have met come from. Later I spent several months in Tokyo and got to know the city for the first time. Akasaka became a regular stomping ground. Because of its very familiarity, I did not think of the area then, or even more recently, as particularly bright or fancy, even though it was and is the home of many discos, geisha houses, and exclusive clubs. This time around, however, I am dazzled by the color and the crowds. I resist the urge to linger.

6:30 p.m. Back in San'ya. I have returned via Minowa Station, rather than Minami Senjū, in order to make a pilgrimage to Jōkanji, also known as Nagekomi-dera, a temple with a memorial to the twenty thousand courtesans of various ranks who were literally dumped at the temple gate after having taken ill and died in Yoshiwara during the Tokugawa period. Average age: twenty-three. Opposite this memorial is the Himawari ("sunflower") Jizō, erected in 1982 by the San'ya Rōyūkai, a senior citizens' association founded in the mid-1970s. The statue is dedicated to deceased Yama men who have no relatives or acquaintances to claim their ashes and for whom memorial services are conducted twice a year. The inscription on the plaque reads: "The sunflower works hard and long its entire life under the sun. It is the symbol of the day laborer."

From Jōkanji I head east as far as Namidabashi but then double back to Iroha Arcade rather than return to my doya. It is too early to be cooped up inside that cubicle. In the arcade, I run into Kagawa and tell him about my unplanned holiday. He says he also did not work at the expressway and ended up at another *genba* where he got twenty-six thousand yen for his trouble working as a *tobi*. I ooh and ah. He treats me to a large, cold can of beer from the vending machine outside Nodaya. I had promised myself to stay dry today. Alcohol is not cheap, and I am unemployed right now. It is also not particularly good for me. But it is his treat, and I succumb to temptation. We talk strategy. Kagawa promises to fix me up with a job tomorrow if Minami-san fails to come through. Just show up here at the arcade by five-fifty a.m., he says. Even as we drink, he has an eye peeled for the *tehaishi* he knows. He has another peeled for his cohort Arakawa.

7:00 p.m. I excuse myself and visit an office in the recently completed San'ya Workers' Hall to ask when the Sōgidan portion of the Summer Festival begins. I am told to check directly with the Sōgidan headquarters up the street, which I do. On the way there, I run into Arakawa, whose face looks puffy and hung over, and tell him Kagawa is waiting for him near the arcade entrance.

7:30 p.m.   Kagawa, Arakawa, and I are squatted down and making small talk in front of Nodaya, where I was imbibing *shōchū* cocktails just the day before with my American colleague. I am now working on a vending-machine version of the same cocktail, also Kagawa's treat, along with some peanuts, dried cuttlefish, and other snacks. We are using a couple of broken-down cardboard boxes as mats. With each sip of alcohol the frustrations of this morning and afternoon fade a bit farther away. I am on the verge of blurting out some of the afternoon's frustrations in particular to Kagawa and Arakawa but then check myself; delving into that kind of personal history is simply not the thing to do here. We continue to make small talk.

A Nodaya employee steps over us on his way to a storage space facing the street between the tavern and the liquor store. A few minutes later, the proprietor of Nodaya tells us impatiently that he is closing up shop and wants us to move. He glares at us. He glares at me. Kagawa tells the proprietor that I am "cool" and that I can speak the language and am one of "them." "I know who he is," the proprietor snarls. His look is one of utter contempt.

8:00 p.m.   We move into the arcade as far as a store front across from Sen'nari, the stand-up bar, which is closed. The arcade is asleep, Tuesday being the weekly holiday for most shops here. Kagawa buys another round of canned *chūhai* for everyone. I have had enough. I push my can onto Arakawa, who finally accepts after several refusals. Kagawa scolds him for drinking too much and tells him to go easy. Arakawa looks glum but continues sipping. We are joined by a couple of others: a tall man who claims to have been a pilot in the Self-Defense Forces, and a short man who used to be a painter. Both, particularly the ex-pilot, seem well oiled.

8:30 p.m.   The proprietor of the shop we are lounging in front of appears on his bicycle with his young daughter in tow. She looks at me strangely. The proprietor looks at all of us strangely. He asks me to move off the threshold, which sticks out beyond the closed shutter, and make room for his bicycle. I ask him if it is all right to linger awhile longer. "I don't want you people making a mess," he says. "Don't worry," Kagawa replies, "we'll clean up after ourselves." I make a pitch of my own, promising to take personal responsibility for the bicycle. The proprietor is skeptical, but I am persistent. The point I am trying to make—that all three of us are trying to make—is that we are not a bunch of common drunks.

As for drunks, well, there are plenty of those around, too. Right across from us, in fact, are two or three men whom the label would fit perfectly. One of them, a very large man who walks about on unsteady feet, cannot seem to keep his pants up; they continually slide down his massive behind. Too drunk to remain standing, he eventually collapses to the ground, but once horizontal his pants slide down even further, exposing everything. We laugh audibly. He is a blight on the neighborhood, we agree. I have seen him around more than once. I recall him defecating in the street near here just the other day. Sure, we are drunk, but not *that* drunk. I recount for the group a scene I witnessed earlier this evening, when I returned from Akasaka and saw a man zigzagging about Meiji Boulevard in a thricefold attempt to cross it, completely out of sync with the traffic lights, and nearly getting hit by several honking cars. No, we are *definitely* not that drunk, we guffaw, and applaud our self-control.

8:50 p.m. I excuse myself and return in a bit of a fog to my doya before its bath closes for the evening. I feel down but not out and am confident of getting a job the next day. Kagawa has cheered me up. "Minami-san thinks you're doing good work," he told me. "I heard him say so myself." Anyway, if the Shinden job fell through, he would arrange something else. All I had to do was show up next morning at the arcade. "You can depend on me," he had said as he bid me good night.

WEDNESDAY, JULY 31.

5:20 a.m. I show up early at the usual corner east of Namidabashi. Minami-san is there and says that he is working today but that he cannot use me. They need fewer men now at Shinden, he explains. Fewer, perhaps, but not none, I want to tell him. Why not me? Perhaps the company policy on foreign workers, or at least the ones that look obviously foreign, has changed. I reverse my tracks and head down Old Streetcar Boulevard in search of Matsui-san, who sounded promising yesterday. He is not there.

5:45 a.m. Down to my last course of action, I head for the arcade entrance as Kagawa told me to do. He is there. We march straightaway to the boulevard in search of the labor broker he knows. Kagawa assures me there is work but warns me that the broker may be leery about taking on a foreigner. That is in fact what happens. I excuse myself and look for Matsui-san once again. He is still nowhere to be found. Then I cross back to the Nihonzutsumi side and approach the Gijintō labor broker near Yamagata-ya I ran into ten days ago with Tottori and who seemed to have work available, although at a lower wage. It turns out that he does have a job today and he needs someone to fill it, but it is work ordered directly by the Ministry of Construction and hiring a foreigner would therefore not do. Not in this business, maybe. But I recall my days as a freelancer without a permit in the mid-1970s, working through agents and translating among other things speeches into English for various government ministries. No problem then, apparently, as long as I remained out of sight.

6:00 a.m. Defeated, I head back to my doya, resigned to another day without work. As I cross Old Streetcar Boulevard back into Kiyokawa, however, I run again into Kagawa, with *jōbi* in tow. He turns his back to me and talks quickly to the *jōbi*. Yes, I can work. Hooray! We hurry to the minivan parked on Meiji Boulevard. The job is in Fuchū, a suburb in west Tokyo. Kumamoto, one of the "fearsome foursome," joins us on the way. He is hung over and not his usual talkative self. I rush to buy a portable breakfast (*onigiri* and hard-boiled eggs) at a shop across the street to eat in the minivan on the way and race back to the van, only to be told by another *jōbi* accompanying the group that he will not have me, period.

6:20 a.m. Breakfast in Tamahime Park. I try to map out the day, but my mind will not focus. I return to my doya and unpack my shoulder bag and fail to find the extra egg and rice ball I was saving for lunch. I must have inadvertently thrown them out with the wrapping material at the park. This is proof enough of my fatigue. I unfold my futon and sack out.

10:00 a.m. After a two-hour nap I rise a second time, do my laundry in a coin-operated machine, and chat with the doya manager.

12:45 p.m. I eat some rolls and fruit I have bought for lunch and then write out some notes I had been taking for the last week or so. An occasional day off can be quite useful, I tell myself. Then I count the money in my wallet. Yes, very useful—as long as it is only occasional. But I am still confident that something will come up, if not tomorrow, then the next day for sure.

6:00 p.m. Await another visitor near Namidabashi, a professor I have known since graduate-school days. Another tour of San'ya. It turns out that this is not his first visit, and it shows. His demeanor fits the surroundings; he neither swaggers nor cowers. He overnighted in a doya long ago, he tells me. We drink at Nodaya. I apologize to the proprietor for the previous evening, wondering why I even have to say I'm sorry. He mutters a grudging acknowledgment. The conversation with my professor friend is an animated one. "You are picking up where I left off, you know," he says. "I wish you luck."

6:30 p.m. On tour. I have several encounters near Tamahime Park. First, with Akita, who offers me a job on the spur of the moment at a *hanba*. One part of me regrets having a guest in tow, which prevents me from taking Akita up on his offer. Another part breathes a sigh of relief, well aware as I am of the miserable conditions that prevail at most construction camps. It might be a *takobeya*—an "octopus trap" from which there is no escape. Then with Koshigaya, whom I have not seen on the job lately. "I've been tapering off," he explains. "It's too damned hot." He is accompanied by a woman I have seen on occasion in San'ya and who is perhaps a few years younger than he. A hat adorns his balding head. Finally, with Wada, who is on his way to the toilet but is cut off by a truck when trying to dismount his bicycle. He swears. I do not recognize him at first. He is clean shaven, and his hair has grown back. Only the red, luminous eyes are the same.

THURSDAY, AUGUST 1.

4:45 a.m.   Rise and prepare for work.

5:20 a.m.   On Old Streetcar Boulevard. Matsui-san is nowhere in sight. Maybe he is out of town. I run into Kumamoto, who offers to talk with Minami-san about work. He takes off looking for him. Keeping an eye out for Matsui-san and Mitaka, I follow along halfheartedly, convinced that this route will lead nowhere. Then I abruptly shift my course to Yamagataya and ask the Gijintō *tehaishi* again about a job. I get the same story: no work for foreigners at the site he is recruiting for. Resigned, I head back to Namidabashi and beyond to the corner where Minami-san holds forth, but there is no sign of him or Kumamoto.

5:50 a.m.   Proceed to Iroha Arcade to look for Kagawa. He is not around, but Kumamoto is there. He tells me he has arranged everything and has been looking for me. I return triumphantly to Minami-san's corner. Minami-san says sorry, no job.

6:00 a.m.   Completely drained, I abandon the hunt and think about breakfast. Whom shall I have send me off with an *"Itte'rasshai"* this morning? In my masochistic despair I choose Tatsumi, whose head waiter is the most vociferous of the lot.

6:30 a.m.   I walk across Old Streetcar Boulevard into Nihonzutsumi as far as the Welfare Center, which is just opening up. Men crowded before the motorized door are crawling through the widening crack as it rises in hopes of being first in line. A lone Sōgidan officer sits at a table outside the Center, the time hanging heavily on his hands, reading a newspaper. No one is taking his fliers.

6:45 a.m.   I recross Old Streetcar Boulevard and head east for the Shokuan, which opens now. Hundreds of men are gathered at the entrance and in the street in hopes of getting work, or just to chat with friends. A strict order is followed here, according to the number on one's white card. Today's first number is 5,400, out of a roster of some eleven thousand.

7:15 a.m.   Head south to Kobe's apartment, where I unburden my woes and take a rest. On the way there I pass by a group of local residents doing "radio calisthenics" on the street. I am reminded of the regimen at the Shinden construction site and curse my fate.

10:00 a.m.   Venture north of Namidabashi and across the tracks into Minami Senjū for a change of scenery. Wend my way westward through a lane lined with shops until I hit the main drag near Minowabashi. There I spy a vacant lot with a sign announcing the imminent construction of a large business hotel and a banner next to it protesting the influx of "bad elements" into the neighborhood. Just across the street I encounter a man lounging in a tiny park but who springs to life at the sight of me. When I tell him I am working as a day laborer and getting my jobs out of Namidabashi, he duly informs me that the corner just down from the park is a mini-yoseba in the mornings and that I should give it a try. The work he knows of is in Fuchū, about an hour's drive or so west of here by minivan. The wage is considerably lower than what I can get out of Namidabashi, however. I decide I am not that desperate and simply file the information away for future reference.

12:00 noon.   Return the way I came down the lane of shops, where I get to chatting with a tofu maker I have heard about from a friend. Back in San'ya, I buy a lunch of rice balls and fruit and dine in Tamahime Park, where I am lectured by a madman on noodles and Japanese history. Then, because the pay phone I can use for international calls is just down the street, I phone my wife. I have been meaning to do this for some time, since it is I who must call. After being reprimanded for the long silence, she tells me that an offer is about to be made on the house. The prospective buyers like our neighborhood and are looking for a place to start a family. I have learned not to be optimistic in such situations, however. If something can go wrong, it will. The trick is to anticipate what can go wrong beforehand and work to set it right. But this time I am not around to do that. I am here in Japan enjoying myself, as my wife says. I'm not sure I agree that "enjoying myself" is the right word for what I am doing, but I have to admit that the freedom of movement here is a palpable luxury. To go where you want and be accountable only to yourself; to think no further than the present: these are very real attractions. It will be hard to give them up. I am beginning to wonder why I should ever have to give them up. There must be some way to work all this out. But that requires long-term thinking. And I am in the habit now of thinking only of today. Or at the outside, tomorrow's job.

2:00 p.m.   Kill time at the coffee shop in Nihonzutsumi. The proprietor tells me more about the shop's history.

4:00 p.m.   Race through a sudden downpour to a meeting at the Santōrō headquarters I heard about earlier from Kobe. I pause during the worst of the storm under the protective metal awnings of Asahi Street, where I meet a man who claims to have seen me breakfasting this morning at Tatsumi. He insists on celebrating this fortuitous encounter and buys several large cans of beer from the vending machine next to us. He then insists on giving me all the change in his pocket: a total of thirteen hundred yen. I refuse, saying that I'll gratefully accept the kind thought, but not the cash. He presses the coins on me with a stern firmness, however, saying that he felt sorry for me because I had to eat at such a place. I tell him he needn't feel sorry, because I enjoyed it. That is the truth—the food is good and the portions generous—but he will not take "No" for an answer. I walk away incredulous, thirteen silver coins jangling in my pocket and laden with an armload of beer cans.

4:30 p.m.   I am a hit at the Santōrō headquarters, where I relate my encounter and distribute the largess. Tottori and Osaka are present along with several others. We start the party off with the beer I brought, and then go to work on the saké and plum brandy already in stock. Tottori is stir-frying vegetables of the season for hors d'oeuvres. The meeting has its serious side: the men are here to plan the Santōrō-sponsored portion of the Summer Festival. I tell Tottori of my difficulties getting work. He immediately calls the *tehaishi* who initially got us the job at Shinden and learns that I-gumi has told Minami-san not to hire me anymore. As a light-skinned foreigner from the West, I am too conspicuous and a potential cause for trouble. Tottori then takes the opportunity to complain about working conditions in general, wearing the hat of union lobbyist. "You really ought to add a thousand-yen bonus for the workers who pour concrete. It's hell in that heat. I know. I worked in it myself for two days straight earlier this week." Tottori hangs up and tells me that my days working at Shinden are over, but not to worry because jobs at other work sites should be available. I thank him and yield to the mood of the moment: it is time for another beer. This party is just what I need to get my mind off unemployment.

FRIDAY, AUGUST 2.

5:30 a.m.   On a street near Namidabashi, not far from the corner where Minami-san holds forth, I am waiting for Tottori, who has promised to intercede on my behalf. After talking with T-san, a *tehaishi* recruiting workers for a job in Shiba, he says it's a "go" and wishes me luck. T-san asks one of the older men going to look after me, but it is Ebisu, another day laborer picked for today's job, who volunteers to show me the ropes.

7:20 a.m.   Arrive at the *genba* with Ebisu, who has worked here before. We work as a pair the entire day.

8:00 a.m.   Work commences without ceremony. This is a tiny operation compared to the one at Shinden: a small, well-appointed office building, nearly finished, in what was once an established residential section just west of Dai-ichi Keihin, a major thoroughfare linking Tokyo with Yoko-hama, but which is now being overrun by commercial interests because of the skyrocketing price of real estate. Most of the neighborhood's office buildings and condominiums are much larger than this one. The two-story wooden house next door, one of the few remaining single-family dwellings, has a well-manicured garden that provides the area's only greenery other than a few sickly trees and clumps of shrubbery in the small park opposite the building. It is summer vacation, and children play baseball in the park all day. Among the work crew of perhaps twenty there are half-a-dozen day laborers, and among the latter are two I know from the job at Shinden, including the quiet man from Akita. I marvel at the circulation of labor in this vast city.

8:10 a.m.   Our first job is to haul thirty-five heavy boxes of carpet tiles to every floor in the building—a total of 175 boxes in all. There is no wheelbarrow. We lug the boxes to the elevator and deliver them to all five floors, working down from the top floor and resting frequently. Ebisu, a chain smoker, constantly looks for an excuse to light up.

9:30 a.m.   A man from Toshiba Equipment arrives and says he is here to do preventive maintenance on the elevator. No more free ride up the building. We protest, but our arguments fall on deaf ears. We decide to take an early break. On our way out the building, we are asked to help relocate a small truck parked in front and standing in the way of everything. It is locked, however, and we manage to push it only about five feet. "Shit— worse than the carpet tiles!" is Ebisu's only comment.

9:45 a.m.   On break. Sweltering though it is, the air outside is positively refreshing compared with that inside the stuffy, dusty building. It is no less noisy, however. Inside, a man has been cutting marble (part of the interior decoration) with a huge power saw; outside, several men are chiseling away at the asphalt in front of the building with jackhammers. Nearby a small crane and power shovel are tearing up another part of the street. The ferroconcrete high-rises that tower over the neighborhood serve as an echo chamber. The clamor is deafening.

10:30 a.m.   Our next job is to sweep out the entire building floor by floor, in preparation for the laying of tiles. We also remove the plywood boards protecting the marble floors in the lavatories. The air is even stuffier than before, and the sweat pours off our faces.

11:50 a.m.   Lunch break. At this *genba* we are on our own. We buy *onigiri* and tea in chilled cans at a nearby convenience store and eat at Shiba Fudō, a tiny temple at the far end of the park. An elderly woman makes her way between us two reclining laborers to pray at the altar. Later two other day laborers from our crew ascend the steps right up to the altar and take a snooze. No room for worshipers now. We don't care. We are worn out.

12:30 p.m.   Continue sweeping. We finish the fifth floor and move down to the third. Another team is in charge of the even-numbered floors.

3:00 p.m.   Break. The foreman buys snow cones for us day laborers. That is our only amenity. We are not served any beverages, and there are no thermos jugs.

3:30 p.m.   Resume work. Ebisu and I are charged with cleaning up the flat roof. We fill countless hemp bags with debris. Masons are putting up a tile face on the front.

4:30 p.m.   Time to quit. We descend the stairs, wash up at a faucet in the park, and collect our wages along with the others in the basement, acknowledging payment with signature and finger print. There is a moment of tension when the site manager handing out the money, whom I have not seen during the day, claims he did not know that I was on the job. After receiving assurances from the other workers, however, he borrows fifteen thousand yen from a coworker to pay me. I breathe a sigh of relief.

5:30 p.m.   After a leisurely change of clothes and a chat with Ebisu, I decide to accompany him to the office of an acquaintance who works for a trading company within walking distance of the *genba*. An introduction might be useful, he says. All is for naught: the friend is not there. Our walk back to the station is in near silence. I have no words to console him in his failed attempt to show off his connections. I am too lost in my own failure to be where I am needed, and taken aback by my seeming inability to care.

It is still very warm. I can think only of how good the *chūhai* I'll be ordering will taste tonight and can hardly wait to get on the train. I celebrate today's successful job hunting at Ōtsuboya, a tavern right next to Minami Senjū Station. The *chūhai* is every bit as good as expected—too good, really, to have just one. I have no interest in the food. Cooled off at last, I make my wobbly way back to the doyagai, pleased with my ability, once again, to gear down my mental activity to zero.

WEDNESDAY, AUGUST 7.

6:00 a.m.   Having had no luck whatsoever getting a job out of San'ya since Friday, I have decided to try my luck farther afield. I visit some friends in western Japan whom I have not seen in years, then head for Kamagasaki in Osaka, where I know someone I think can help land me a job.

12:40 p.m.   Arrive in Osaka. Take the Loop Line to Shin-Imamiya, the gateway to Kamagasaki.

1:45 p.m.   Leave note at Tabiji-no-Sato, a volunteer organization run by Jesuits where my acquaintance Tajima works part time, and inform him I will be there in the evening to talk about a job.

2:00 p.m.   Brave the heat and search for a doya, starting with a business hotel close to Tabiji-no-Sato. Lodging is somewhat cheaper here than in San'ya. But so are the wages, I hear, which start at ¥12,500 a day. Hotel rooms are priced from ¥1300 to ¥1800, substantially less than their Tokyo counterparts. Bunkhouses that go for ¥800 in San'ya cost only about ¥500 in Kamagasaki. Before I can inquire about a room, however, a man on the street strikes up a conversation with me and offers a cigarette. I am in a hurry and refuse politely, hoping to get on with my search, but he continues to ply me, this time with a soft drink from one of the vending machines that line the street. "Fate must have brought us together," he says. I resign myself to an obligatory chat. We are overheard by another man who merely repeats the question, "Why did you come here?" I tell him that I am here to earn money, that I am not fond of teaching English, and that I hope to see an acquaintance at Tabiji-no-Sato. Whether it is because he is satisfied with my answer or has some other business, he hands me the pack of imported cigarettes he has just bought from a machine and departs.

3:00 p.m.   I have looked up and down Kama Ginza (the area's main drag and the site of many business hotels) for a place to stay: Hisa, Kikuya, Ryokufūsō, Manyō, Fukusuke, New Plaza, Palace, and even Esukarugo ("Escargot"), Kama's most renowned (and most expensive) hotel and favorite haunt of *tobi* and other *shokunin.* Wherever I go, either no one appears at the desk or I am informed that there is no room at the inn. In the midst of my search, I am confronted by a yakuza-type who asks me my business here. When I tell him I am here to work and looking for a room, he points in the direction of the Sun Plaza, the hotel that caters to foreign migrant workers and charges some of the steepest rates in Kamagasaki. I explain that I am not interested in spending two thousand yen per night if I can help it. No problem, he says. He knows where I can stay for just three hundred yen, and we start walking south down the Ginza toward Triangle Park (Sankaku Kōen), the Kama equivalent of Tamahime Park. It is an even grimmer spot, with not a hint of green. He then asks if I am alone and if I want him to fix me up with a girl. First things first, I tell him. I need a place to stay. He mentions in passing that the doya we're headed for has lice. I demur. No wonder it is cheap. I could end up spending a lot more than three hundred yen on insect powder alone. I am admittedly curious about a place that could cost so little, but I am running out of patience. As for that other offer he was talking about—she'll probably have lice, too, I decide. We part company.

3:30 p.m.   I spot a cheap doya near the Kama police headquarters, just off the Ginza behind Rectangle Park (Shikaku Kōen): the Royal. The man on duty says that he has one private room available. Take it or leave it. On the sixth floor. No elevator. No bath. No air conditioning. I take it, and pay the bill in advance: nine hundred yen, plus a five hundred-yen key deposit. There is an eleven-thirty curfew—good to know for occupants like myself who plan to bathe late. I pay for two nights, so that I may keep my bags here all day tomorrow. This is no small convenience, because a locker costs good money. Besides, I am hoping to get work and stay at least a couple of days anyway. The manager ascends the stairs in slippered feet like mine and shows me my room. We pass a bulletin board with mug shots of Red Army members and other wanted figures, a monthly TB check-up schedule at the nearby Airin Welfare Center, a few missing-persons ads with photographs, and a request for information about a hatchet murder, body unidentified, that was discovered on July 30.

I place my shoes, which I have carried up with me, just inside the door and survey my lodging. The room is functional. It is about four or five feet wide and nine feet long, or about two tatami worth. There is a shelf below the window and an open space below which a small TV and electric fan sit. At the other end is a strip of wooden flooring some eighteen inches deep and on which is placed a tray holding a glass cup and an ashtray. The futon is already spread out and nearly fills the room. This is no *kaiko-dana*, however: the dry-wall ceiling stands a good six-and-a-half feet above the floor. A naked fluorescent lamp is suspended from the ceiling; you cut the electricity by rotating the bulb by hand, because the switch is on the corridor wall outside the door and you lock the door from the inside. A clothesline is suspended above the shelf. Given what I see on the street below, it would appear that the window is used as a sink and waste basket as well as a lens on the world. From this, the top floor of the building, I can see Tsūtenkaku, an Eiffel Tower-like structure standing above Shinsekai, the amusement park, in the distance.

My room is one of a dozen lining one side of a long corridor that runs the length of this dreary ferro-concrete building. Half a dozen larger rooms line the other side. One of them is occupied by a woman who, by virtue of a furtive glance through the open door, I make out to be in her forties and a long-time resident. She has her own plaid, cotton-cloth slippers, not the plain, vinyl variety I pushed my feet into at the doya entranceway. One toilet and one urinal serve our floor. The urinal is out of order. The floor also has a couple of natural-gas burners for those who wish to cook a simple meal. I see one man preparing some stew. There are cigarette burns on the mats and the raw concrete walls of my room, and cockroaches skitter away at the approach of this new intruder. But at least there are no lice.

4:00 p.m.   Go to Welfare Center for a prearranged visit with Airin. On the way I purchase a pair of *gunte* for good luck.

9:15 p.m.   Return to the doya after dinner with Airin and relax at a nearby public bath. Make contact with Tajima, who suggests that I join him at the Kamagasaki yoseba on the Welfare Center's ground floor tomorrow morning. I tell him I will be there without fail.

10:15 p.m.   Lights out. I toss and turn on the hard futon, then dream of my wife, who suddenly appears with me in Osaka. It is the first dream I recall having had of anything since arriving in Japan. What is she doing in this doya? Then I remember the woman in the room down the hall.

THURSDAY, AUGUST 8.

5:00 a.m.   Rise and prepare for departure.

6:00 a.m.   Meet Tajima.

6:10 a.m.   Eat breakfast under the Nankai Shin-Imamiya tracks near the Welfare Center and then wait for a *tehaishi* whom Tajima knows. Unfortunately, he has no work for me. Tajima tries another *tehaishi*, again without success. We extend our search to an area west of the tracks, where many young men, and many Asians, especially Filipinos, are recruited for lifting and hauling jobs. I note the "punk-rock" types Airin told me about during yesterday's conversation.

6:30 a.m.   Head east to Minami Kasumi-chō Station, which was burned out in last October's riot. Kamagasaki had been quiet for many years until this disturbance, which began when workers found out that a police officer in charge of yakuza investigations had been on the take from the yakuza themselves. Meet a young, blond "all-American" type from Atlanta who says he does day labor on occasion and who suggests a couple of places down the street where I might test the waters. We immediately go our separate ways, the chance of landing a job being more important than comparing notes.

7:00 a.m.   After several vain attempts to get work for me, Tajima decides to take me to his own *genba* east of Osaka where he has been working alone for the past several days. He takes his envelop of wages, which are typically paid in advance here in Kama, from the labor broker who assigns the work and hands it over to me. Tajima cannot get hold of the foreman, but he is gambling that there is in fact enough work for the both of us.

8:00 a.m.   Arrive at the *genba,* a modest, four-story apartment barely fifty feet wide and forty feet deep with just four two-bedroom units per floor and to be rented, I am told, at ninety-thousand yen per unit. It is located in Kayashima, a lower-middle-class residential community about a thirty-minute train ride northeast of Kyōbashi Station in central Osaka. The work has been farmed out three times: from the general contractor to the subcontracting firm, then to the labor broker, and finally to Tajima. We are the only workers present. Tajima's job is to put up cinder-block walls that will separate each room on the ground floor. I help out by doing the odd jobs: shoveling piles of sand used for mortar, mixing cement, and moving stacks of cinder blocks—250 in the morning alone, and a total of some 400 for the shift. My wrists, especially my left wrist, ache by the end of the day. I note that asbestos is being used to seal the ground-floor ceiling girders. We choke on the dust as we wedge a board above the girders in an attempt to anchor the plumb line.

10:00 a.m.   Morning break. We drink coffee at a nearby café.

12:00 noon.   Break for lunch at a nearby restaurant.

3:00 p.m.   Afternoon break.

4:00 p.m.   The foreman arrives just when Tajima has decided to call it quits. He chats while I make as though I'm hard at work. The foreman coughs up the extra money for Tajima's tag-along and swallows the argument that an upcoming deadline necessitates more help for the next couple of days.

5:00 p.m.   Leave the *genba*. Tajima and I split up at Kyōbashi Station. I telephone an acquaintance I know in the suburbs. He is unavailable this evening but can see me tomorrow. It seems like an eternity until tomorrow. I feel uprooted in these unfamiliar surroundings and am just plain lonely. I take the Loop Line to Tennōji and alight there, one station shy of Shin-Imamiya, and cruise the area: first north, to the seedy, Asakusa-like entertainment district of Shinsekai and its theaters, shops, taverns, observation tower, and noisy *shōgi* (a board game) and mahjong dens along "Jingle-jangle Alley" (*Jan-jan yokochō*); then south, for a look at the brothels of Tobita. Prostitution is illegal in Japan, but loopholes abound here. Because beds are outlawed, oversized cushions adorn the anterooms, I am told. The only business of these "teahouses," the management would have the authorities believe, is serving food and drink. The cuisine is clearly not the forte around here, though. Indeed, when I overhear a madam inquire of two visitors in business suits at the entranceway to a house a few steps ahead of me what they wished to order, one simply answers, "A Coke, please." Tobita Association rules prohibit the main attractions from presenting themselves up front, but the rules are flagrantly violated by some houses. I notice a university-student-aged man, who has just overtaken me on the street, hurriedly peer through an entranceway curtain at a scantily clad woman sitting in the wings, quickly move on to the next house, and then, finally seeing someone he likes at a third house, step inside.

The foyers are all decorated in what might be dubbed the neobrothel style: subtly colored woodwork on the walls which clashes hilariously with the crimson-and-purple carpets. All the women who are visible are heavily made up and dressed in revealing gowns done in bright, primary colors. Dolls in cases or flower arrangements provide the final touch. The decor does have its charm, and the buildings themselves, mostly two-story affairs made of concrete but done in the style of the Meiji Period, look more like something out of the old Yoshiwara licensed quarter than anything to be found in the Senzoku soapland district today. Like Yoshiwara, Tobita is flanked by what used to be an execution ground, located on the hill above; it is now a large cemetery owned by the city. Many of the madams turn away when I glance in their direction. A few beckon tentatively. One is not at all tentative. I stop in my tracks. What am I doing here, anyway? Am I deliberating over whom to give the nod, just as I was waiting myself to get the nod this morning, and on previous mornings, in Kamagasaki and San'ya? Whisking by the entrance, I notice through an open window in the same building two young women changing clothes inside. Their satin slips fit snuggly about their bodies. One of them sees me and winks. I do not wink back, but simply rub my eyes and move on, thinking of the unsold house in North Carolina.

7:00 p.m.   Return to Kamagasaki. Dine at a restaurant near Triangle Park recommended to me as an eatery with a wholesome set menu along with the alcohol. I order a *chūhai*. Then a second. Then a third.

7:30 p.m.   Less than steady on my feet, I make my way to Triangle Park past a building that houses a local yakuza gang—one of a dozen in the area—its name neatly lettered in gold at the entranceway. At least a hundred men are gathered in the park, some watching a television set mounted on a high post, others stretched out on a stagelike concrete slab, and still others just milling about. I am attracted by the noise on the park's west side and discover the local casino where men are engrossed in dice games at three makeshift tables. The betting is furious. It is interrupted temporarily by the advent of a police patrol. *"Akan, akan!* [Bad news!]," the men yell as they clear off the dice and tin cans and turn over the plywood boards, making as though nothing has been going on. It has taken them about twenty seconds to effect this change of scene. The four-man patrol arrives in perhaps another thirty seconds. Sixty seconds later, it is business as usual. The police no doubt can hear the racket.

8:00 p.m.   Have tea at a nearby coffee shop with a man in his mid-forties I met in Triangle Park, where I was digesting dinner and my liquor and waiting for I don't know what. Our conversation is dull and unrevealing. We feel each other out but get nowhere. He hints of a complicated personal history that he is finally unwilling to divulge. He merely informs me, with no little pride, that he has been in Kama for twenty-six years. He then informs me that his younger brother is a bartender and that I ought to be quitting work as a *dokata,* if I know what is good for me, and work as a bartender myself. I do not mind the lecture. At least he doesn't insist that I teach English. Suddenly he is in a hurry to leave. He has not even finished his coffee. Because he has paid for the drinks, I press on him the pack of imported cigarettes I received yesterday from the man I met near Tabiji-no-Sato. When he reaches out to take them, I notice the body tattoo under his shirt—part of the complicated personal history, no doubt.

9:00 p.m.   At the public bath: Suemori-yu, a spacious, brightly lit facility with plenty of hot water and showers at each stall for washing hair. The man next to me wears a brilliantly colored tattoo that extends from his neck to his buttocks. He washes himself meticulously, using a pumicestone "sponge" on the heels of his feet and other areas where the skin is rough. A man in the tub strikes up a conversation with me. Americans are gentlemen, he says, when he finds out where I am from—not like those Asians who have been invading Japan of late. A smile comes to my lips when I recall the proprietor at Nodaya glaring at me. No doubt he would disagree.

11:00 p.m.   Go to bed thoroughly exhausted. The day's labor and the liquor have their desired effect, and I sleep very soundly.

FRIDAY, AUGUST 9.

8:00 a.m.   At the *genba* again in Minami Kayashima. Much the same work as yesterday. My wrists continue to ache, and I try to haul the cinder blocks in a way that does less damage. The way is simply to take things easier. I spend more time chatting with Tajima, whom I first got to know a year ago during an earlier visit to Kamagasaki. The son of a farmer, he arrived in Osaka after finishing middle school on the the Japan-Sea side of Hyōgo Prefecture. Soon after his arrival, Tajima converted to Catholicism and met his wife-to-be through church-related activities. He settled in Kamagasaki two decades ago, when still in his mid-twenties, and has been here ever since. He lives with his wife just to the west of Kama in a two-bedroom apartment, which at seventeen thousand yen a month is a fraction of the rent for this new condo. They are childless, and his wife also works, currently at a child-care center in Kama. She has just returned from a three-day excursion with her ward to the countryside north of Kyoto. Pictures of deceased children formerly under her care adorn the center's entranceway. One was kidnaped and then murdered, her body pierced by multiple stab wounds; another was run over by a car; and so on.

The organization for which Tajima volunteers has many wealthy patrons who are tapped regularly. Its funds go to support educational seminars and night patrols as well as rehabilitation of disabled workers. No less than a dozen volunteer organizations, with special interests in alcoholism, labor issues, care of the elderly, child care, housing, soup kitchens, foreign laborers, and so on, operate out of Kama. Each supports its own activities, and there is no transfer of funds. As for his own finances, the money he makes as a day laborer is his own, and he spends it as he pleases. He works for the church in his free time. It is a frugal life, but he seems content, wanting nothing.

5:00 p.m.   Leave the *genba.* I avoid all distractions and head straight for the home of my friend in the suburbs. As when visiting acquaintances in western Japan before my arrival in Osaka, however, I feel overwhelmed by the outside world. Living in the drab confines of San'ya and now Kamagasaki, I am no longer accustomed to the bright lights and conspicuous wealth that characterize so much of urban Japan.

SATURDAY, AUGUST 10.

The visit with my friend has turned into an overnighter. My left wrist has frozen up and work is out of the question. I decide to take it easy before returning to Tokyo. There is much catching up to do anyway, and I do not regret the time off.

MONDAY, AUGUST 12.

4:30 a.m. Back in Tokyo, my wallet a little fatter and my wrist a little better, I prepare once again to work out of San'ya.

5:30 a.m. It is very quiet on the street, with less than half the usual number of workers. Construction firms are already shutting down for the holidays. T-san, the *tehaishi* who got me the job in Shiba earlier this month, tells me that the pickings are slim and that the earliest I might expect to find work is after the Obon holiday ends, which is to say the nineteenth.

6:00 a.m. Abandoning any hope of getting a job, I think about breakfast. On the way to Iseya I run into Ebisu, who is standing on Old Streetcar Boulevard. When I tell him I was in Osaka and actually got work there, he replies that I should have stayed on. Perhaps. But things would be slow now in Kamagasaki, too, and besides, I am back in San'ya for another reason: the Summer Festival, which begins today.

6:30 a.m. Swing by the Welfare Center and later the Shokuan. Today there are almost no jobs to be had at either place, but the buildings are mobbed anyway. Just about everyone at the Shokuan is turning in his white card for this afternoon's unemployment dole. Sōgidan members are busy passing out fliers on the Summer Festival.

7:00 a.m. Return to my room, go over notes, and catch up on my sleep.

11:00 a.m. Write a letter and do some shopping on Asahi Street. At a stationery store the proprietor reminisces expansively about his experience in China during the Pacific War. He assures me that the Japanese presence there was a benign one. "We knew what we were doing in China," he tells me. "I lived there for many years, and I ought to know. If the Chinese were as hostile to us as people say, then how do you think I survived? I was part of a five- or six-man platoon, and we lived deep in the mountains far away from any outside help. We were entirely on our own. We had no choice but to make friends with the local people. And I made many. That phrase—'the whole world under one roof' (*hakkō ichiu*)—wasn't just so much propaganda. We sure didn't go about our business the way you did in Vietnam.

You brought in the big guns and just tried to blow people away. But it didn't win the war for you, did it?" Nor did the way that the stationer spoke so highly of win the war for Japan, I thought to myself. Saying nothing, I buy some envelops and leave the shop.

1:30 p.m.   After splurging on tempura for lunch, I swing by Tamahime Park to observe preparations for the Summer Festival, which will take place in the caged playing field. It is the only time the field is open to use by day laborers. A two-level platform is being erected in mid-field for folk dancing, and a stage is going up on the far side. A matted sitting area is being laid next to the platform, and an altar memorializing deceased Sōgidan members and their supporters, including the two men slain by yakuza in the mid-1980s, stands next to the stage. The fence on the cage's north wall is lined on one side of the gate with large placards urging solidarity, and on the other side with booths that will sell everything from *chūhai* and beer on draft—plus a variety of hors d'oeuvres to go with them—to shaved ice and pickles. This year, Sōgidan has the first shift: August 12–14. Santōrō holds forth from the sixteenth. The two unions have alternated shifts over the years. The Obon holiday itself is observed from the thirteenth to the fifteenth.

On my way out of the park, I pass a day laborer who stops, waves his hand, and begins talking to me as if he's known me all along. He launches into a treatise on the state of the nation. "You know that Japan's in a very bad way," he begins. "You've seen the newspapers." "Oh, really?" I reply. "The view from the outside is that Japan has it pretty good these days." "Well, don't you believe a word of it," he says. "Japan is rotting at the core. I just wanted to let you know." The man has a sickly look about him, and he has a deep cough. He wipes his face furiously with the cotton towel draped about his neck.

I decide that I had better call my wife and walk the short distance to the phone booth near Tamahime Park. I quickly regret making the call. The offer made on our house has fallen through. I am given to wonder what I could have done to prevent such a turn of events had I been there. I am also reminded of the impending move from North Carolina, sale or no, and of the need to be home well before the scheduled departure date to assist with packing. There is much to do already and I am not around to help. I give a noncommittal reply and curse under my breath every possession I own.

When I hang up, however, it is as if the conversation never took place. I reflect on how simple the act of disengagement has been: merely place the receiver on the hook. I exit the phone booth. An exciting world awaits me outside. The air is thick with the voices of men already streaming toward the park in anticipation of the Summer Festival, and I am caught up in the fervor. I have few things I can call my own here and very little money, but my needs for the moment are amply filled. My hopes for improving my livelihood, moreover, are undaunted by recent setbacks. When the spirit is light and the body strong, the sky is the limit, or so I feel. As I make my way to the cage entrance, however, past the slumbering bodies of at least a dozen men who look either drunk or sickly, I am reminded of the chimera of spiritual lightness and bodily strength.

4:50 p.m. At Tamahime Park. Scores of men are milling about the cage already, and dozens more are headed this way. At five o'clock sharp the gates are opened, and will remain so until nine. Soon several hundred men are gathered inside. I celebrate my new-found sense of freedom with a beer bought at one of the stalls lining the cage's north side. The atmosphere is festive and the enthusiasm contagious. Sōgidan officers deliver speeches from the stage, and men test their mettle in contests of arm wrestling, watermelon cutting, and karaoke singing. The stalls teem with customers buying food and drink. Later, after dark, the platform tower sways with dancers. The crowd has swelled to five or six hundred. A couple hundred more men mill about outside the cage, peering down through the wire mesh. Some eventually venture inside and join in the festivities, but many simply stand for hours, literally above it all, and just watch.

Others watch, too. Plainclothes detectives are on the job: the ones standing on short ladders behind the public toilet outside the cage are taking notes and snapping pictures; those farther away are observing through binoculars and communicating with other units on walkie-talkies. They in turn are being watched by Sōgidan members and sympathizers, bandannas over their faces, from their posts on the park's north side. The police are backed up by riot-control units in armored buses and minivans parked near the Mammoth box. The plainclothesmen's get-ups are no disguise: the caps, vests, and shades they wear are their own kind of uniform. One of the workers barks epithets at the detectives, but the latter ignore him and pretend to be invisible. The festival ends abruptly half an hour early when a squall drenches the park.

TUESDAY, AUGUST 13.

5:00 p.m. No work again today. This evening, too, the festivities begin at five sharp. The caged area is spotless: a clean-up crew has picked up after yesterday's rain. The weather is fine and there is a good crowd. Today's activities include a tug-of-war, more karaoke singing, an *onnagata* show (a kind of dancing-in-drag contest), all capped by folk dancing on the platform tower. There is one disturbance. A man is sleeping off his drink right next to the cage entrance, blocking traffic. Another man takes offense and lifts the sleeping man by the pant legs and scruff of the neck and proceeds to carry him off. He loses his grip after a few steps, however, and the sleeping man falls to the ground, hitting his head with an audible thud on the pavement. The latter rouses himself and goes after his would-be caretaker, wrestling him to the ground and throwing wild punches. Several others, including a man who has been serenading me with an expert rendition of the theme song to the television western "Rawhide," rush to intervene. The fight over, I return to the caged area in search of a drink. Beer in hand, I am greeted at one of the booths by a man who gives me a gentle, flirtatious peck on the cheek. "How do you like that?" he whispers invitingly. "Not much," I answer testily. It has been a long dry spell, I admit, but I am not ready for this sort of activity, which I am told San'ya has plenty of. There are no women among the festival's celebrants, with the exception of one local bag lady I see on occasion, plus a few nonresidents—a handful of students from a women's college here as volunteers and the wife of the faculty member who has brought them. That is all. I slip away to another booth in search of hors d'oeuvres to go with the beer.

6:00 p.m.   I leave the park early today to meet an acquaintance at Minami Senjū Station. He is not here to tour San'ya but to talk business: he has been helpful with another project I am supposed to be working on having to do with Japanese literature in translation but which I have neglected for some time. On the way I run into a man who refuses to let me go until I tell him my business in San'ya. I answer that I am here to work and that I haven't had much luck of late. "Don't waste your time here," he says. "Go work in a *hanba*. If you get your jobs off the street and are paid by the day, you'll spend your money right away and won't save any of it. That's my problem. I bet on the horses and the bicycles any chance I get. Now I don't have a yen to my name." The man then asks me to "lend" him a couple of hundred yen for a drink. He shows me the contents of his coin purse—three copper ten-yen pieces—and says that even one hundred yen would do. I show him the contents of mine, which is nearly as empty. Tonight's dinner will be my acquaintance's treat. "Then to hell with you," he says, and walks off. "Likewise, I'm sure," I reply, and march off to Minami Senjū.

WEDNESDAY, AUGUST 14.

4:00 p.m.   Another day off. I walk by a tiny stand-up bar in Kiyokawa on my way to the Summer Festival. "Hey, look at that foreigner!" I hear someone exclaim inside. "What's he doing here? Do you suppose he can drink *shōchū*?" "Sure can, if it's your treat," I shout at the open doorway. I am beside him in a jiffy. I learn that the man who invited me is the son of a Kyoto priest in charge of a small temple near the Kamo River. A few minutes later, and now feeling very good about life, I head once again toward the park. At some point I sense that I am being followed from behind. Before I can turn around I am tapped on the shoulder by a self-identified (with cheek-slicing gesture) yakuza. Kanamachi Ikka, no doubt. He is built like a bull and looks nearly twice my size. "Who are you, anyway?" he yells. "America? Okay, scram. Beat it. Get out!" I do not oblige him, but I do quicken my steps toward the park.

5:00 p.m.   This is the final installment of the Sōgidan portion of the Summer Festival. The skies remain clear and the crowd is the largest yet. I have a visitor today, a fellow student of Japanese literature doing research in Tokyo, who is very conspicuous here. The visitor is female and for that reason alone sticks out in this neighborhood, and she is a foreigner to boot—the only one other than myself on the premises. For the previous two days, dressed in my workman's garb and speaking nothing but Japanese, I have clung to the illusion that I am a member of the group. Today, with this particular visitor at my side, I stick out like a sore thumb. It is assumed that we are a couple, and we are swarmed from all sides by admirers. When the men realize that she, too, is fluent in Japanese, they begin plying her directly with questions and volunteering comments about her figure. She answers with a restraint worthy of a diplomat.

The tour over and having our own talking to do, we leave the park and head toward Iroha Arcade. We do not stop and end up across the street in Yoshiwara. We note the fliers pasted on a fence halfway down the main drag advertising well-paying jobs in the bathhouses for female college students, and we browse with nervous amusement through the racy magazines on display in front of a tiny shop on a street corner nearby. My companion wonders out loud what it is like to work in a bathhouse. I respond with what little I know, but do not get very far into my explanation before realizing the folly of bringing her here. After a meal of poorly cooked pork cutlets at a cheap restaurant just outside the quarter, we part company, she heading back to her apartment in west Tokyo, I back to my doya in San'ya. The air in my room is oppressive. I toss and turn.

THURSDAY, AUGUST 15.

It is the last day of Obon, when spirits visiting relatives for three days return to the other world. San'ya being between festivals—the Sōgidan shift having ended yesterday and the Santōrō shift starting tomorrow—I travel to Yokohama and take in the Summer Festival at Kotobuki-chō, which is in high gear. The center of activity is an eight-story apartment complex that also houses the local hiring office and welfare center. The neighborhood lacks a park even approaching the size of Tamahime in San'ya, but the atmosphere is by no means grim. Here at least there is no cage, and there are music, dancing, and a dozen stalls selling food and drink. There are also many women in the crowd, and not a few children. I run into Miyazaki, who notes with pride the familial atmosphere that obtains here in marked contrast with San'ya or Kamagasaki. He himself lives in Kotobuki with his wife and children.

FRIDAY, AUGUST 16.

5:00 p.m. The Santōrō-sponsored portion of the Summer Festival begins, for which preparations have been going on all day. The layout is similar to that by Sōgidan, and the appointments, if anything, are on an even more elaborate scale. Santōrō is not to be outdone by its rival. Several of the rank-and-file, with Matsui-san in the lead, were hard at work this morning erecting a platform tower. Once again a stage, an altar (commemorating a completely different group of deceased persons), a matted sitting area, and food stands have been set up from scratch, the Sōgidan building supplies having been removed entirely. Four or five waist-high cauldrons are lined up in a corner and bubbling with rice, stew, and curry sauce, which will be served gratis to all comers.

It is a warm evening. The speeches by union officers are mercifully brief, but the affair as a whole is less well organized than Sōgidan's. The gates open at five o'clock sharp, but most supplies arrive late. Only the shaved-ice booth is in operation, and its product is eventually distributed free of charge to placate a long line of very thirsty men. The beer stand is the next to open up, but its supply of twenty-five cases sells out in no time, to the disgruntlement of all concerned. I work the veggie stand from six until nine o'clock as a volunteer along with three others, selling tomato slices, cucumber with miso relish, and steamed soy beans in the pod. The festival-goers are tough customers. Our product moves slowly until we fatten the portions. All four of us peddle the goods as though our lives depend on it (profits fund the union's operations), and we soon grow hoarse.

On stage several Yama men serenade the crowd karaoke-style. Later the Bridge Band, a semiprofessional group that has become a local institution, makes an appearance. Osaka gives a welcoming speech, and one of the rank-and-file delivers a testimonial to the union's leadership. The dancing on the platform tower tonight, by the same familiar figures who by now have had three days of practice, is livelier than ever. There are only two or three plainclothesmen about, and no riot units in front of the Mammoth box. There is only one walkie-talkie in operation, and there are no cameras. Clearly, the police are less worried about Santōrō than they are about Sōgidan. And the Yama men are less worried about the police. While strolling through the neighborhood during a short break I notice that the open-air gambling, which had taken a three-day holiday, is going strong again just up the street from the park at the usual intersection, next to the shop selling horse-racing newspapers.

After the festival I treat myself to some sushi at a tiny stall near my doya, and then sack out.

SATURDAY, AUGUST 17.

I spend the earlier part of the day in Asakusa, enjoying *rakugo* at the variety hall and generally getting my mind off things. Later, while cruising the area near the hall, I run into the proprietor of the Matsubaya in Yoshiwara, Tokyo's last traditional teahouse and a living museum that twice monthly hosts a special *rakugo* program I have attended several times in the past. He invites me to the *oiran* show, which I have heard offers a sense of the attractions of the licensed quarter in its heyday. Walking back to San'ya through the Iroha Arcade, I get to talking with a sixty-five-year-old man who is going in the same direction as I am and who works out of the yoseba, not as a construction worker but as a security guard doing duty at various *genba* around the city. When the subject shifts to a recent operation, he suddenly unzips his pants and proudly shows me the suture marks near his groin—the spot where a blocked artery was removed. He claims that he has a wife in Saitama to whom he sends money every month. They have lived apart for years, he says, but he still supports her hobby—gardening.

5:00 p.m.   Things are somewhat better organized today, although the stalls still do not get going until about five-thirty. Today I man the beer stand, taking in through the corner of one eye the tug-of-war and later the Bridge Band and a couple of other groups playing Japanese golden oldies. Forty cases of beer are on hand this time, but only twenty-five sell. You can't win. Just after seven o'clock, I excuse myself and head straight for Yoshiwara—not for the bathhouses, but for the licensed quarter of yesteryear, the beneficiary of a free pass courtesy of the proprietor of Matsubaya I met earlier today. The *oiran* show is a true spectacle. Professional dancers don the wardrobe of high-ranking courtesans and display the coquetry that won the hearts of dandies in the Edo period. A man in the audience is invited on stage and duly coquetted. It is all in good fun.

The evening's entertainment is very good. I needed the break. As I emerge from the teahouse, however, I come face to face once again with the present-day Yoshiwara and am taunted by the garish neon lights, the glitzy architecture, and the clusters of bow-tied men in front of the bathhouses beckoning me inside. Each wants my business. I cannot say I would mind being a customer. Money, among other things, is a problem, however. Ten to fifteen thousand yen will get me in, but all I'll get for it is a soaping down.

I can do that myself for ¥330 at a public bath. I would have to add another twenty thousand yen or so, depending on what I want, for anything extra. But I have worked a total of just three days in the last two weeks. I return to my room for another fitful night's sleep.

SUNDAY, AUGUST 18.

8:00 a.m. After breakfasting on *onigiri* at a stand-up eatery near Namidabashi following a halfhearted attempt to get a job off the street, I run into a man in his late forties who claims to have seen me in Kamagasaki when I was there ten days ago. It is indeed a small world. He talks about his work as a *tobi* and reminds me to stay out of trouble: it is a fool who gets into a fight, but it is an even bigger fool who jumps in and tries to stop one.

Later in the day I am approached suddenly by a man in his late thirties who addresses me in my native tongue. His eyes are glassy, his legs wobbly, and he is missing all his front teeth. He claims he used to teach English at a high school in Aomori Prefecture, and he takes a sheet of printed English I have in my hand and proceeds to read a paragraph in a wavery voice but, virtually without mistakes. He tells me he has worked in San'ya for four years. "Do you know three 'M's'?" he asks. "Men, material, money. In America you have three 'M's.' In Japan, only one 'M.' Money. Yes. Goodby." With that he walks off as abruptly as he approached me, and does not look back.

5:00 p.m. It is the last installment of the Santōrō-sponsored Summer Festival. There is a good turnout once again. Five hundred men are already waiting at the gate. Kobe, whom I have accompanied to the park, is pleased. I do not man a stall this evening, but simply wander about the caged area, about the park, and about the immediate surrounding area, enjoying the festivities and the atmosphere. During my walk I am approached by a small man who is missing the front teeth in his lower jaw. I greet him automatically in Japanese. "So, you're an American!" he replies when I tell him where I am from. "Well, I'm glad you're here. This is the age of internationalism, even here in San'ya. Welcome!" Near festival's end, I chat with Tottori, who was so instrumental early in my stay in helping me get a job. This may be his last Summer Festival, he tells me. The pressure on him to return to his home in the country and help care for his aging parents is mounting by the month. The man who pushed the idea that San'ya can be a true home for day laborers is about to leave.

9:30 p.m. The festival over, the Santōrō officers and several rank-and-file members gather in a tiny children's park just east of Tamahime, which occupies a nook of the apartment complex that also houses the Shokuan, to celebrate a successful conclusion. Osaka is master of ceremonies. Each man reports on the job for which he has had responsibility: stalls, communications, electrical equipment, entertainment, finances, food, materials, rentals. Total out-of-pocket cost of the festival, including all supplies: ¥1,500,000. Total income from booth sales and contributions: ¥1,300,000. Santōrō is ¥200,000 in the red and will have to raise more money. But not tonight. Several large bottles of saké, plus plum brandy, beer, and juice for nondrinkers are quickly dispensed and greedily downed. There is nothing but good cheer for a big job well done, and done on their own, without help from the city or any major sponsors.

MONDAY, AUGUST 19.

4:20 a.m. I finally rouse myself after a long night of tossing and turning. Having spent a leisurely week, I shall be back on the street again looking for a job in earnest. This morning is the first real opportunity for work since the Obon holiday began ten days ago. My wallet is nearly empty.

5:10 a.m. Wanting things to work in my favor, I am on the street early. The crowd is small. But it is not because I have gotten the jump on the rest. It is because they already know what I am about to find out: the pickings are still slim. I make my way toward the corner where I have seen T-san (the one who arranged my job in Shiba and who told me not to expect any work before the nineteenth) holding forth in the past. He is there, thank heaven, but my joy is short-lived. Work is not available. It's still the first day after holiday, he explains. I can't just fritter the days away like this, I decide. I recall the possibility of work through the mini-yoseba near Minowabashi, but opt instead for a completely different venue: Takadanobaba, about an hour's commute away. This is a major gamble, because I may arrive too late to do any good.

5:20 a.m. As I hurry across Meiji Boulevard, I pass Arakawa and Kagawa, who say they are waiting for a contact who has yet to arrive. I board the 5:29 train on the JR Jōban Line for Nippori, where I transfer to the Yamanote Line bound for Ikebukuro and Shinjuku. Having visited the yoseba at Takadanobaba when I was in Tokyo last year, I know exactly where to go. I take the south exit, a hundred yards away from the main exit I have taken countless times during previous stays when visiting Waseda University. Same station, different world.

6:20 a.m. I am moving against traffic and pass scores of men walking toward the station from a small park near the tracks. Many are foreigners, mostly from China and the Philippines, it would appear. They are all young, but so are the Japanese compared with the men in San'ya. Some of the latter sport punk-rock hairdos of the sort you see in Kamagasaki. Three minivans drive up and empty their precious cargo of *tehaishi* just after I arrive. Perhaps I am not too late after all. The yoseba here is positively intimate compared to the one in San'ya. There are perhaps one hundred workers and a dozen *tehaishi*. They stand in a circle which is broken only by a line of parked cars and minivans on one side. The *tehaishi* work the crowd, eyeing all of the men, talking with some of them, and giving the nod to a select few. I find that I have positioned myself among the Japanese laborers. The foreigners stand in a group opposite me and the parked cars. Two of them get picked. "This man is a serious worker," is a comment I hear voiced about one of them by a *tehaishi*. The rest of the work, what little there is at this hour, goes to Japanese laborers. Many jobs have to do with scaffolding. One *tehaishi* hands out a couple of one-hundred-yen coins to each of the men he has hired for their breakfast.

I do not know the protocol here. Do I say something or just stand about, hoping to get noticed? I work myself into one *tehaishi*'s line of sight, and am patently ignored. I finally ask, in my most obsequious Japanese, if there is any work. The answer is "No." Or rather, the work available is not for me. The *tehaishi* seem to know every man here. They are in the market for specific skills and know who can offer them. Once they find their man, they hail him from afar and offer him a job. The rest continue to stand and wait. The lucky ones load themselves into one of the parked minivans or walk toward the station, map of *genba* in hand.

7:00 a.m. As if the clock had actually struck the hour, one *tehaishi*, perhaps a *jōbi* and himself dressed in day-laborer garb, announces, "Okay, that's it for today. No more work." The announcement is unquestionably for the sake of the foreigners in the crowd, and especially for the new face— he has come up right to me and practically shouts in my ear. Seeing the Japanese leave the parking area, the group of foreign workers breaks up. I walk up to the employment agency, a rude shack situated on a slight rise above the parking area. The jobs provided by the agency go on the block just as I arrive. Only five offers are posted, and they are taken in a matter of seconds. Wages are much lower than in San'ya, ranging from eight thousand yen to fourteen thousand. The rest of the men shove their cards through a single window (rather than a whole wall of windows, each marked off by the thousand, as in San'ya) marked *abure teate*. By 7:10, everyone is retracing his steps back to the station, and the park is quiet. A passerby could not have imagined the bustle just minutes earlier.

I chat briefly with a *tehaishi* as I leave the yoseba. "Try again tomorrow," he says. "Maybe something will come up." Clearly, it helps to have your face known. A few mornings here, I tell myself, and I, too, can land a job.

The problem is that my mornings in Tokyo are numbered, and the date of my scheduled return to the States is drawing near. I am very tempted to extend my stay, now that I am finally getting a feel for the work. Even if I fail to land a job out of Takadanobaba, I am reasonably confident of success again in San'ya. I have built up a network that sooner or later will pay dividends. It seems a shame to quit now when things are just kicking into gear. How much more time would I need? A few more weeks, maybe, or months, perhaps. It is hard to say. The one thing for sure is that I must settle in for the long haul if I am serious about getting to know the place.

I cannot afford to dwell on these matters, however. My family awaits me in the States, and I am obliged to help them, however belatedly, prepare for the move to California. We will be driving across country and setting up house—or apartment, rather, because we are in no position to buy a house, the offer having fallen through on our home in North Carolina.

I reflect on the rigors of family life, and wonder if I will be up to them. I seem to have a knack for acquitting myself poorly of my duties even in the best of times, and this is clearly not the best of times. It is all too easy for me to give in to the urge to abandon everything, and in doing so cast off possessions of real value. I must steel my resolve to resist that urge. I have bought a present for my son as promised and will give it to him, of course. I have yet to buy a present for my wife. I do not know what to get. I flatter myself to think that my return to the States is itself a kind of gift. Not that I could tell her this. I wonder if she would understand.

The thought of returning home is worrisome; the thought of moving, utterly daunting. It is difficult for me right now to fathom the notion of settling in either a house or an apartment. I feel positively done in by the prospect of living on such a large scale. A three-mat room is not ideal, perhaps, but the upkeep is minimal and the privacy very appealing.

I decide to table any decisions for the time being and simply enjoy my day of unemployment, visiting a garden and a shrine in a neighborhood close by that I have known since my exchange-student days and returning to San'ya via Nihombashi, where I browse the shelves at Maruzen for books on the yoseba. After lunch I visit the Welfare Center and have a long chat with Nerima. Supper is at Makotoya, where I talk at length with a day laborer from Akita who is surprised to learn that I know the section of the city he lived in. From there it is on to Takara, the karaoke bar I visited early on with Tottori. This time I am alone, but the manager recognizes me and offers me the microphone along with a *chūhai*. I am still a bit self-conscious, and my repertoire is limited, but I am ready to sing and my selection is an easy one to make: "*San'ya burūsu* [San'ya Blues]," by the folk singer Okabayashi Nobuyasu, followed by "*Kyō de o-wakare* [Today We Say Good-bye]," to the accompaniment of the five-foot pillar of laser equipment and monitor. The audience is impressed—not by my voice, which has never recovered from puberty, but by my selection. Both songs are two decades old. The men know, without my telling them, that I have been around. And that, as much as anything, may be why this neighborhood has the appeal it does for me.

To live in San'ya is in many ways to live in another era, despite the modern conveniences and gadgetry, such as the electronic orchestra backing me up, that are ubiquitous even here. It is a reminder of what Japan was as well as what it is, where the Japanese have been as well as where they are going. It is a reminder, too, of my own history in this country, at first young and single on an exchange program in the provinces, then as a married man making a living in Tokyo, and now older and "single" once again, at least for the time being. I marvel at the tenacious bond I have with this country, outsider though I am, just as I marvel at the intimate connection between San'ya and the rest of the city, isolated though the neighborhood seems at first glance from its surroundings.

It is late. I exit Takara a bit unsteadily and direct my steps toward the doyagai. Traffic is light now on Old Streetcar Boulevard, and pedestrians are few. I spot a couple of men camped on a street corner, where they will sleep, no doubt, until the sunlight and the yoseba crowds rouse them in the early morning. The prospect of a tatami-covered room in which to spend the night, even if a mere three mats in size, is a pleasant one indeed, as is the prospect of securing a job once again somewhere in this city. In the meantime, I shall live frugally, stay out of trouble, and continue tapping into the story that San'ya is trying to tell.

EPILOGUE

No pick to wield—
I contemplate the quiet
Of a winter day.
                    —Homma Takashi (haiku inscribed on a
                    stone in Hōju Inari Shrine, San'ya)

The San'ya I visited in the summer of 1995 was a far more somber place than the one I left in 1991. In the four intervening years, the deepest recession in Japan's postwar history, which came on the heels of the most sustained postwar boom, had thwarted the dreams and stunted the incomes of nearly all the day laborers living there. More men than ever cannot find work, and the homeless population, which had numbered in the dozens in and around San'ya, now numbers in the hundreds. When added to the hundreds living in cardboard boxes and tents beneath the expressway along the Sumida River and the hundreds more in the tunnel leading from Shinjuku's west exit to the Tokyo Metropolitan Government building, the homeless in Tokyo are said to total some three thousand altogether—a small figure by U.S. standards, perhaps, but still representing the severest such condition since the war.

The formula for hard times had already been written in the 1980s: a building spree in San'ya and other yoseba that converted many bunkhouses and single-room apartments into far more expensive "business hotels"; the failure of any institution, public or private, to provide anywhere near the requisite number of shelters for those in need (the idea of converting the Parcel Post Distribution Center into a shelter, for example, has been tabled more or less permanently); and an aging population, plagued by illness and infirmity, that is far less able to work even when jobs are available. All that was needed was for the economic "bubble," inflated by a reckless investment mood focusing on highly speculative real-estate ventures, to burst finally in the winter of 1991–92, with repercussions that continue to the time of this writing.

The morning yoseba was a quiet affair compared to that of four years earlier. Jobs off the streets were down to less than half of what they were during the "bubble" years. Men appeared around Namidabashi as early as four o'clock in hopes of being one of the lucky few to get work. The *tehaishi*, meanwhile, were looking for men they knew, and rarely picked workers sight unseen. With jobs so scarce in San'ya, many men had opted for life in a *hanba*, despite the notorious drawbacks. They were often stranded at a site, working only a few days out of the week but getting charged throughout for room and board. A common practice was for men to work alternately in pairs, getting paid every other day.

Other workers had moved to Kamagasaki in search of opportunity, especially after a major earthquake struck the Kansai district in January 1995. Matsui-san, the *tobi shoku* I knew in 1991, was one of these. For a man of his energy, skills, and connections not to get work out of San'ya was the clearest indication to me just how serious the situation had become.

The city administration, through the Tamahime Shokuan, has responded to the high rate of joblessness by lowering the required number of working days needed for unemployment compensation from twenty-eight days to twenty-six in a two-calendar-month period and by increasing the amount of daily compensation (for up to thirteen days per month) from ¥6200 to ¥7500. At the same time, it has computerized its operations in an effort to reduce fraud. Not surprisingly, the chief beneficiaries of this new regimen on the part of the bureaucrats are the yakuza, who sell insurance stamps on the black market. In addition to charging ¥1000 for a stamp (the face value is now ¥176), they also charge a ¥500 premium for a seal of the firm for which the white-card holder claims to have worked. Even in this neighborhood, it takes money to make money, and the truly indigent are of course untouched by these various ploys.

With so little work to be had out of San'ya and many men trying their luck in the *hanba* or some other yoseba, the doya population has plummeted, by some estimates to six thousand or less, or barely 60 percent of present capacity. The doya at which I stayed in the summer of 1991 is doing relatively well, operating at about 70–80 percent. Occupants may leave Tokyo temporarily to work elsewhere, the manager told me, but they continue to patronize his doya upon their return to San'ya. Not surprisingly, the business hotels have been the hardest hit; few men can afford the higher rates for a bed. A ten-story business hotel, which opened its doors in 1992, just as Japan entered recession, charges ¥4100 per night. The owners do not seem overly concerned, however, if an interview on a television documentary is to be believed. They claim to be catering to businessmen from out of town—the short-term guests who stay over in San'ya for no other reason than the price, which, when compared to other parts of Tokyo rather than other business hotels within San'ya, is very competitive indeed.

Lodgings for clients who do not work by the day, many observers believe, is very likely the wave of the future in San'ya and other doyagai. It may never have been desirable, and it is becoming less profitable, to treat day laborers as the principal clientele. Whereas day laborers are said to have comprised as much as a quarter of the construction industry's total labor force as late as the mid-1960s, the number had shrunk to well under 10 percent in the mid-1990s. Even allowing for the current recession, the writing is on the wall. With increased mechanization, the movement of capital offshore, the influx of cheap foreign labor, and a decreasing (and aging) domestic day-laborer population, the consensus is that the yoseba will never reclaim the prominence it enjoyed in the first three decades after the war, even with the full recovery of the business cycle.

The inevitable counterpart to the decreasing demand for day laborers is a rapid increase in homelessness. As one old-timer told me, there may have been more homeless in the immediate postwar years in terms of absolute numbers, but then nearly everyone was scrounging about desperately for a living, and those without roofs over their heads did not particularly stand out. Now they do, because the gap between the nation's poor and the affluent middle class has become immense. The day laborer is society's castoff twice over now that Japan has become a service-oriented economy, relying less and less on the kinds of industries and the level of technology which once provided him jobs. Here Japan is merely mimicking a trend to be found in other postindustrial societies. Former day laborers and other homeless men in Tokyo, themselves unrecyclable, are reduced to pulling hand carts loaded down with broken-down cardboard boxes destined for the recycling bin—just as vagrants in the United States push shopping carts filled with aluminum cans. That the most prominent homeless population in the city is to be found not in San'ya but lining the gateway to the towering Tokyo Metropolitan Government building west of Shinjuku is not so much an irony as it is simply typical of what is seen in a great many cities in the so-called developed world.

A number of volunteer groups, all privately funded, are engaged in activities directed primarily at feeding the homeless. In San'ya, a man in need of food can now avail himself of a soup line nearly every day of the week. A man in need of shelter, however, is in dire straits, for none of these groups has the real estate or wherewithal to put a roof over anyone's head. (In the meantime, the Asahi Street proprietors have removed the rigid metal awnings from their shop fronts and replaced them with retractable cloth awnings in an effort to shut out the dozens of homeless who used to sleep in the protected area every night.) The institutions that do have the wherewithal, such as the local shrines and temples dotting the neighborhood and the entire city, are too busy making money from the parking lots and nursery schools on their property to direct their attention to the homeless. The tradition, well established in the United States, of converting churches or synagogues into temporary (and sometimes not-so-temporary) shelters in the evenings is nowhere to be found in Japan. The volunteer organizations with religious connections in this "land of the gods and buddhas," it should be noted, are almost entirely Christian (both Catholic and Protestant) and not Shinto or Buddhist.

Will the doyagai disappear entirely? That seems unlikely, according to another of my old-timer acquaintances, as long as there are men who have reason to leave their families and strike out on their own. That the yoseba will change over time no one doubts, but that it will continue in some form seems equally certain. Symbolic of both the change and continuity at work in San'ya, the Mammoth box, formerly nestled under the wing of the Palace House (which, by the way, has installed air conditioning and charges a thousand yen per bunk), now guards the Nihonzutsumi side of Old Street-car Boulevard at the corner nearest the Iroha Arcade's east end. Standing four stories high and replete with "retro" clock and tiled exterior, it looks from the outside more like an upscale condominium than a police box, except for the high-tech antenna that dons the roof. The relocation may have pleased shopkeepers in Nihonzutsumi, but it has not reduced the number of vagrants lying about the arcade entrance.

Another change is the complete demise of the Gijintō, once a powerful yakuza group in San'ya, the victim of recent legislation against "violent groups" (bōryokudan) which has forced some yakuza to close up shop or go underground. The Yamagataya, near which the Gijintō-related tehaishi operated, is now out of business. No one believes that the yakuza are on their way out, however. When one group stumbles, others are waiting in the wings to take its place.

Still another change is the disappearance of the Santōrō labor union, which disbanded in 1994. Some of its supporters have gravitated to an organization called Furusato no Kai, in existence since 1990 and part of what one of its leaders calls the network of welfare and volunteer services which now plays such a large role in the yoseba. Sōgidan, the group connected with the national day laborers' union (Hiyatoi Zenkyō), has split up into factions which are vying for control and which have occasionally engaged in violent confrontations. The era of union activism appears to be on the wane, and San'ya awaits new leadership to negotiate the vicissitudes of yoseba life during this most difficult time.

In the meantime, life goes on for those who make or have made the yoseba their home or place of work. The Santōrō officers have gone their separate ways. Tottori has returned to his family's home in the country. Osaka now drives a taxi in another section of Tokyo. Kobe, who sought a seat in the Taitō Ward Assembly in 1991, ran again in 1995 with the backing of another national party (the Shintō Sakigake), and missed by a mere fifty votes. He attributes his narrow defeat to the mistrust that Shitamachi residents have for outsiders, especially one without family, which he ultimately could not overcome. Not that Kobe has completely abandoned family connections. His son, now attending a provincial high school, was in San'ya for a visit during the 1995 Summer Festival, manning one of the food stands. Nerima, who quit her post at the Welfare Center after twenty years, now teaches at a journalism school and is active in groups concerned with alcohol abuse in Japan. Sendai continues to manage Maria, which is now open only in the evenings. The price of dinner has actually gone down, to ¥150 for the set menu and ¥220 for the meal of the day—yet another sign of how seriously the recession has hit San'ya. Hakuba has been to Indonesia twice working on charcoal kilns, and Nihonzutsumi has added homemade bread to the complement of cakes on the menu to be enjoyed along with the fresh-roasted coffees.

The day laborers I have kept up with are simply trying to manage from day to day in a time of great change. Others I have not been able to keep up with, either because they have moved away or because I have lost track of them or because they haunt the yoseba in another world. Shiga, I am told, is trying his fortunes in Kamagasaki. Sakata is no longer in San'ya and now makes Kawasaki his stomping ground. Aizu, Sakata's nemesis, is no longer alive—the victim of a murder in Tamahime Park which has yet to be fully accounted for. A relative refused to accept the remains. Naga-san is also no longer alive, having been killed, apparently, in a fight in Kamagasaki. Staying alive in the yoseba, which was never easy, has become even more difficult with jobs off the streets at a premium and welfare being granted largely on a case-by-case basis. The men who helped Tokyo rise from the ashes are themselves headed, far faster than any other population within Japan, for the funeral pyres.

As for the fruits of my own labor, the office building in central Tokyo and the apartment in the Osaka suburb are long since finished, and automobiles now speed up Ramp No. 2 of the Jōban Expressway, Sōka Interchange—its sleek sound-proofing wall arching over the pavement—and pass over the Tōbu Isezaki Line train tracks near Shinden Station. I can appreciate, however infinitesimally, the feelings of day laborers who utter with conviction, "We have built Japan."

MEMORY AS ORAL HISTORY

In retrospect, it seems as if the degree to which one becomes a participant [in the course of field work] is as much a matter of perceiving oneself as a participant as it is of being accepted as a participant by others.
—Elliot Liebow, *Tally's Corner*

All ethnography is part philosophy, and a good deal of the rest is confession.
—Clifford Geertz, "The Cerebral Savage"

A note about the method of transcription used in Chapter 2 ("Lives") and in parts of other chapters is certainly in order. The interviews presented as written texts are not oral histories in the ordinary sense. No tape recorder was used, and the words as they appear on these pages, therefore, are in the strict sense not transcriptions, or edited transcriptions, of the speaker's actual words. Rather, they are reconstructions of conversations held with San'ya residents—as faithful to the letter and spirit of each individual's utterances as I could make them, but reconstructions nonetheless.

What I have offered the reader, then, is not so much a documentary history as a fictional retelling: utterly nonfictional in intent but certainly novelistic in method. Without the use of a tape recorder, I was at the mercy of memory. If the conversation was a short one, I would usually make notes to myself soon after the exchange. If I was engaged in a more extended conversation, I would sometimes take advantage of natural breaks—the speaker's visit to the toilet, for example, or brief exchange with an acquaintance passing by—to note on a scrap of paper topics and key words that would aid the process of recollection. On the train home from San'ya (or before bedding down in my *doya* when staying overnight), I would make more detailed notes. I would then spend my free hours afterward writing out a draft of the one or more conversations I had had, which in turn became the "transcript" for what appears here in print.

If the method outlined above sounds somewhat tedious, it is hardly without precedent. It was probably the norm, in fact, before the age of the tape recorder. Indeed, my method resembles less that of the modern anthropologist in the field than that of James Boswell in the salon. We know that the biographer reproduced his conversations with Dr. Johnson from elaborate notes, which, however, he did not take down during the conversations themselves, realizing full well that doing so would have brought them to an end.[1]

Short or long, conversations with San'ya residents tried my powers of memory to the limit. To the question any oral narrator, lacking written notes, must face—that of how to enable recollection—Walter J. Ong offers the only logical answer: "Think memorable thoughts."[2] To which I, in my sometime role of field worker forced to rely on his powers of recall, shall boldly add: Ask memorable questions. Although my initial encounters could be characterized by their complete ethnographical haphazardness (as I shall explain below), due to the initial lack of any clear anthropological purpose on my part, my conversations with people began to take on a certain pattern over time. The questions I posed (or, to put it more accurately, the topics I encouraged each person to volunteer information about) were more or less set: descriptions of the person's home town or village, family, and childhood; reflections on work, living conditions, and reasons for working in the yoseba; thoughts on the person's acquaintances and relations, interests, avocations, and other activities.

To confine myself to these categories may have been as limiting as it was liberating. Yet within the confines of the descriptions prompted by such questionings and encouragements, memory, I feel, served me at least as well as, say, questionnaires or more structured interviews.[3]

I have observed the convention of most oral histories and present the conversations as first-person monologues; however, I have let the narratives retain traces of their conversational origins. Each monologue represents the utterances of a discrete individual. Only in two or three cases did I collate two conversations with the same individual, for the sake of convenience, into a single monologue. Under no circumstances did I collate conversations with different individuals into a composite monologue by some San'ya "everyman" in the interest of narrative fullness or for any other

1 A brief description of Boswell's recording method can be found in M. H. Abrams, gen. ed., *The Norton Anthology of English Literature*, rev. (New York: W. W. Norton, 1968), 1:1873.

2 Walter J. Ong, *Orality and Literacy: The Technologizing of the Word* (London: Methuen, 1985), p. 34. See also pp. 57–68 for an important discussion of oral memorization.

3 Hindsight makes me appreciate how similar my approach was to that of Elliot Liebow in *Tally's Corner: A Study of Negro Streetcorner Men* (Boston: Little, Brown, 1967). See pp. 10–12.

reason, however tempting that possibility might have been. Each individual represented here speaks only, and entirely, for himself or herself.[4]

The resulting collection will perhaps be forgiven its nonreliance on mechanical memory because of the circumstances that availed themselves to me—not in the strong sense of the end justifying the means, but in the weaker (yet no less urgent) sense of there being no viable alternatives. Given the specific circumstances and milieu, a tape recorder would, I am convinced, have presented an overwhelming obstacle to communication. Indeed, it would have been as great an imposition on residents as the camera I had slung over my shoulder during earlier visits in a vain attempt to capture once and for all the "reality" of the area on film.

The use of a tape recorder assumes the fulfillment of certain conditions during an interview which were rarely operative in my case: the possibility of leisurely reflection by the speaker, the maintenance of some privacy, and the privileging of the interview format itself over the relationship between speaker and listener, to name the most obvious. To begin with, the conversational mood was often anything but reflective. Residents typically spoke to me while engaged in other activities: celebrating (drink in hand) during festival time, rallying constituents, arguing with peers, waiting on customers, serving clients or patients. The speaker was often quite excited or upset and in such cases would certainly have been most unwilling to have a leisurely chat on the park bench, let alone sit down across a table with a microphone on it.

The presence of a microphone, moreover, would have resulted in the regularizing of a speaker-listener relationship that was in fact utterly protean and subject to sudden and unpredictable change. To confine the conversation mechanically to the format of recorded interview would have defeated one of the main purposes of my conversations, which was to track the very nature of my rapport with the resident—over and above documenting the resident's specific personal circumstances.

The degree of privacy in my talks with day laborers varied considerably. Some conversations were held in a doya room, but they were the rare exceptions. In most cases, speaker and listener were situated in a public space—a park, an arcade, a work site, a tavern, a shop, a clinic—and typically surrounded by many others, who were active listeners of, and occasional participants in, the conversation. Such settings actually helped the men pre-

4 Thus my method differs from that of both Oscar Lewis, *The Children of Sanchez: Autobiography of a Mexican Family* (New York: Random House, 1961); and Marion Benedict and Burton Benedict, *Men, Women, and Money in Seychelles* (Berkeley: University of California Press, 1982), two well-known anthropological studies that employ collation. See the introductions to both studies.

serve what they cherished most: their anonymity. As I trust this book makes clear, a great many men have come to San'ya and other yoseba after severing all previous social ties, whether to family, acquaintances, employers, loan officers, or underworld connections. A tape recorder would be perceived as a threat to that anonymity, not because the speaker has been called on to answer incriminating questions, but because he has been singled out publicly and made vulnerable by that fact alone.

Yet another way in which my conversations diverged from the paradigm of oral-history "interview" has to do with the relationship between speaker and listener, which differed fundamentally, in form if not in content, from that between a typical interviewer and his subject. I walked the streets of San'ya, generally on my own, in hopes of making acquaintances. I succeeded beyond my wildest dreams. While the oral historian generally seeks out individuals to interview, it was the San'ya day laborers who, noting my presence, often sought *me* out (whether I was prepared or not) and proffered their views on work and life. Relying almost never on introductions (knowing that they succeed in opening doors in mainstream society precisely because they are meant to do away with anonymity), I simply made myself available on the street—at the local clinic, on night patrol, in the park, on the job, at a festival—in hopes of spontaneous interaction. Those hopes were nearly always fulfilled.

I describe my initial forays into San'ya as ethnographically haphazard. There is no question, however, that as time went by I began thinking about people and place more and more like an anthropologist. Yet in no case did I present myself as an anthropological researcher doing field work. When I was commuting to San'ya in 1989–90, I replied, when questioned, that I was a student of literature and popular culture whose casual interest in the day-laborer situation in Tokyo had deepened with each successive visit to the yoseba. This answer had the dual advantage of being more ambiguous and much closer to the truth. When I was actually living in and working out of San'ya in the summer of 1991, I replied, upon questioning, that I was interested in earning money in a hassle-free environment and did not enjoy teaching English—also close to the truth, albeit hardly the whole truth. Vestiges of this sort of give-and-take are purposefully left in some of the interviews in "Lives" and in certain sections of "Work."

Early on, many men asked me, often in a derisive tone, if I was a journalist and appeared visibly relieved when I answered in the negative. Some explained to me on separate occasions, in terms so similar as seemingly to express a collective memory, that journalists were to be despised because they were at bottom more concerned with their readerships than with the subjects of their articles and that they merely fed like jackals off the lives of others in the name of news gathering.

This view of journalists is understandable. The yoseba is given sparse coverage except when there are disturbances;[5] the daily lives of the laborers otherwise go virtually unnoticed and without comment. Foreign journalists, mindful of their limited sojourns and on the lookout for the unusual during their stints abroad, might feature stories on the yoseba at any time, despite a lack of turmoil. But once having made the obligatory visit to a place like San'ya and having noted that even Japan has its "slums," they feel little compunction to return and even less need to link what they have seen there with what goes on in the rest of society.

I can appreciate how a tape recorder, in certain circumstances, can act as a kind of guarantor that a message will get across and actually encourage the speaker to be more forthright and articulate.[6] But its presence could also tempt the speaker into exaggeration or rationalization or other means of self-justification which would not have been contemplated in its absence. The use of a tape recorder, moreover, both presupposes and encourages a certain fullness of production and properness of delivery. Many of my "conversations," on the other hand, were little more than spontaneous exchanges. I believe that they were no less sincere or valuable for that. Indeed, as suggested above, once I became conscious of the ethnographic potential of this project, I worked hard at being in the right place at the right time; spontaneity, therefore, should not be confused with accident. In any event, the mechanics of setting up a conventional interview would only have gotten in the way of the kind of spur-of-the-moment communication which is so typical of daily life in the yoseba.

The surreptitious use of a tape recorder, which might seem to have afforded greater accuracy of transcription with a minimum of mechanical bother, would in fact have been unworkable as well as unethical. A tape recorder, if not hidden well enough, would cause embarrassment, to say the least; yet if too well hidden, would no doubt defeat the purpose. It would be difficult, if not impossible, to change tapes during a conversation, and it would certainly be well-nigh impossible to catch the many ephemeral and spur-of-the-moment but nonetheless essential exchanges that I continually engaged in and that, even though they may not appear in print as "interviews," have added much to my overall understanding of the area. In retro-

5 The media coverage of the October 1990 riots in Kamagasaki typifies the swing in the level of attention from lackadaisical unconcern (which is the usual situation) to frenzied obsession (in times of "crisis").

6 Daphne Patai makes this point in her *Brazilian Women Speak: Contemporary Life Stories* (New Brunswick, N.J.: Rutgers University Press, 1988), p. 4. Patai also makes an eloquent case for oral history, even when duly recorded by machine, as literary artifact. See her "Introduction: Constructing a Self," pp. 1–35. I thank Daphne Patai, who was a fellow at the National Humanities Center in 1990–91, and members of Asian and African Languages and Literature at Duke University, to whom I gave a faculty seminar in 1990, for encouraging me to consider further the ramifications of my "interviewing" method.

spect, exercising my memory was highly preferable to taxing my mechanical ingenuity.

Another crucial (albeit typically overlooked) issue related to interviews when not conducted in English is that of translation. Interviewers who voice concern over the accuracy of transcription often fail to demonstrate equal concern over the appropriateness of their English-language renderings. I do not subscribe to the belief that the transcribed interview remains as "unmediated" in its translated as in its untranslated state. The act of translation—which is, after all, one of cultural transference—is neither neutral nor transparent; and the process of editing begins with, rather than follows, the rendering of one language into another. The use of a tape recorder does not in itself make the Japanese speaker's words more accessible, or comprehensible, to an English-speaking audience.

An even more serious issue is the use of a person's words without that person's permission. To tape a conversation in secret and then offer it to the public domain is unconscionable. The words I present here—representations of the speech of those who quite possibly would never have wanted to see themselves in print—are, finally, my own words, for which I must take full responsibility. Although each speaker is clearly etched in my memory, I have taken steps in nearly every case to ensure that he or she remains unrecognizable to anyone else. In those cases where the anonymity of the speaker could not be completely protected, or where the relationship between speaker and listener became a long-standing one, I sought permission to use the specific conversation in question and present it only when permission was granted.

That San'ya day laborers especially do not take lightly an invasion of privacy has been documented in the Prologue. To those who feel that my crime of stealing faces with a camera was simply transformed into one of stealing words, I offer the following defense. The faces of these men I did indeed "steal," without permission or advance notice. Their words, however, were offered freely and willingly—sometimes in confidence, to be sure, but also as open pronouncements to an outsider. Would those who were so free with their words have been less so had they known that they would appear in print—albeit in a different language? To that question I shall never know the answer, except in the cases of those, whose anonymity could not be fully guaranteed, I asked directly and who gave me permission. But the feeling—call it a kind of faith if you will—that their words as I have recorded them, uttered at times with much pride and at times in much pain, have both done them some justice and preserved what they desire most—their anonymity—is what has driven this project.

In addition to the question of the accuracy of any individual account is the accuracy of the accounts taken as a whole. Together, the "interviews" presented in these pages offer one possible cross-section of San'ya residents. They are far from random, however, and do not reflect in numerical terms San'ya's actual demographic make-up.[7] Randomness is actually far more difficult to achieve than might be thought in an area where one can so easily strike up casual acquaintances on the street (not to mention in the taverns and shops). I have tried to correct for overrepresentation of this type by presenting a variety of other groups—day laborers on the job as well as shopowners, union leaders, bureaucrats, and missionaries, whose perspective on life in San'ya is invaluable to an overall understanding of the area—without, I trust, overemphasizing any of the latter. Yet in the final analysis, my claim to any sort of representativeness must be a limited one. The sheer diversity of those I came into contact with dictates otherwise; my method itself militates against it.

In sum, the risks of the very unscientific variety of ethnography I have attempted here are admittedly great. I would like to think, however, that the rewards are potentially even greater. I agree with Michael B. Katz's criticism of quantitative methods for studying poverty in the United States, which can actually blind researchers to the urgency of their subject. His observations seem as germane to the study of a day-laborer neighborhood in Tokyo as to that of the African American ghettos he describes: "The method of ethnography contrasts vividly with quantitative studies of poverty. Its minimal contribution is the destruction of stereotypes; its signal achievement, in the work of its most able practitioners, is a portrait of the world from the vantage point of its subjects. The best ethnographies always break down conventional categories and reassemble the lived world of their subjects in the terms of the subjective experience."[8]

It should be clear from the above discussion that I am skeptical about the possibility of presenting a "portrait of the world from the vantage point of

---

7 The difficulty of coming up with the proper "sample" is commented on by Liebow in *Tally's Corner*, a classic ethnographic text (see p. 8 and p. 20); however, I find inspiration in the writing of Amos Oz, who in his physical and psychological probing of his own nation renounces the "representative" in favor of more limited yet powerfully individuated revelations: "None of the conversations presented here were taped. . . . I do not consider these articles to be a 'representative picture' or 'typical cross-section' of Israel at this time; I do not believe in representative pictures or typical cross-sections. Every place is an entire world and every man is a world in himself, and I reached only a few places and a few people, and even then I was able to see and to hear only a little of so much" (*In the Land of Israel*, trans. Maurie Goldberg-Bartura [New York: Harcourt Brace Jovanovich, 1983], p. viii).

8 Michael B. Katz, *The Undeserving Poor: From the War on Poverty to the War on Welfare* (New York: Pantheon Books, 1989), pp. 170–71. It is not my purpose here to disparage more scientific studies or to privilege the grossly imprecise ethnographic method I happened to have stumbled onto in getting to know the yoseba, but simply to make a space for the latter in the discourse of sociological/anthropological/literary studies. That more traditional social-science studies have their use, not simply in the abstract but in the specific case of San'ya, I do not doubt. See Suggested Readings.

its subjects," given my belief in the highly constructed nature of the "portrait" and the concurrent necessity of filtering it through the presenter's own subjectivity. Nevertheless, I believe just as strongly in the ideal of portraiture and consider it an eminently worthy goal even as a fictional construct. The failures encountered in attempting to represent individuals are of infinitely greater value to me than any success in quantifying faceless groups in exactitude.

GLOSSARY

This list contains most terms used in the text. A few terms not appearing in the text are also included for those wishing to learn more about yoseba argot.

Abure. Argot for unemployment; specifically, not getting a job off the streets in a yoseba (or from a government agency operating in the yoseba). Thus: *abure teate,* or unemployment dole.

Anko/ankō. Argot for day laborer, derived from the angler fish, which waits for a meal to drift its way.

Aokan (short for *aotenjō kantan*). Sleeping out in the open. Thus: *aokansha* (person who sleeps in the streets).

Beddo hausu. Bed-house; here translated as bunkhouse: a lodging house (doya), typically accommodating eight men per room on four double-decker bunks.

Buraku. Lit., "hamlet," but often referring to a section of a village or city where outcastes (*eta, hinin*) and (after 1871) descendants of outcastes reside. Thus: *burakumin* (hamlet residents, i.e., outcastes). Also known as *hisabetsu buraku* ("hamlets that are discriminated against").

Chikkō. The yoseba in Fukuoka. Has no doyagai.

Chūhai. A highball of *shōchū* and seltzer water, said to have been invented in San'ya and now popular throughout Japan.

Dezura. Argot for wages earned by a day laborer.

Dokata. Common term for day laborer. Less formal than *hiyatoi rōdōsha.* Derogatory in some contexts.

239

Doya. Argot for lodging house (*kan'i shukuhakusho; kichin'yado*) in a yoseba, the syllables of the usual word (*yado*) being reversed. Sometimes translated as "flophouse."

Doyagai. Lodging-house district, often with a yoseba. In San'ya, the principal doyagai is in Kiyokawa/Nihonzutsumi.

Edo Period. 1603–1868. Named after the shogunal capital (present-day Tokyo). Ended with the Meiji Restoration.

Enka. A variety of popular song, often in the style of a melancholy ballad.

Eta. Outcastes; Japan's "untouchables." Worked with leather and performed other tasks, from slaughtering to grave digging, which were considered unclean or polluted by social and religious custom. They were ostensibly incorporated into the mainstream after 1871 by legal fiat, but discrimination remains. Known today as *burakumin.*

Genba. Construction site; work site.

Geta. Traditional wooden footwear with thonglike straps that secure feet. Still popular in hot weather.

Gijintō. A formerly prominent yakuza group in San'ya.

Gunte. Work gloves, usually white, made of coarse cotton cloth.

Hachimaki. Headband; esp., a small towel, usually made of plain cotton or terry cloth, which is customarily twisted and wrapped around the head to absorb sweat during strenuous physical activity.

Hanba. Construction site; specifically, one at which workers, including day laborers, spend a period of days, weeks, or even longer, lodging on the site in barracks. Also, the barracks at the site.

Harappa. The yoseba in Kawasaki, just south of Tokyo.

Heisei Period. (1989–). Named after the Heisei emperor (Akihito).

Hibakusha. Victims of the atomic bombings in Hiroshima and Nagasaki at the end of World War II. Many survivors suffer the effects of radioactive fallout.

Hinin. Another group of untouchables in pre-Meiji Japan, which included executioners, prostitutes, and entertainers. Unlike *eta,* whose status was hereditary, *hinin* could be reinstated as commoners.

Hisabetsu buraku. See *buraku.*

Hiyatoi rōdōsha. Lit., "laborer hired for the day." Standard term for day laborer.

Horumon-yaki. Grilled or sautéed pig's guts, richly seasoned. A common dish in the yoseba.

Itte'rasshai. Short for *Itte irasshai;* lit., "Go and come back." A common sendoff.

Jikatabi. The flexible split-toed footwear worn by gardeners, construction workers, and so forth on the job. Rubber-soled for sure footing.

Jin-pato. Short for *Jinmin patorōru.* Citizens' patrol.

Jōbi. Quasi-foreman. A day laborer who is elevated to the role of recruiter and who leads a group of workers on the job.

Kaiko-dana. A tiny, cubicle-like lodging space with just barely enough room for one person to sleep in. Now refers to the "bunkhouse" type of lodging.

Kamagasaki. The yoseba in Osaka, and the largest in Japan. Has a doyagai.

Kanamachi Ikka. The most prominent yakuza group in San'ya.

Kan'i shukuhakusho. Lit., "simple overnight accommodation." The bureaucratic term for doya. Also, *kan'i shukusho.*

Kanpa. Donations, either in the form of money or materials. A word heard especially at festival time.

Kenchinjiru. A stewlike dish containing burdock, carrots, daikon radish, pork, tofu, and *kon'nyaku* ("devil's tongue").

Ketaochi. A work site (typically a *hanba*) that flagrantly violates labor laws and/or contracts, or which has particularly poor conditions or low wages.

Ketsuwari. Quitting (one's job) halfway through, whether out of laziness or because of some legitimate reason, such as a false job description.

Kichin'yado. Cheap lodging house; doya. Less formal than *kan'i shukuhakusho.*

Kidōtai. Riot police.

Kotobuki-chō. A major yoseba, located in Yokohama, the port city south of Tokyo. Has a doyagai.

Meiji Period. 1868–1912. Named after the Meiji emperor (Mutsuhito).

Meiji Restoration (1868). Marked the end of shogunal rule in Japan and the beginning of the modern state under the reign of the emperor.

Min'yō. Traditional folk song.

Mogaki. One who preys on men sleeping outdoors (*aokansha*).

Nikoyon. Lit., "two [one-hundred-yen] plus four [ten-yen] coins." Nickname for a worker's daily wage, set by the government hiring agencies in the 1950s. The term can also refer to a day laborer himself.

Ninpu. An older term for day laborer.

Ninpu-dashi. Another word for *tehaishi*, esp. one who sends day laborers to work at a *hanba.*

Ninsoku. A historical term for day laborer. Thus: *ninsoku yoseba.*

Nomi kōi. A kind of informal betting, common in the doyagai, which places a ceiling on the possible winnings. Thus, a bet placed on a horse that wins ten thousand yen in the doyagai might yield much more at the track. Certain shops serve as fronts for this type of betting, and the proceeds go to the yakuza gangs.

Obon. The Buddhist Festival of the Dead. The principal summer holiday and along with New Year's one of the two major holidays in Japan. Traditionally celebrated in the seventh month of the lunar calendar, but now usually observed in August (13–15).

Okera. Flat broke, either because of no income or from gambling losses.

Onigiri. Rice ball, often garnished with fish or pickles inside and seaweed on the outside. A popular lunch item.

Oyabun. Boss; leader.

Pachinko. A very popular pinball game, found in *pachinko* parlors everywhere in Japan, including San'ya.

Pinhane. Wage skimming, in yoseba jargon. The *tehaishi*'s cut of the day laborer's wage.

Pūtarō. A derogatory term for day laborer.

Rakugo. Comic monologue. A traditional narrative art.

Sasajima (or Sasashima). The yoseba in Nagoya, located close to Nagoya Station. No longer has a doyagai.

Senjū Kawara-chō. A small yoseba to the north of San'ya in Kita Senjū, Adachi Ward.

Shichibu. The flared knickers worn by *shokunin*, especially by the many day laborers who are *tobi*.

Shinkansen. Commonly known as the "bullet train." The superexpress that connects Tokyo with the major cities of Honshu and Kyushu.

Shiro techō. "White card." A popular appellation for *hiyatoi rōdō hihokensha techō*, or logbook for insured day laborers. Used by day laborers registered with a municipal government to obtain unemployment compensation.

Shōchū. A distilled liquor made from potatoes, barley, rice, or other grains. Generally about fifty proof.

Shokunin. Skilled workers, including carpenters, electricians, and *tobi*.

Shōwa Period. 1926–89. Named after the Shōwa emperor (Hirohito).

Soapland [sōpurando]. The name given to bathhouses in Yoshiwara and other quasi-brothel districts after the Turkish government, in the 1980s, protested the use of "Turkish baths" in this context.

Suiton. A thin broth containing flour dumplings and flavored with daikon radish and onions.

Tachinbo/Tachinbō. A term for day laborer. One who stands and waits for a job.

Taishō Period. 1912–26. Named after the Taishō emperor (Yoshihito).

Takobeya. A descriptive term for a particularly poor *hanba*, likening the cramped accommodations to an octopus trap (a pot that is easy to slip into but virtually impossible to escape), and where one is forced to do hard labor.

Tatami. A thick, woven rush mat used for flooring in most rooms of a traditional Japanese house. The size is roughly three feet by six feet but can vary considerably. Rooms are often measured by the number of tatami mats they accommodate.

Tehaishi. Labor broker, who supplies day laborers with work off the street. Usually under the employ of the yakuza.

Tobi. Also *tobi shoku.* Skilled, highly paid workers who assemble and disassemble scaffolding on buildings. Many work as day laborers.

Tonjiru. A stewlike dish in a miso broth similar to *kenchinjiru.*

Tonko. Escape, typically from a *takobeya.*

Umeshu. Plum brandy. An alcoholic beverage made with Japanese plums (*ume*) fermented in sweetened *shōchū*, with roughly the alcoholic content of a sherry or port.

Yakuza.   Generic term for gangster or group of gangsters in Japan. The latter is known more formally as *bōryokudan*. Originated from itinerant peddlers (*tekiya*) and gamblers (*tobakushi; bakuchi-uchi*).

Yama.   Another name for San'ya, taken from the first character of the two-character compound (*yama* [lit., "mountain"] and *tani* [lit., "valley"]). Thus: "Yama man."

Yamaguchi-gumi.   The largest yakuza syndicate in Japan. Based in Kansai.

Yoseba.   The place (such as San'ya) where day laborers gather to get work. It may or may not have a lodging quarter (doyagai).

❋

SUGGESTED READINGS

In the interest of a less encumbered reading, I have elected not to use notes (except in the Postscript) in this book. My debt to oral and other informal sources, such as fliers and handouts, is prodigious, as should be clear from the text itself. At the same time, my debt to formal written sources, both in English and Japanese, is by no means small. Readers interested in scrutinizing the materials are referred to the bibliography appended to Edward Fowler, "San'ya: Scenes from Life at the Margins of Japanese Society," *Transactions of the Asiatic Society of Japan*, 4th ser., 6 (1991), 141–198; and to two annotated bibliographies, one compiled by Matsuzawa Tessei, the second by Kakiage Manzō et al., in *Yoseba* [journal of the Yoseba Gakkai], no. 3 (May 1990), 164–186, 187–207. Some works cited in these bibliographies, however, deserve elaboration here, along with other selected titles. All Japanese-language texts are published in Tokyo, unless otherwise indicated.

A good deal of writing in English exists on San'ya. See Brett de Bary, "Sanya: Japan's Internal Colony," in *The Other Japan: Postwar Realities*, ed., E. Patricia Tsurumi (Armonk, N.Y.: M. E. Sharpe, 1988), pp. 112–118, for a comprehensive description of the yoseba scene in Tokyo which, two decades after its original publication in 1974, is still very useful. See also Matsuzawa Tessei, "Street Labour Markets, Day Labourers and the Structure of Oppression," in *The Japanese Trajectory: Modernization and Beyond*, ed. Gavan McCormack and Yoshio Sugimoto (Cambridge, Cambridge University Press, 1988), pp. 147–163, which is a summation of his earlier work. (For other articles in Japanese by

Matsuzawa, a prolific writer on the yoseba, see the bibliography in my article in *Transactions*.) More recently, Tom Gill has written an article titled "Sanya Street Life under the Heisei Recession," *Japan Quarterly*, 41 (July-September, 1994), 270–286. See also Roman Cybriwsky, *Tokyo: The Changing Profile of an Urban Giant* (Boston: G. K. Hall, 1991), pp. 182–86, for a brief but effective description of contemporary San'ya; and James Fallows, "The Other Japan," which views San'ya through the eyes of Masahiko Katori, director of San'yūkai, and which appears in the *Atlantic Monthly*, April 1988, 16–20. My citation of Fallows in the Prologue comes from an article titled "The Japanese Are Different from You and Me," also in the *Atlantic Monthly*, September 1986, 35–41.

I relied extensively on Japanese-language publications, including Kanzaki Kiyoshi, *San'ya doyagai: Ichi man nin no Tōkyō mushuku* [The San'ya 'doya' district: Tokyo's ten thousand vagabonds] (Jiji Tsūshin Sha, 1974); Kojima Kazuo and Aramaki Masayuki, *Shin San'ya burūsu* [The new San'ya blues] (Hihyōsha, 1983); Miyashita Tadako, *San'ya nikki: Aru iryō sōdan'in no kiroku* [San'ya diary: The record of a clinic worker] (Ningen no Kagakusha, 1977); Kaji Daisuke, *Saikasō no keifu—San'ya no sengoshi o ikite* [A genealogy of the lowest stratum: Living in postwar San'ya], 2 vols. (Sekibundō, 1977); Eguchi Ei'ichi et al., *San'ya—shitsugyō no gendai-teki imi* [San'ya: The meaning of unemployment in the modern era] (Miraisha, 1979); and Imagawa Isao, *Gendai kimin kō* [Reflections on modern-day outcastes] (Tabata Shoten, 1987). I should not overlook the biweekly magazine *Jidai*, which has published several special issues on San'ya over the years.

Kanzaki's book provides a detailed account of San'ya's early and postwar history and of the process of job procurement in the morning yoseba. Kojima's book, handsomely illustrated with photographs by Aramaki Masayuki, contains vivid portraits of key individuals and numerous San'ya landmarks. Miyashita's book offers important though somewhat dated information on job procurement and work content, as well as vivid descriptions of the rampant abuse of alcohol in the yoseba. See also her *San'ya Namidabashi—doyagai no jibunshi* [Namidabashi, San'ya: Oral histories from the *doyagai*] (Banseisha, 1978); *Omoikawa—San'ya ni ikiru onnatachi* [Omoikawa: The women of San'ya] (Chikuma Shobō, 1985), for collections of fascinating oral histories of men who worked as day laborers and women who worked as prostitutes in San'ya. Miyashita's most recent book is *Yama mandara* [San'ya mandala] (Taishūsha, 1995). Kaji, the dean of day-laborer activists who first set foot in San'ya in 1946, offers a rich description of San'ya's postwar rise as a yoseba and an impressive, if polemical, account of his own career and the early day-laborer movement. The book compiled by Eguchi et al., based on a series of comprehensive surveys, contains helpful statistics concerning the San'ya doyagai, day laborers' backgrounds, livelihood, and job procurement, as well as dozens of revealing individual case studies. Imagawa's book presents an incisive history of official treatment of vagrants throughout Japan's modern period.

I consulted all six of the above-cited books, as well as the *Jigyō gaiyō* (see below), when writing my book. Imagawa's book also provides perhaps the best history of day-laborer activism in San'ya. The fold-out chart after page 388 well illustrates the postwar San'ya day-laborer movement's complex lineage. See also the inside of the dust jacket of *Damatte notarejinu na—Funamoto Shūji ikō shū* [Don't die meekly in the gutter! The writings of the late Funamoto Shūji], ed. Zenkoku Hiyatoi Rōdō Kumiai Kyōgikai (Renga Shobō Shinsha, 1985), for a time chart on San'ya day-labor activism.

The single most important source of statistical information on San'ya is *Jigyō gaiyō* (Summary of activities), compiled by the Jōhoku Welfare Center and published annually. I have used the 1989 and 1990 editions. Numerous charts and graphs on demography, geography, job procurement, and livelihood combine to offer a detailed portrait of the San'ya day-laborer population. It also contains a chronology of events that have affected the area in the postwar period, as well as an introduction to the services offered by the Welfare Center. The Center also publishes a newsletter (*Hiroba*) and two literary magazines, including one that specializes in haiku written by members of the day-laborer community. These and other magazines and tabloids (now defunct) published by various day-laborer activists, are listed and critiqued in Imagawa, pp. 239–242.

In addition, the Center publishes a pamphlet, revised yearly, titled *Kurashi no benri-chō*, a survivor's guide for day laborers new to San'ya. A similar publication, although with very different ideological objectives, is put out by Hiyatoi Zenkyō and is titled *Rōdōsha techō* (Workers' handbook). It includes descriptions of all the country's yoseba in which the Hiyatoi Zenkyō has offices (San'ya, Kotobuki-chō, Kamagasaki, Sasajima [Nagoya], and Chikkō [Fukuoka]), histories of the various yoseba-related labor movements, and biographies of numerous deceased activists. Hiyatoi Zenkyō also publishes the monthly newsletter *Hiyatoi Zenkyō nyūsu*, which covers events at the major yoseba.

Hayashi Kōichi has written no fewer than three books on the so-called lumpen proletariat. His first, *Runpengaku nyūmon* [Lumpen-ology: An introduction] (Peppe Shuppan, 1976), includes extensive coverage of life in the San'ya doyagai. Ikeda Michiko has published two collections of short stories on San'ya day laborers: *Muenbotoke* [An unclaimed body] (Sakuhinsha, 1979), and *Kain to sono nakamatachi* [Cain and his comrades] (Fukutake Shoten, 1983), as well as several volumes on the lives of San'ya prostitutes in the postwar period.

There are many writings on the other two major yoseba. Three of the most accessible are Rey Ventura, *Underground in Japan* (London: Jonathan Cape, 1992), which describes Kotobuki-chō from a Filipino immigrant's point of view; Elizabeth Strohm, *Kibō no machi—Kamagasaki ni ikite nijūnen* [Town of hope: Twenty years in Kamagasaki] (Nihon Kirisutokyōdan Shuppankyoku, 1988), which describes Kamagasaki from a German missionary's point of view; and Kōsaka Toshio, *Nagoya Sasashima: Shunkashūtō* [Sasashima, Nagoya: The four seasons] (Nagoya: Fukushinkan, 1995), a dual-language photo essay on homelessness in Nagoya. Also very useful are the collections of comic strips by Arimura Sen depicting life in Kamagasaki, two of which are available with

English glosses. See *Kamagasaki "doyagai" manga nikki 3, 4* [Comic journal of the Kamagasaki doyagai, parts 3, 4; English subtitles: "The Alternative Side of the Rising Sun" and "The Art of Laughing at Japan Inc."] (Osaka: Nihon Kikanshi Shuppan Sentā, 1989, 1993).

My account of Tokyo's history and physical aspect has benefited enormously from the writings of Edward G. Seidensticker and Paul Waley. For a history of Tokyo that focuses with particular attention on the Shitamachi district, see Seidensticker, *Low City, High City: Tokyo from Edo to the Earthquake* (1983); and *Tokyo Rising: The City since the Great Earthquake* (1990), both published in New York by Alfred A. Knopf. For an introduction to the city which will reward social historians as well as serious travelers, see Waley, *Tokyo Now and Then: An Explorer's Guide* (New York and Tokyo: Weatherhill, 1984). A fascinating description of the premodern city, including the area around San'ya, is to be found in Yoshikawa Eiji, *Miyamoto Musashi,* trans. as *Musashi* by Charles Terry (New York and Tokyo: Harper & Row/Kodansha International, 1981), in the novel's second half, where the action shifts from Kyoto to Edo, the shogunal capital. A treasure house of information about the Edo *buraku* can be found in the volume of source materials *Shiryō, Asakusa Danzaemon* [*Danzaemon of Asakusa: Documents*] (Hihyōsha, 1988), prepared by Shiomi Sen'ichirō for his monumental trilogy on the hereditary leader of the *eta;* see esp. chap. 2. Readers can learn more about Yoshiwara, the licensed quarter next to San'ya, in Cecilia Segawa Seigle, *Yoshiwara: The Glittering World of the Japanese Courtesan* (Honolulu: University of Hawaii Press, 1993), and about its more recent incarnation as a "soapland" district in Nicholas Bornoff, *Pink Samurai: Love, Marriage, and Sex in Contemporary Japan* (New York: Pocket Books, 1991).

The reader will find many books that describe the Japanese experience of World War II and the subsequent "Allied" (but in fact almost exclusively American) Occupation. Particularly recommended is Haruko Taya Cook and Theodore F. Cook, *Japan at War: An Oral History* (New York: New Press, 1992). See also Otis Cary, ed., *War-Wasted Asia: Letters, 1945–46* (Tokyo, New York, and San Francisco: Kodansha International, 1975); John W. Dower, *War without Mercy: Race and Power in the Pacific War* (New York: Pantheon Books, 1986); Thomas R. H. Havens, *Valley of Darkness: The Japanese People and World War Two* (New York: W. W. Norton, 1978); and Kazuo Kawai, *Japan's American Interlude* (Chicago: University of Chicago Press, 1960).

The following titles are offered as a guide to topics related to the yoseba experience. Gary P. Leupp, in his *Servants, Shophands, and Laborers in the Cities of Tokugawa Japan* (Princeton: Princeton University Press, 1992), devotes two chapters to Tokugawa-period day laborers, who formed a substantial portion of Edo's commoner population. The novelist Natsume Sōseki offers a now-dated but nonetheless illuminating account of *hanba* life in *Kōfu* (1908; trans. as *The Miner* by Jay Rubin [Stanford: Stanford University Press, 1988]). Although it does not deal with Japan or other non-Western cultures, *Drinking: Behavior and Belief in Modern History,* ed. Susanna Barrows and Robin Room (Berkeley: University of California Press, 1991), does shed light on the use and abuse of alcohol; a number of essays, moreover, underscore the public nature of drinking (of the kind to be seen in San'ya and other yoseba) among the working classes.

A concise review of postwar economic trends in Japan can be found in Laura E. Hein, "Growth versus Success: Japan's Economic Policy in Historical Perspective," in *Postwar Japan as History*, ed. Andrew Gordon (Berkeley: University of California Press, 1993), pp. 99–122. In the same book, Koji Taira examines the costs of economic growth in "Dialectics of Economic Growth, National Power, and Distributive Struggles" (pp. 167–186). A valuable account of an often overlooked sector can be found in Matthew Allen, *Undermining the Japanese Miracle: Work and Conflict in a Coalmining Community* (Cambridge: Cambridge University Press, 1994), which presents the little-told story of the demise of the coal-mining industry in the Chikuhō region of Kyushu in the late 1950s and early 1960s.

Capital and Countries Report: Japanese Construction Industry, ed. John Bennett et al. (Reading: Centre for Strategic Studies in Construction, University of Reading, 1987), provides much useful information about the construction industry in Japan. I consulted the chapter "Construction's Role in the Japanese Economy" when writing my Chapter 1. See also Sidney M. Levy, *Japan's Big Six: Inside Japan's Construction Industry* (New York: McGraw-Hill, 1993), for a view of the construction industry from the top. Much is written about Japan's dual-structure economy. David Friedman's *The Misunderstood Miracle: Industrial Development and Political Change in Japan* (Ithaca: Cornell University Press, 1988), is one book that argues against the dual structure theory of industrial development in Japan, particularly in manufacturing, but the construction industry is conspicuously absent from his discussion. I borrow Friedman's English rendering of *shin'yō kumiai* as "credit association."

For a review of Christian-sponsored activities in Japan's major yoseba, including San'ya, see Koyanagi Nobuaki, "Yoseba no kirisutokyōsha-tachi—sono ayumi to kadai" [Christians in the yoseba: Progress and problems], *Yoseba*, no. 4 (May 1991), 131–147, esp. 137–141. For an account of the growing number of migrant workers in Japan, see Edward Fowler, "Minorities in a 'Homogenous' State: The Case of Japan," in *What Is in a Rim? Critical Perspectives on the Pacific Region Idea*, ed. Arif Dirlik (Boulder, Colo.: Westview Press, 1993), pp. 211–233. For a description of syndicated crime in Japan, see David E. Kaplan and Alec Dubro, *Yakuza: The Explosive Account of Japan's Criminal Underworld* (Reading, Mass.: Addison-Wesley, 1986), at times a somewhat sensationalist but still useful account of gangster activity. A more ethnographically sophisticated although less accessible account will be found in David Harold Stark, "The Yakuza: Japanese Crime Incorporated" (Ph.D. diss., University of Michigan, 1979). A very useful introduction will also be found in Jacob Raz, "Self-presentation and Performance in the *Yakuza* Way of Life: Fieldwork with a Japanese Underworld Group," in *Ideology and Practice in Modern Japan*, ed. Roger Goodman and Kirsten Refsing, (London: Routledge, 1992), pp. 210–234. Popular conceptions of yakuza as portrayed in Japanese cinema are discussed in

Ian Buruma, *A Japanese Mirror: Heroes and Villains of Japanese Culture* (London: Jonathan Cape, 1984). Information in my book about gang operations in San'ya not obtained off the streets was gleaned primarily from Imagawa, op. cit.

A number of valuable studies stressing the diversity and contentiousness of Japanese society are available. A short sampling in English: David E. Apter and Nagayo Sawa, *Against the State: Politics and Social Protest in Japan* (Cambridge: Harvard University Press, 1984); Mikiso Hane, *Peasants, Rebels, and Outcastes: The Underside of Modern Japan* (New York: Pantheon Books, 1982); Dorinne K. Kondo, *Crafting Selves: Power, Gender, and Discourses of Identity in a Japanese Workplace* (Chicago: University of Chicago Press, 1990); Margaret A. McKean, *Environmental Protest and Citizen Politics in Japan* (Berkeley: University of California Press, 1981); Rob Steven, *Classes in Contemporary Japan* (Cambridge: Cambridge University Press, 1983); and Frank K. Upham, *Law and Social Change in Postwar Japan* (Cambridge: Harvard University Press, 1987).

The situation of day laborers and migrant workers, as well as of the homeless, in the United States differs greatly from that in Japan. Still, a number of sources may provide useful comparisons. See, for example, Peter Rossi, *Down and Out in America: The Origins of Homelessness* (Chicago: University of Chicago Press, 1989). *The Homeless* (Cambridge: Harvard University Press, 1994), by Christopher Jencks, offers a detailed description of and prescription for the massive problem of homelessless in America. See also Jencks's double-issue review article in the *New York Review of Books*, April 21 and May 12, 1994, for a survey of recent writings about the homeless. Tony D. Guzewicz has published a photo essay titled *Down and Out in New York City: Homelessness— "A Dishonorable Poverty"* (Commack, N.Y.: Nova Science, 1994). Benedict Giamo offers an instructive comparison of homelessness in the United States and in Japan (in the case of the latter, focusing on the yoseba, especially Kamagasaki), in his "Order, Disorder, and the Homeless in the United States and Japan," *American Studies International*, 33 (April 1995), 19–41. Finally, Aoki Hideo carefully distinguishes between yoseba, skid rows, and slums, using a wealth of English-language sources, in *Yoseba rōdōsha no sei to shi* [The lives and deaths of yoseba workers] (Akashi Shoten, 1989), esp. pp. 40–69.

All said and done, this book is what it is thanks to the wealth of information—from items displayed at the "morning market" to the going doya rates—I got off the streets, either with my own eyes or from conversations with others. When relying on orally transmitted information, I made it a point to check and double check with as many sources as possible. No doubt errors have crept in, and I must assume responsibility for any misunderstandings that have arisen because of them. I remain convinced, however, that the book is richer for this information, unsystematic though its method of gathering may have been.

This book went through numerous stages in manuscript, and it benefited from a reading of other books that explore the ethnographic process. Several important texts have already been noted in the Postscript. In addition,

Fieldnotes, edited by Roger Sanjek (Ithaca: Cornell University Press, 1990), reminded me just how complex the process of transforming notes into published text is; and I recalled more than once Clifford Geertz's injunction that "all ethnographic descriptions are homemade, that they are the describer's descriptions, not those of the described" (in his *Works and Lives: The Anthropologist as Author* [Stanford: Stanford University Press, 1988], pp. 144–145), even as a I labored to inscribe the voices of those I observed.

GENERAL INDEX

Note: Technical terms and place names appearing in the glossary and maps are listed in the index only when there is substantive discussion of them in the text. Page numbers in boldface denote photographs.

INDEX OF PSEUDONYMS

Note: Conversations in "Lives" are indicated in bold type

INDEX OF PSEUDONYMS